Prime Times

Prime Times

A Handbook for Excellence in Infant and Toddler Care

**Jim Greenman and
Anne Stonehouse**

Redleaf Press
a division of Resources for Child Caring

Published by: Redleaf Press
                a division of Resources for Child Caring
                450 North Syndicate, Suite 5
                St. Paul, MN 55104

Distributed by: Gryphon House
                P.O. Box 207
                Beltsville, MD 20704-0207

Edited by: Jan Grover

Book Design and Production
David J. Farr, *ImageSmythe*, St. Paul, MN

Permissions
The following publishers and authors have generously given permission to use materials from copyrighted works. (pp. 38, 42, 89-91, 142) Gonzalez-Mena, J. and Eyer, D. *Infancy and Caregiving.* Mountain View, CA: Mayfield, 1980, 1989, 1993. (p. 75) Olds, Anita. Quoted in "Fine Details" Organizing and displaying materials." *Beginnings* (Summer 1984): p. 13-16. (p. 113) Giovanni, Nikki. "let's take a nap" from *Spin A Soft Black Song.* NY: Farrar Straus & Giroux, Inc., 1971. (p. 141) Gonzalez-Mena, Janet. *Multicultural Issues in Child Care.* Mountain View, CA: Mayfield, 1993. (p. 196-201) Post, Jackie. "High Scope's Key Experiences for Infants and Toddlers." *Extensions* 9:4 (January/February 1995): 1-4. (p. 307, 309) Bloom, Paula. *A Great Place to Work.* Washington, DC: NAEYC, 1988.

Library of Congress Cataloging-in-Publication Data
Greenman, James T., 1949-
    Prime times: a handbook for excellence in infant and toddler care /
    Jim Greenman and Anne Stonehouse.
        p. cm.
    Includes bibliographical references.
    ISBN 1-884834-15-9
    1. Child care--Handbooks, manuals, etc. 2. Infants--Care--
Handbooks, manuals, etc. 3. Toddlers--Care--Handbooks, manuals,
etc. 4. Child care services--Management--Handbooks, manuals, etc.
I. Stonehouse, Anne. II. Title.
HQ 778.6.G74 1996
362.7'12--dc20

Table of Contents

Acknowledgments

Bits and pieces of this handbook were published previously in *Child Care Information Exchange* and in Jim Greenman's book: *Caring Spaces Learning Places: Children's Environments that Work,* both published by Exchange Press. The support, encouragement and friendship over the years from Bonnie and Roger Neugebauer, publishers of *Child Care Information Exchange* and Exchange Press have enriched our lives and careers. Material in this book was also published originally or adapted from Anne Stonehouse's book *A Good Beginning for Babies* (with Henry Ricciuti, NAEYC, 1975).

Janet Gonzalez-Mena has been an inspiration and source of wisdom. Her books have influenced our thinking and we appreciate her generosity in allowing us to use her material.

A good portion of this handbook was originally developed for programs operated by Resources for Child Care Management, now CorporateFamily Solutions. Bob Lurie, Mariene Weinstein, Susan Brenner, and Gigi Schweikert have been a source of ideas, support, and here and there, original versions of material printed here.

Our families endure both the time and egocentrism that writing requires. Jim Greenman is indebted to the patience of his daughters, Anne and Emma, and his wife, Jan. Anne Stonehouse to her sons, Daniel and Eric.

We would also like to note that more than anyone, our respective children—Anne, Emma, Daniel, and Eric, taught us about the joys and challenges of young children. They have always been and continue to be a constant reminder of two things: When it comes to doing the right thing by children, it is a lot easier to talk, teach, and write about it than to do it, and that sensitivity and sensibility come more from reading children than reading books.

JIM GREENMAN
ANNE STONEHOUSE

Photographs Photographs came from a number of centers over the past 15 years. Photographers include: Pam Jonas, Jim Greenman, Steve Moore, Jean Wallach and Shawn Connel.

Foreword

I am heartened by the publication of *Prime Times: A Handbook for Excellence in Infant and Toddler Care*. Undoubtedly, one of the single most important changes in our society is the increase in the labor force participation of mothers of infants and toddlers. In 1965, 21 percent were in the labor force; by 1995, that number had gone up to 59 per cent (United States Bureau of Labor Statistics, 1966). In addition, more and more families are seeking early social and educational experiences for their young children (Hofferth, Brayfield, Deich & Holcomb, 1991).

I remember the first time that I even saw infants and toddlers in a child care center. Although I was a veteran preschool teacher, it was truly shocking to see tiny infants circled up, covered by blankets, asleep in their cribs. It was equally shocking to see toddlers in high chairs being fed their lunch or practicing the newly acquired skill of walking, holding a teacher's hand. This was the time—the mid 1960s—when just one in five mothers with young children was employed.

Less than five years later, I became part of the surge in employed mothers. After bouts with less than satisfactory child care for my son, Philip, I joined forces with others to establish an infant/toddler center for my daughter. The Family Center at Bank Street College opened its doors in 1974. No longer was the thought of infant/toddler care frightening to me; it was the way I wanted to raise my children. But it was still frightening to others. I was told by a well-respected authority that group care for infants would harm their brain development.

Sadly, more than 20 years later, few young children have the fantastic experience in child care that my daughter did. Three multi-site observational studies of both center care and family child care conducted between 1988 and 1994 indicate that 12 to 14 percent of the children are in child care arrangements that promote their growth and learning while 12 to 21 percent are in child care arrangements that are unsafe and harmful to their development. For infants and toddlers, the proportion in unsafe settings is even higher: 35 to 40 percent (Whitebook, Howes & Phillips, 1990; Galinsky, Howes, Kontos & Shinn, 1994; Kontos, Howes, Shinn & Glainsky, 1994; *Cost, Quality, and Child Outcomes in Child Care Centers*, 1995).

Research has identified the factors associated with good quality early education and care. In center-based settings, studies have found that children fare better emotionally, socially, and cognitively when they are in arrangements that have:

◆ a sufficient number of adults for each child—that is, high staff-to-child ratios;

◆ smaller group sizes;

◆ higher levels of staff education and specialized training;

◆ low staff turnover and administrative stability; and

◆ higher levels of staff compensation.

Studies of center-based arrangements reveal that these characteristics of quality are interrelated (*Cost, Quality, and Child Outcomes in Child Care Centers*, 1995; Phillips, Mekos, Scarr, McCartney & Abbott-Shim, 1995; Whitebook, et al., 1990).

In addition, recent studies also show that it is possible to improve the quality of early education and care in ways that affect children's development. In one study, for example, we found that when centers moved to higher staff-to-child ratios and when staff engaged in more training and education, the changes in children's development were impressive; they were more securely attached, exhibited better cognitive and social development, were more proficient with language, and had fewer behavior problems (Howes, Smith & Galinsky, 1995).

Thus, it is with a great deal of hope that I welcome the publication of *Prime Times*, written by two well-respected experts in infant/toddler care; Jim Greenman and Anne Willis Stonehouse. This book is practical and well researched. It will help all of us come closer to our dream of "excellence in infant and toddler care."

Ellen Galinsky

Introduction

Our experience with infant and toddler care spans three countries, two continents, twenty-five states, two territories, and a combined total of over fifty years. Small programs, large programs, rich programs, and poor programs. Programs in homes, church-based centers (above and below ground), centers in both ramshackle and multimillion dollar "state of the art" (a grossly overused term) buildings. We have worked with programs sponsored by universities, nonprofit agencies, government agencies, employers, for-profit chains, and mom-and pop-centers. Both of us have been teachers, directors, consultants, trainers, and last, but certainly not least, parents in child care settings. We have learned from hundreds of dedicated professionals, parents, infants, and toddlers about what works and what doesn't.

Prime Times: A Handbook for Excellence in Infant and Toddler Care is intended as a general handbook for programs serving children under the age of three and as a text for students intending to work with infants and toddlers in child care. We have tried to include enough material to help program developers and directors set up and manage a program yet retain the focus for an audience of caregivers.

About Our Language

Language is a tricky business in child care because of general perceptions about the relative values of caring and providing education. In a just world, *care* would be recognized as the all-encompassing term and given considerable status; *education* would be understood as a critical component of care. That is not our world. Today, one derives status and legitimacy primarily as an educator, more specifically as a teacher. Many centers feel driven to identify as schools. However, quality child care does not look like school and staff do not behave like our preconceived notions of teachers. So where does that leave us in terms of nomenclature?

We strongly prefer the terms *center* to *school*, *homebase* to *classroom*, and *caregiver* to *teacher*. *School* is a more narrow, institutional, and deceptive term than the all-purpose term *center*. We prefer the term *homebase* to *classroom* because it better describes what a child care room should be: a homelike place and a base for children's daily activities. A base connotes that it is just that—a starting place for their daily experience of life, not merely the room in which they spend their time.

We use the term *caregiver* to describe everyone responsible for the care of children. However, we also use the term *teacher* as a job title, in recognition of the above-mentioned status concerns and the knowledge that most programs will use that title. Like it not, no other term gives staff the recognition they deserve as educators as well as more pay (if not decent compensation). *Educarer*, the term promoted by Magda Gerber and others, has not gained wide acceptance.

We also struggled with the terms *baby* and *toddler*. In that hypothetical ideal world, we believe that *baby* would apply to children up to two years old and that the act of toddling should not cost a child its status as a baby in today's headlong rush to grow up. However, recognizing that the term has become virtually synonymous to *infant*, we generally used it the same way, using the term *toddler* to describe older babies from about a year old to around two and a half.

As to the issue of gender, we bowed to reality and used the feminine for caregiver and director (fully understanding that there are males in those roles) and alternated between male and female when referring to children.

About the Book

This book is fueled by a number of convictions about how quality care for infants and toddlers actually happens.

The Importance of a Good Organization

Good care does not happen simply because of good people. It happens when good people are hired and then provided with the organizational supports necessary to do the job: a decent environment, good working conditions and compensation, and a program culture that respects and develops people and values active intelligence. As centers grow larger, organizational quality assumes an even greater importance.

Good care is always the product of both sensitivity and thought. Juggling the needs of individual children and families and the individual and collective needs of caregivers is complicated. There are endless trade-offs to be made and hourly balancing acts—everything from weighing the value of exuberant exploration against safety concerns to balancing staff/child ratios, parent fees, and teacher salaries. Directing and caregiving involve brains as well as laps, good minds as well as good hearts.

Quality is always a balancing act. We have laid out a vision of what we consider the principles and practices that lead to excellence but at the same time have made clear that there is rarely if ever a "right" way to do things. We tried to include the "why" of things, not just the "what" and "how" of policies and practices. It is invariably true that those who develop and implement programs have to shape and twist practices to fit their circumstances.

Prime Times

Is it odd to think of babies being in the prime of their lives? Not when *prime* means fundamental and primary. The first years are when our lives are launched: The people we will become are developed, and our sense of self, security, and what the world has to offer are shaped. These years are truly prime.

We use the term PRIME TIMES to signify the critical importance of care and one-to-one interactions in the child's life in the program. Caring times are PRIME TIMES. These are the times when the child's primal human needs for food, sleep, disposal of bodily waste, bathing, clothing, nurturing, and learning from others are addressed. These times occupy a large part of both the child's and the caregiver's day in care. With a relaxed pace and gentle one-to-one contact between caregiver and child, full of language, interactions, and real give-and-take, these are PRIME TIMES for developing a strong sense of personal worth and power, language, and a basic trust in the world as a good place. If the child is actively involved and respected as a person while having his or her personal needs met, these are PRIME TIMES for developing a sense of autonomy. And when a caregiver and child intimately share a moment of delight, these are PRIME TIMES for discovering the joy of being human.

Rushing through diaper changing, dressing, consoling a child in distress, or sharing a child's concern in order to get back to teaching or managing children is exactly the opposite of what should happen. Those are the times to draw out, talk, listen, touch, and reassure. The often-heard complaint of some caregivers, "All we do is care for the kids, we never get to the curriculum," fails to recognize that those caring times are *the* prime teaching times: the times that the child has his or her caregiver alone and learns through responsive care, "I am somebody, I am important."

The Importance of an Environmentally-Based Program: A World at Their Fingertips

We believe strongly that while the most important ingredient in good care for babies is the quality of the staff who work with the children, what often separates high-quality programs from others when staff/child ratios, group size, and staff qualifications are relatively equal is not the caregivers but the overall environment that supports the caregivers and that promotes good care. A good environment *works for* the caregiver and the child and helps further goals.

Our book emphasizes a learning environment approach as opposed to an activity-oriented curriculum. We call this "a world at their fingertips." The educational program does not happen in the environment; rather, the environment is the program.

An all-day program has many hours in which to build learning experiences into the program. An environment set up to allow the child to explore independently, to discover and play, also allows the staff to focus on PRIME TIMES. A rich, responsive learning environment set up to engage the other children with valuable learning experiences allows each child to have the full human presence of a caregiver to encourage and share the delight of discovery.

Neither infants nor toddlers benefit from large groups. Three is a large group for an infant or a toddler. An environmentally based program allows simultaneous individual play, pairs, and small group play and minimizes the times when all children are doing the same thing or spending time as part of a crowd.

An environmentally based program assumes that children learn from the entire experience the day provides. The ways that time and space are structured, the routines, the furnishings, the equipment and materials, and all the ways adults and children behave teach young children what the world is like, how it works, what they are capable of, and their place in that world. Much of a caregiver's planning revolves around how to build learning into the environment. What furnishings will in themselves provide learning, such as a couch that serves as a walking rail? What equipment will create a sensory or reaching/kicking activity center? While adult-initiated and -led activities take place, such as a simple cooking experience or sensory play with fingerpaints, the program is not activity based: that is, structured around activity times or groups. Music may take place anytime, as may some large motor experiences. Activities take place individually and in small groups within an environment rich with built-in learning.

The Importance of the Parent/Staff Partnership

Only when parents and staff work in partnership is quality possible. Parents' experience of child care is as important as their children's experience. Quality inherently includes parents feeling satisfied, competent as parents, and in control of their children's care. Child care, unlike school, serves families and recognizes both the similarities and differences in needs, concerns, and values that families bring to the program. There is no such thing as good centers or good caregivers that dictate the "right way" to parents or that exclude parents from influence over their children's care. Excellence is a true partnership of mutual respect and power sharing that results in individualized care based on parental values and concerns.

Using the Book

Our book is designed to be a handbook for both training and program development. It offers a logical sequence and functions as a reference that can sit on a caregiver's shelf and answer questions about practice. *Part 1: The Context of Good Care: Good Organizations for Infant and Toddler Care* explores the real world of child care that every program operates in—a world in which child care is not completely understood and is undervalued. *Chapter 1: Child Care in the Real World* opens the book and is appropriate for caregivers as well as administrators because both need a broad perspective on the range of program alternatives. Quality comes in different packages, there are a number of thorny issues, and very few simple or right answers exist. It is important for everyone to understand the complexity of child care and to avoid simplistic views. Teachers should understand the issues facing directors no less than directors must understand and respect the daily difficulties that teachers confront. We have witnessed many instances in which narrow thinking in a program created divisions when individuals refused to respect the challenges faced by people in other roles. Excellence is an outgrowth of a team effort.

In *Part 1*, we also examine how centers work, the characteristics of good organizations, and, in *Chapter 3: Goals, Characteristics, and Assumptions in a Quality Program*, what quality care for infants, toddlers, and their families really is.

Part 2: Organizing the Program begins with a chapter on understanding infants and toddlers: what to expect and what is most important for us to keep in mind about their development and needs for care. The rest of the section addresses the structure of a high quality program: how children are grouped and how time and space are structured to achieve the personalized care, individualized education, and relaxed, happy days characteristic of quality care.

Part 3: Quality Caregiving describes the what, why and how of good programming: the policies and practices that lead to quality. *Chapter 7* describes in detail what good care is, *Chapter 8* analyzes caring routines, *Chapter 9* looks at socialization and guidance, and *Chapter 10* addresses the critically important issues of how to ensure the health and safety of every child.

Part 4: Quality Learning focuses on the learning environment a quality program provides for infants and toddlers. We recognize that for infants and toddlers, care and learning are inseparable. But it is useful for program development and planning to detail the learning environment, both indoors and out.

Part 5: Good Places for Adults covers the policies and practices that lead to quality in the adult dimension: a place where parents and staff are true partners and both feel respected, valued and empowered. A center of quality has to be a great place to be a parent and to work.

Part 6: Staying Good and Quality Control recognizes that "good enough never is," and quality depends on monitoring and evaluation. *Chapter 16* offers useful tools for program evaluation and discusses the importance of NAEYC accreditation.

A Final Word

Group care for infants and toddlers, particularly toddlers, is inherently a challenge. The usually less than optimum budgets and facilities in the real world that readers of this handbook inhabit increase that challenge. A handbook is more a guide than a script; it needs to be used wisely and adapted to the particulars of each setting. All of us still have a lot to learn about how to make quality happen.

Prime Times

Part One
....
The Context of Good Care: Good Organizations for Infant and Toddler Care

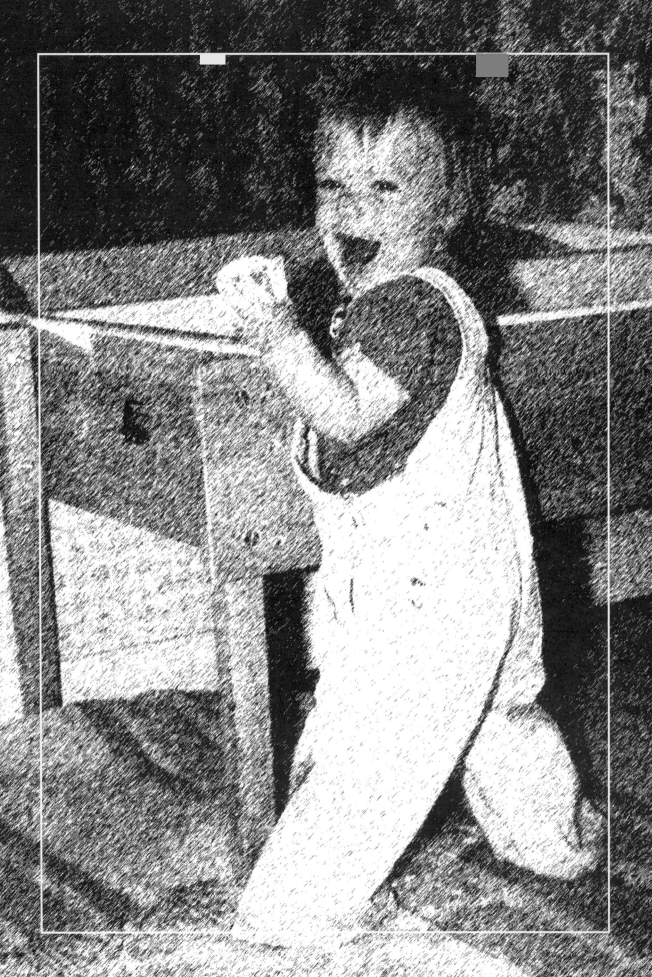

Chapter 1
Child Care in the Real World

excellence

Caregivers achieve a realistic perspective on the world of child care and an understanding of the forces that shape it, recognizing the various forms that quality and mediocrity assume in a range of settings.

Introduction

People come to infant/toddler programs from a variety of backgrounds; their experience ranges from baby-sitting to student teaching in college laboratory schools. Chances are that few readers of this book were enrolled in child care as infants or toddlers. Most of us don't arrive with a breadth of experience that helps us place issues in perspective and get a solid grasp on what quality care is and isn't. But that perspective is critical, for caregivers as well as directors. Without perspective, we are apt to narrow our ideas of what does and doesn't work, and equally important, what we can and cannot work with.

Infant and toddler group care on a mass scale is still relatively new. As recently as 1980, most centers did not include infants or toddlers. Enrollment of infants and toddlers has grown dramatically over the past decade. Before getting to the nuts and bolts of good care for infants and toddlers, it is useful to tour the real world of child care centers and homes and look at the issues that providers face.

Infant/Toddler Care in Centers Is Now Mainstream

While it's not true that everyone uses group care, nearly every sort of family is found at child care homes and centers: rich, poor, professional, single parents, extended families, rural and suburban, all cultures. That is a big change from the past, when child care existed on the margins of society as a social service for families considered "broken" or for children who were "disadvantaged," or as a cottage industry of largely unregulated homes and small mom-and-pop centers for low- and moderate-income families.

But babies are in centers to stay, and the world of child care centers has changed in other ways. It now encompasses a wide range of programs. Centers range from the small mom-and-pop centers to large centers of up to 200 children (or more), some sponsored by Fortune 500 companies like Johnson & Johnson, Ford, and Citibank. Small owner-operated centers have expanded into local chains. Large child care companies like Kinder Care are facing competition from rapidly growing regional chains. Some nonprofit, community-based centers have gone out of business, but many have expanded.

What is likely to happen in the next twenty years in the world of infant and toddler care? It's clear that the number of parents using group care will continue to grow, and if current trends are an indication, more and more of these parents will choose centers than in the past. Barring major changes in economic conditions or sociopolitical thinking, the current mixture of large and small, for-profit and nonprofit, public and private auspices will continue. Employer-sponsored care will grow slowly but steadily. Quality is likely to remain uneven unless public financial support increases.

A Note about Family Child Care

Regulated and nonregulated family child care—care in the home of a nonrelative—still provides the majority of child care for infants and toddlers in the United States.

Family child care probably provides some of the best and worst care available. At their best, family child care homes are wonderful places for young children: The small scale, informality, and richness of the home environment allow for personalized care, experiential, active learning, and enduring relationships that provide the next best thing to home. Homes are undervalued as learning environments for young children. A typical home offers a rich variety of sensory-motor learning—different textures, sounds, sights, lighting, props, and furniture to crawl on, over, under, around, and in. When children are involved in the life of the home—in cooking, cleaning, walking, doing laundry—as well as in planned activities, opportunities for language and other developmentally appropriate experiences abound.

At their worst, family child care homes are dispiriting places subject to little outside regulation. They may offer infants and toddlers little except confinement and the hypnotic stimulation of the television. When caregivers are uninterested, motivated primarily by money or obligation to family or friends, homes offer little to children.

The High Cost of Quality

Care for infants and toddlers is always going to be costly because it is labor intensive: you need low staff/child ratios to provide quality care. There's no good way around this. Because continuity of caregivers is as important as good ratios, using volunteers, student interns, or other short-term staff to keep the cost down is a good idea only to supplement, not supplant, regular staff.

High personnel costs and desire to keep parent fees down usually lead to tight budgets. Center fees are also subject to a downward pressure in most communities because other child care options for infants and toddlers (in-home care by friends and relatives and family day care) are undervalued and usually cost less. Tight budgets lead to relatively low salaries, at or close to minimum staff/child ratios, and limited spending on furnishings and equipment.

Caregivers and families experience the results: minimum regulations—supposedly floors below which children may be harmed—also serve as ceilings that many programs struggle to achieve. Somehow, quality is supposed to spring forth from minimum staffing, minimum salaries, minimum space, and minimum support. It usually doesn't.

Sketches from the Real World

Visit as many programs as you can. You are likely to make a number of discoveries:

◆ Quality comes in a lot of shapes and sizes, and so does its dismal cousin, mediocrity. Both are seen in large and small programs, new facilities and church basements, college-trained staff and experienced staff with vocational training, for-profit and nonprofit programs. Some programs look good and feel bad (to a baby or parent). Some programs may not look so wonderful but feel great to a baby or parent.

◆ Mediocrity is a lot more common than quality. Most programs are victims of the minimums: minimum funding, wages, facility, ratios, and training. For the most part, the people involved—aides, directors, family day care providers, trainers, and support services—make terrific efforts. But in a sense, they are often asked to construct child care shantytowns, creating good places for babies out of the underpaid staff, found and purchased spaces and materials they can afford, and to offer all the energy, love, and commitment they can muster.

Here are some sketches of what you are likely to encounter in the real world of child care.

Nelson's Family Child Care

Karen has been taking care of five or six children for the last eighteen years; in fact, she has her first second-generation child. She usually has two or three children under three years old. Her own children are grown and help out occasionally. Karen's child care children are swept up into the life of her home. Their cooking, cleaning, running errands, and "helping" Karen's husband Jerry with projects add richness to the planned activities, toys, and games that Karen provides. Karen's training over the years has led her to make a conscious effort to build language, math, and self-help skills into the children's participation in home life.

Preschool children have "jobs," and the school-age children help with the youngest. Clearly, each child is treated like an individual family member, and infants and toddlers are on individualized schedules. The multiage setting allows the infants and toddlers opportunities to interact much of the time with older children. Karen always has a waiting list for children under two.

The YWCA Children's Center

The YWCA Center is licensed for ninety-five children, and while it has been renovated, the wear and tear shows. The rooms are ample and most have windows. Most of the staff have been there for years (pay scales are high for the area), are well trained, and have degrees or certificates. Funding from the United Way and the county supports the center. While quality has fluctuated over the last fifteen years, the program is in good shape and is in the process of being reaccredited by NAEYC.

The infants and toddlers are in rooms with experienced staff, and the atmosphere is both quietly nurturing and active—children are crawling over and under various pieces of equipment, sloshing at a water table, and preparing for a walk. Parents and children are greeted warmly.

The center has a mission to serve low-income and single-parent families, but because of cuts in subsidy funding for poor families, many of the families are instead middle-class. Parent support and education are built into the program budget.

Barbara's Babes

Barbara's Babes takes only children under three and is licensed for forty. Barbara owns and runs the center, which is adjacent to her house. Open for six years, the center has a good reputation: "Barbara cares about kids and families." She has staff who have been with her since opening, although turnover is a problem with aide positions. Staff/child ratios are at state minimums, but Barbara's constant presence helps alleviate problems.

Children in Barbara's program get a lot of loving, and there are ample supplies of toys and materials, some designed by Barbara. Parents are enthusiastic, and many rely on Barbara as their advisor on a range of child-rearing questions.

Barbara is unabashedly entrepreneurial and has another center in the works. Active in the local child care community, although occasionally at odds with the nonprofits, Barbara is something of a model for the successful small businesswoman in child care. She understands that her "market niche" is middle- and upper-income child care. She knows what her customers want and provides it for them.

Kinder World

The Oak Park Kinder World is part of a regional chain of twenty centers (with more on the way). At first glance, the center is appealing, with a homelike sloped roof, lots of windows, and a fenced yard with swings and a climber. The center is licensed for 150 children in a compact building of under 10,000 square feet. Inside, it is crowded and noisy, and the voluminous amount of artwork on the walls of the bright colored, narrow corridors combines with harsh florescent lighting and gleaming tile floors to make you feel as if you are walking through a kaleidoscope. Each room is filled with kids and two staff, some of whom look very young, some of whom seem overwhelmed. Ratios are at state minimums and sometimes less at the beginning and end of the day. Salaries are low and staff turnover is high.

The infant room has lots of toys, rocking chairs, high chairs, and cribs. Babies seem to be held and soothed more than stimulated. Older babies are often discouraged from motor exploration. Schedules are only partially individualized. By nine or ten months old, all the children seem to be on the same schedule.

The toddler room is hard to be in as a visitor: Fourteen toddlers and two staff try very hard to do activities mostly suited to the older two year olds in the group. Biting and general distress seem to be common. Neither staff nor children seem particularly relaxed or happy.

For the most part, parents are happy with the center, except for staff turnover and biting, when the latter reaches epidemic levels. The moderate rates are a big attraction compared to the higher rates of the YWCA Children's Center and Barbara's Babes.

A couple of miles away, the same chain has a center that feels quite different. A new building has slightly more room and better lighting, giving it a homier feel. The young, enthusiastic director has managed to motivate the staff despite the low salaries. She has gotten the staff some training on developmentally appropriate care and the center is planning to try for NAEYC accreditation next year.

XYZ's Corporate Kids

The XYZ'S Corporate Child Care Center serves around 200 children and is housed in an 18,000-square-foot, state-of-the-art new building designed for child care. Parents enter with their children using their security badges. The building is new and impressive with lots of natural light, wide corridors, and bathrooms in each room; support space (offices and a staff lounge/workroom); a full kitchen; and a large, wraparound playground. There are two infant rooms, three toddler rooms, and two two-year-old rooms, all in a separate wing. The center also has six preschool and school-age rooms. Staff love the building except for one thing all too reminiscent of the less-advantaged programs they came from: small classrooms and cramped storage. New buildings are expensive per square foot, and once you add the support space, something has to go. Here it was classroom space and storage. There is multipurpose space available to reduce the number of children in the classroom.

Staff/child ratios are generally higher than state minimums, and group sizes are small. Salaries are the highest in the area except for the University Center. Staff have breaks and planning time built into their days. The program plans to be accredited by NAEYC.

The program feels good, if a bit formal and very large. Staff and children seem happy, and there is a lot of active learning taking place. Staff are well trained and enthusiastic. Some staff and parents wish that the center could be smaller and more informal, while others wish that there could be more interactions between children of different ages.

"How Can You Make Money off of Children?"

That question is asked both in outrage by some advocates and in curiosity by entrepreneurs. The United States has a market economy. Unlike schools but like health care, child care has always depended on a mixed system: for profit, nonprofit, and public child care. Some believe that for-profit child care is inherently negative; others believe that nonprofits and public child care offer unfair competition.

Is there a moral issue here? Perhaps for some, but the more important issues are quality for children and parents and good employment for care-givers. Providing low-quality services, exploiting staff, or gouging consumers to increase profits is indefensible. But so is the similar practice of some nonprofit agencies of assessing high overhead and indirect costs to child care departments. Whether you believe that we should have a national child care system like Sweden's or a completely market-driven system, it is important to judge child care providers by their practices, not their auspices.

Park Methodist

Established for low-income children, almost all Park Methodist's families receive subsidy to attend. The director at Park Methodist is constantly searching for potential support to supplement unpredictable state funding. Although the center is lodged in the church's basement, its rooms are good sized and renovated. The core staff have been there for over five years and live in the community. Staff/child ratios are at state minimums. Furnishings and equipment are adequate, although there is no playground area suitable for infants and toddlers.

The children seem to be prized by the caregivers, although there is more holding of infants than encouraging of active exploration. Young toddlers are treated much like the infants, and older toddlers much like the threes. There is quite a bit of correction and redirection.

Parents and staff are from the same community and often have relationships outside of child care. This is both a source of support and a problem because little that goes on at home or in the center is a secret for long.

Key Issues in Child Care

Cost, Quality, and Affordability

Obviously, there is a direct relationship between cost, quality, and affordability. Few centers can offer quality care without some source of support: public, an employer, United Way, a staff that stays despite minimal wages, or the unpaid "labor of love" that goes into a mom-and-pop center. It is also usual for the preschool rate to subsidize the infant and toddler rates. At XYZ Center and the YWCA, the cost of care is high ($190 weekly for an infant), and it shows in the quality of the program. XYZ and YWCA parents pay only $140 a week, still a very high rate for their area, although it is supplemented further by tuition assistance for moderate-income families. Barbara's Babes costs less ($150 a week), and her rate is also $140. Oak Park Kinder World has moderate rates—$120 weekly—and the program's struggle with untrained staff and turnover reflects the low rates. Nelson's Day Care home is certainly the best value ($130 weekly), but only a tiny, select group of families hear about the home and actually get in. Park Methodist's rates are on a par with Kinder World, but it has few private-pay families; most receive subsidy from the county.

"That's not Quality!"

"I thought that this center believed in quality and you are changing that," said the veteran teacher to the new director after hearing of the proposal to change the staff/infant ratio from one to three to one to four, a change suggested to cope with a budget crisis and to avoid falling further behind on staff salaries. "How can you do this to us?" she complained, refusing to listen to the director's explanation—that the recent extensive facility renovation may have boosted quality significantly enough to more than compensate for the ratio change.

"That's not quality" is sometimes hurled as a charge when change is suggested. In the real world, quality is a moving target. One program element—even one as important as ratios—is not a cast-in-stone quality determinant. The director ended up taking the teacher to visit two similar NAEYC accredited programs with one to four ratios and less supportive facilities to calm down the teacher. The visits moderated the teacher's feelings somewhat.

Quality is an outcome that is achieved through determination, creative thinking, and use of resources. It doesn't happen or look exactly the same way in all programs.

"We Are Not Just Day Care, We Are Educational!"

"We are not *just* day care!" is a refrain used by many homes and centers as well as by Head Start, nursery schools, and schools to enhance their image or set themselves apart from their competition. The five centers described above go to considerable lengths to assure parents that they are indeed early education centers. They want to make it clear that family child care and many other centers offer little more than custodial care. But is there such a thing as *just* day care? All child care is educational: Children learn something in every setting, whether we acknowledge it or not. That learning has implications for future learning. Is it all good education? No, some is actually quite awful. Many centers and homes are not adequately funded to provide good early education. Others may suffer from lack of understanding or ambition. Poor, underfunded learning environments provide poor educational experiences and, most often, poor care as well.

The program name or sponsor is no sure indicator of educational value. Good and bad care and education take place in child development centers, day care homes, academies, nursery schools, learning centers, and Montessori programs.

Individualized Care and Special Needs

Individualized care is a critical quality outcome for infants and toddlers (and parents). Recognizing, addressing, and appreciating differences are essential and will be stressed throughout this book. Children are all special, with special needs that occur as they participate in the child care program. Whether the special need is the result of a sleepless night, illness, separation problems, growth spurts, an injury, culture shock, individual differences in temperament and physiology, or a more serious and permanent condition, the result is the same: the program needs to fit the child.

Caregivers in most programs are likely to encounter infants and toddlers with special needs that are beyond the range of what is typical developmentally for the child's age: children with physical, emotional, or family needs that require even more individualized attention. Because infants and toddlers are so new to the world and in the first

stages of development, their special needs may not be suspected or identified prior to child care.

Caregivers have to understand that these children belong in child care; because of family need, because it's good for society not to isolate and segregate children with differing abilities, and because it's the law. The Americans with Disabilities Act (ADA) entitles people with disabilities to equal access to public services and public accommodations. Working parents of children with disabilities have the same need for child care that other parents do. Under ADA, programs have the responsibility to make reasonable accommodations to serve children and parents with disabilities. What is reasonable is in part determined by program resources, but it may involve extra training, facility accommodations, or changes in program operations, including staff/child ratios.

Providing child care to children with special needs is not the same as providing therapeutic or remedial services. The goals are the same as for any other child: high-quality care and education that fits each child's individual needs when the parents require child care. While some centers may be able to provide special therapeutic or developmental services by specialists, all programs should partner with parents to identify resources that allow the child access to services beyond child care.

Mainstreaming children with special needs (integrating them into regular programs) certainly makes sense for all the children in the program. They will learn more being around other children and are more likely to be seen as full human beings with different abilities. The other children benefit as well, both by being exposed to all sorts of children and by taking part in a program that recognizes and adapts to the special needs of all children.

Keep in mind when serving children with special needs that they will thrive in the least restrictive environment—that is, an environment that allows them to have experiences much like those of children without special needs.

Not all programs have the resources and expertise to serve all children. But what is important is that child care professionals understand and accept that it is normal and expected to serve children and families with a range of needs.

A Final Word: Quality Child Care Requires Financial Support

Improving child care at a societal level will require more financial support from somewhere, probably from *everywhere:* the public, employers, foundations, and parents. Issues of form of care (home or center); sponsorship of care (private, public, employers); for profit or nonprofit; program ideology; and even training have far less significance than the need for better funding. But funding will probably never be optimum, and all programs have the responsibility to maximize the resources that they have.

EXERCISES

1. Visit centers that represent the types of centers sketched in this chapter. Look for differences in philosophy and approach.

2. Interview three or four early education professionals and ask them what they see as the differences (if any) between "day care" and "preschool."

Chapter 2

Understanding How Child Care Centers Work: The Center as an Organization

The center maximizes both material and human resources by developing an organization and creating a culture that can provide good quality care over time for infants and toddlers.

Introduction

How many times have you heard or thought, "Good care for young children all boils down to good people"? This is certainly true for care in the child's home, fairly true in family day care, but only partly true in center-based care. Much has to be carefully thought through and organized before the "boiling down" that leads to good care for an infant or toddler.

Most people on the street have a simple conceptual model of good child care:

Is It Really This Simple?

good people (women?)
+ toys and books
+ adequate space (above ground, windows preferred but not essential)
_____
good child care

No!

Some of us in child care only elaborate this simple model slightly: "Enough" means good staff/child ratios (and group sizes), "good" people means trained, well-paid people, "toys" are educational materials, and space should be better than minimal. But the simple model is far too simple, at least for centers serving over twenty children.

The Elements of an Organization

What children and parents experience over time in a center is a reflection of organizational quality, not just individual "person" quality. People come and go, but the framework they work within continues. This framework is more than the building and equipment and includes the systems, policies, routines, and cultures of the center— "the way we do things here." Organizational quality ensures that good people are hired, stay, grow on the job, and receive the support to perform well. Children (and parents) are well cared for.

Human Resources

Those good people—where do they all come from? What is the talent pool that the center draws from? Why do staff stay at the center? How do they become good or get better at caring for young children?

Good child care for infants and toddlers is built around good people performing well and staying at the center. The talent pool—the population eligible and available to draw employees from—varies from center to center based on the demographics of the area, the center's requirements for the job, and the desirability of the center as a workplace. When a center is having trouble finding good people, what "good" is may have to be reconsidered; perhaps the definition is too

---

Dimensions of Organizations

Human Resources
people: number, quality
talent pool available,
continuity (turnover)

Physical Resources
facility
outdoors equipment
community resources

Organizational Structures and Systems
distribution of people and things
distribution of responsibility, authority, and information
decision-making process

Organizational Culture
"The way we do things here"
shared beliefs, values, goals
expectations for behavior, norms
myths, taboos
relationships to community, other organizations

---

narrow. Are there good caregivers for infants and toddlers out there who simply lack credentials? Are there older people, people of different cultures or with different backgrounds? Is your center a good place to work if someone is relatively old or young, male, or of a particular ethnic group?

Physical Resources

Infant and toddler care happens in a place filled with furnishings and equipment. That site doesn't exist in isolation. What are its surroundings like? Are there resources to be tapped—sidewalks, parks, libraries? Are there negative elements to be screened out and avoided—toxic land, smells, unsavory people, harmful animals or pests?

Organizational Structures and Systems

Resources have to be distributed. How are people distributed throughout the center? Beyond simple ratios and where people go, what about staff expertise and talent? The distribution of knowledge, authority, responsibility, and information involves choices that may lead to greater or lesser quality. Does a teacher's skill at curriculum or organization go beyond her group of infants and toddlers? Are program and homebase decisions made by isolated individuals, a small team, everyone involved, or often not made at all but merely assumed out of fear of conflict, simple inertia, or unquestioning acceptance of past practices?

The distribution of physical resources obviously involves choices that have implications for quality. What determines the use of particular spaces and equipment: decisions made long ago and not revisited, staff seniority or the force of assertive personalities, interpersonal relationships or staff politics? It is not uncommon to discover that staff who have been there the longest have the most resources and that the use of multipurpose space depends on the relationships between caregivers.

Information always flows. But without systems, communication may be intermittent and follow lines of happenstance or friendship, leading to confusion, misunderstandings, ill will, gossip, and missed opportunities.

Organizational Culture

"That's just the way we do things here." Organizations, like societies, have cultures that shape the way their members think, feel, and behave. One can go to two programs and see very similar people, yet one program feels relaxed and fun loving, accepting and creative; the other, efficient and businesslike, formal and industrious, and rather regimented.

One program may have a drive for excellence; another is just getting by. Programs vary greatly in the way people treat each other:

relations may be respectful and caring or the opposite, formal or informal, collegial or distant.

Some programs have no real culture and little sense of program. Individual caregivers set the tone in their rooms. One room feels very different from another and changes as the people change. Or the overall tone is set by the director and changes when the director changes.

◆ At Babyland Child Care, Mary and Alicia have a fairly low tolerance for noise and bursts of movement, and their toddler room reflects that. They also generally do what they have been doing for the past ten years. They are friendly with other staff and parents but seek little input into their practices. Anne's and Melina's room couldn't be more different. Toddlers are all over—climbing, jumping, hauling—and the teachers are always seeking out new ideas and critical reactions.

◆ At Child's Garden, the center has worked hard for over twenty years to establish a consistent culture. Reading through the parent handbook, looking at signs on the wall, observing in each classroom, sitting in on meetings and reading newsletters, visitors discover that everyone who works there buys into the same basic ideas: Messy, active play is essential. Teachers throughout the center work together, use each other's good ideas, and look for ways to inject fun and humor into the day. Children are treated with respect. Unfortunately, parents are at best junior partners. All staff believe that the

"I Thought It Would Always be Fun!"

Alison worked at the Oak Ridge Center for five years before moving to another highly respected program, the Front Street Center, for a slightly better salary and benefits. A year later, she went back to the original program despite its lower compensation because of the differences in program cultures:

It was a good program at Front Street and I liked most of the staff, but it just wasn't much fun. It's hard to describe. At the new center, we were slightly more formal with each other, less spontaneous, not as loose. I felt that I couldn't be as goofy as I normally am with the children or as free conversationally with the parents. Staff worked well together but in a much more businesslike way. It wasn't bad, the kids were great, it just wasn't as much fun.

The difference in the two programs' culture was real enough to send Alison back to her previous job. Other staff at Front Street loved the culture and what went with the formality. They felt that it was a truly professional place with a sense of decorum and seriousness of purpose that led parents to take staff seriously without being stuffy (although Alison would disagree—"It was a little stuffy," she said).

To an outsider, the differences were pretty subtle and hard to identify. To Alison, they were real enough to make a difference.

Some Dimensions of Organizational Culture

Formality
procedures
communication
use of written documentation
humor and whimsy
appearance

Work Ethic
achievement oriented
fast/slow pace
career/job orientation

Thinking/Doing
analyze-question/just do
problem solving/just do
why not try?/why change?

Maintain Status Quo/Innovation
seek/welcome new ideas
constructive conflict/avoid conflict
make waves/smooth waters
improvement driven
risk taking

Authority/Power
empower/control others
top down/bottom up/mutual
trust/mistrust
grow people

Staff Relations
professional
collegial/individual
team/hierarchical
respect/trust

Parent Relations
individuals
us/them, partners/allies
defensive/open
formal/informal
client/customer/nuisance

Child Relations
people/"cute pets"
teaching/learning focus
control behavior/empower
individual/group focus
value action/value passivity

Reactions to the Outside
open/closed to ideas
open/closed to people
open/closed to community resources

parent role is to support the program, not to offer advice or guidance. The hiring and socialization reinforces the program culture.

Becoming Good

The goal of a child care center or any organization is *organizational quality:* organizational resources, systems, and culture that maximize resources and maintain quality for children and parents as staff come and go. Creative program directors use all four dimensions to achieve quality outcomes, using strengths in one dimension to overcome weaknesses in another.

For example, most child care programs have trouble maintaining quality over the course of the ten to twelve-hour day. Often quality deteriorates in the afternoon. Why? Because most of the senior staff often work early shifts, and children (and staff) may be worn out and anticipating the arrival of parents by late afternoon. What to do? This problem can be attacked in a number of ways, some of which have higher costs, others of which may inspire staff resistance.

◆ Human resources can be added or upgraded. Improve the adult/ child ratios or hire more qualified staff for the late afternoon shift.

◆ Physical resources can be improved. Purchase "special," very attractive equipment that increases the environment's ability to engage the children just for late afternoon use.

◆ Resources can be distributed differently. Reschedule staff for a better balance of expertise in the late afternoon or rethink the use of physical resources, perhaps trading toys between rooms.

◆ Talent and authority can be distributed differently. The afternoon can be made the clear responsibility of the lead teacher as supervisor and planner, whether or not she works those hours.

◆ Cultural change may be necessary: the afternoon hours need to be established in people's minds as learning/caring times just as valuable as the traditional nursery school learning times of 9:30 to 11:30 in the morning.

Nearly every exercise in program design or problem solving benefits from using a multi-dimensional approach because there are different routes to quality. Staff/child ratios, room size, quality of the facility and equipment, staff expertise, leadership, and organizational systems are interactive factors. Budgets rarely permit us to have what we want in all those areas. By using resources strategically, particularly funding, we can maximize our quality.

A Final Word: Staying Good

Quality is most easily maintained if good staff are selected and stay. This usually happens when the center is a good place to work relative to other child care and employees feel valued and fulfilled by the work.

How does a center stay good if good people leave? Obviously, by hiring good people to replace them. Less obviously, by making sure much of what those good people who left brought to the center—their ideas, visions, attitudes—stays with the center. In a quality organization, a number of things happen:

◆ information, ideas, and know-how are not permitted simply to reside in people's heads, lost to the program when they are absent from or leave the others. The ideas are put into charts, handbooks, videos, prop boxes, and scrapbooks.

◆ good systems, routines, and practices are *institutionalized* so that they become a part of center life and don't cease to exist because of the whims of individuals: for example, the diapering procedure, parent notes, staff appreciation days, and collaborative planning of the playground.

◆ *active intelligence* is prized. Issues are brought up, old ideas reconsidered, new expertise, ideas, and ways of doing things are sought to avoid the dark side of institutionalization—stagnation and mindlessness.

◆ program cultures grow out of conscious effort to take those good things that are occurring and build them into the life of the program. That culture shapes the next generation of program employees.

EXERCISES

1. Characterize your organizational culture in terms of
   ◆ authority
   ◆ status quo/innovation
   ◆ openness
   ◆ staff relations

2. Identify a way to better distribute the talent and expertise that exist in your program.

3. Approach your homebase as a substitute might. What expectations are clear? What practices or routines might be viewed as confusing or illogical?

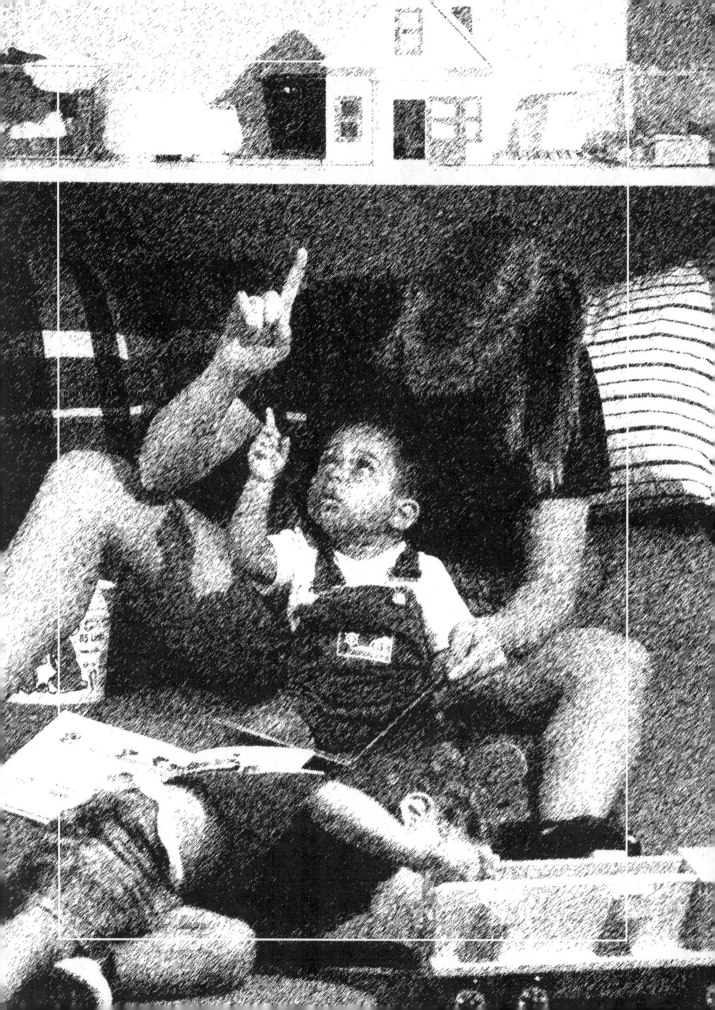

Chapter 3
Goals, Characteristics and Assumptions in a Quality Program

excellence

A clear vision of quality, understood by all staff and parents, that actively guides program practice. This vision is reflected in eight characteristics of quality:

1. Noninstitutional "place for a childhood."
2. Fundamental concern with the health and safety of all children in care.
3. Individualized, personalized responsive care and affection for each child.
4. Active, individualized, developmentally appropriate learning.
5. Flexible, responsive services to parents.
6. Empowered and respected parents.
7. Supportive and professional work environment.
8. Fundamental respect for all people and for the world we live in.

Introduction

Good-quality care for infants and toddlers rests on goals, values, assumptions, and principles that guide the program in all its complexity. The vision of quality extends beyond a concern for good care, education, health, and safety to the children's total development, including the relationship between each child and family and the quality of life during each child's one and only early childhood. The vision acknowledges the fact that children and families exist within discrete as well as overlapping cultures, that cultures differ, and that all cultures deserve respect. The curriculum or program is thought of as encompassing the total experience of the children in care, not just the relatively small portion of the day when they may be engaged in so-called educational activities.

There is another important fact to keep in mind: *Child care can't be good for children without being good for parents and caregivers.* Warm, supportive, and respectful relationships between adults and between adults and children lie at the heart of good care for children. A good center pays attention to *human* needs.

Where Does the Vision of Quality Come From?

Infant group and toddler group care are fairly new as social forms, at least compared to schools and preschools. Because many of us come to them with more experiences with preschoolers and older children, we often don't know quite what infants and toddler groups should be like—sort of homey schools? classrooms with cots and baby toys?

Assumptions for a Quality Child Care Program

Four assumptions underlie the goals of a quality infant/toddler program and bring into focus the critical distinctions that distinguish child care from other early education programs.

Basic Assumption 1: Good homes are good models for infant and toddler group care. The most useful conceptualization is that the best group care setting for a baby's development is one that approximates a good home environment. Keeping this in mind is particularly important in light of continued pressure to provide early education in its narrowest sense. A good home is wonderfully educational, a good place for infants and toddlers to learn nearly all they need to know.

Of course, there are considerable differences between an in-home experience in a child's own family and a group care experience, but it is worth reminding ourselves what a good experience growing up in one's own family is like: the activities and experiences offered as well as the physical and human environments. The good home is a rich, multisensory environment with lots of opportunity for exploration, discovery, and movement. Housekeeping chores, such as preparing and serving food, setting the table, going shopping, helping with younger children, cleaning up, and folding linen, create a sense of belonging through participation in the meaningful work of the home. These same tasks can be incorporated into the daily experience of the children at the center with the same result: a sense of belonging and community.

Basic Assumption 2: Learning and care are inseparable, and both occur nonstop during the day. In schools for older children, learning and care are often considered as separate. Learning is seen as flowing from teaching and as occurring during circle time "work" or playtime. The period from 9:30 to 11:30 is often deemed the best time to learn. In good child care, there is no such separation. The interactions during diapering or mealtime, late afternoon play, cuddling to ease the pain of the latest bump are all learning times.

Basic Assumption 3: Infants and toddlers are very different from older children.   Children under three are sensory-motor beings without the developmental skills for large group living. Most of their learning involves movement and direct sensory experience. Group care is not a necessary developmental experience for babies; it is instead a modern necessity for families. Children under three can thrive in spite of group care because the center has successfully individualized care and learning and broken down the negative institutional effects of group care.

Basic Assumption 4: Child care settings are not schools but places to live.   Child care centers are places where adults and children live together for eight to ten hours a day, most weeks of the year, for a number of years. Are they also educational places? Yes! But formal education is only one part of living, and education is not the same thing as schooling nor is teaching the same thing as learning. With schooling we associate teaching, instruction, and socialization focused on adapting to the requirements of group life. Child care centers for young children are primarily places for learning and discovering, not for teaching.

Goals for Children and Parents

Program goals for children and parents are a statement of what really matters to the program, reference points for assessing whether the policies or practices are achieving what we hope to achieve. What would nearly all parents like to see nurtured in their young children?

◆ a sense of belonging to the family, with primary attachments to the parents and other family members.

◆ the capacity to trust people, to feel secure when away from home and with people other than family members. Security implies that children trust their parents will return when they go away and trust the people in whose care they have been placed by the parents.

◆ enjoyment of other people, sensitivity to people's feelings, acceptance of diversity, the beginnings of a caring and respectful approach that leads to a capacity to interact effectively.

◆ a positive sense of themselves as important persons who are cared about, who are able to control their own behavior to some extent, and who have an effect on the social and physical world (mastery).

◆ the ability to comprehend language and other forms of communication, to give and seek information, to ask questions, to convey needs, wants, and feelings, and to communicate in ways that can be understood by others.

◆ the ability to solve simple problems and the beginning of an understanding of how the world works.

◆ competence in using the body and hands.

◆ autonomy and independence, the ability to think and act with pleasure and competence by themselves.

In addition, what do parents need for themselves?

◆ a feeling of recognition from the program that they are the most important people in their children's lives.

◆ a sense of control over and involvement in their children's care, even when they are not present.

◆ a sense of confidence that they are capable of navigating the complex waters of modern parenthood.

"What About My Values?"

Staff in a program may not always agree about the ins and outs of good care. After all, we don't always agree as parents or as citizens. The more diversity in staff backgrounds, the wider the likely range of beliefs and values. Whether little boys and girls should be treated differently, the value of competition, how much children should be allowed to assert themselves, and how independent they are encouraged to be are just a few of the areas where differences are likely to occur.

It should be okay for staff to be different and to believe different things. However, it is also important that *the program* have a clear, articulated point of view and goals that all staff understand and accept. These may necessitate defining those areas where staff do not have to behave alike. Acceptance means agreeing to follow program guidelines for behavior, including those areas where individuals may have to adapt their own caregiving practices.

Characteristics of a High-Quality Center

These goals are easier to achieve if the care of infants and toddlers is guided by an appropriate vision. The following statement of quality characteristics forms the core of what we regard as a good experience for young children.

A Noninstitutional "Place for a Childhood"

Every child deserves a childhood. Children in group institutional care deserve a time of magic and wonder, of safety and security in which to discover what life has to offer. The center should offer the right mix of freedom and restraint, exuberance and serenity, and an abundance of warmth and laughter. Children are not entirely fenced off from the world of people and nature or regimented into routines and activities based on group or institutional requirements.

Program characteristics include

◆ a place that is warm, soft, and aesthetically pleasing.

◆ a relaxed, home-like rather than school-like atmosphere (with, for example, informality, flexible use of space and time, minimal lining up, waiting, and doing the same thing at the same time).

◆ a variety of places to spend time, places with different "feels" because of light, texture, smell, enclosure; places that allow different movement; beautiful places.

◆ opportunities to spend time with siblings and people of different ages.

◆ connections to the broader community and use of community resources.

A Fundamental Concern with the Health and Safety of All Children in Care

Children deserve a safe and healthy environment designed to allow opportunity to explore, be challenged, and take reasonable risks without threat of serious injury or illness. Therefore, program practices should include

◆ continuous monitoring of the physical environment, equipment and materials, and caregiving practices to ensure health and safety.

◆ appropriate supervision of children to minimize accidents.

◆ appreciation of the tension between providing a totally accident-, injury-, and illness-proof environment and children's need to explore and to take reasonable risks in order to develop.

Individualized, Personalized, Responsive Care and Affection for Each Child

The essential sense of trust and security for children (and parents) is built on care that is responsive, nurturing, and appropriate to each child *when the child needs it*. Each child is viewed in the context of family and culture, and all caring practices and interactions are designed to empower the child and to promote a positive sense of self. Practices that sustain personalized care include

◆ primary caregivers as advocates for child and parents, as quality monitors, and as vehicles for parental influence.

◆ flexible, individualized schedules and routines.

◆ personal rituals between child and caregiver.

◆ caregiving practices tailored to the characteristics of each child.

◆ continuity of caregivers.

◆ consistency of care practices between home and care.

Active, Individualized, Developmentally Appropriate Learning

Children are not the same, and each child deserves a full range of developmentally appropriate experiences, free of stereotypes or limits based on race, sex, and ethnicity. Program practices that promote individualized, appropriate learning include

◆ an emphasis on learning environments and child-choice curriculum (not an activity-based, teacher-directed, or diagnostic curriculum).

◆ an emphasis on natural, authentic experiences and interactions.

◆ an environment rich in written and spoken language experiences.

◆ an emphasis on hands-on, "mind-on," active learning.

◆ a generous allowance for child mobility, messy play, and challenge.

◆ extensive use of the outdoors.

◆ use of caring routines as times for play and learning.

◆ exposure to cultural diversity through materials, interactions, and experiences.

Flexible, Responsive Services to Parents

Child care is foremost a service to parents who need assistance in caring for their children. Because families are not the same, program hours, services, and policies should be designed according to the needs of families. Program practices include

◆ hours and services reflecting parents' needs.

◆ periodic surveys of parents' service needs.

Empowered and Respected Parents

The program respects and understands parents and is sensitive to family beliefs and values. It recognizes the need for a true partnership with parents and is responsive to individual and collective parents' needs, requests, and concerns about the care and education of the children. Parents are encouraged to contribute, make suggestions, and have influence over their children's care. Program practices include

- primary caregivers who are responsive to parents.
- daily written and verbal communication systems.
- individual systems that allow parents to monitor and evaluate quality.
- individual parent conferences and group parent meetings.
- a range of efforts to solicit parent ideas, concerns, and information about family and cultural practices.

A Supportive and Professional Work Environment

Staff feel secure, valued, and respected as professionals doing a difficult job that involves both thinking and doing. Teamwork and collegiality are valued and supported. Individual strengths and needs are acknowledged, respected, and addressed. Program characteristics include

- clearly articulated roles and responsibilities.
- supportive supervision.
- communication mechanisms for program planning, evaluating, and problem solving.
- mechanisms for regular staff input into policies and procedures.
- times and places for planning, meeting, and time away from children.
- professional development experiences.

A Culture of Respect for All People and for the World We Live in

Good child care develops good people and a vision of a good society. It strives to serve the widest range of children and families. It is important that policies, practices, and curriculum promote

- a nonsexist, nonbiased approach that understands, values, and respects other cultures and individual differences.
- conservation and respect for the physical environment and preservation of the natural world.

A Final Word: Quality Comes from a Comprehensive Vision

Every program needs its own vision of quality that becomes reflected in the child's day, the daily interchange between parents and staff, and the way participants feel about themselves and each other as they go about the business of living and working in the world of child care. Everything about the center should be considered in light of this vision of quality: how it looks, sounds, and what it expects from its members.

The Logic of an Environmentally-Based Program

While the most important ingredient in good care for babies is the quality of the staff who work with the children, what separates high-quality programs from others, if staff/child ratios, group size, and staff qualifications are relatively equal, is often not the caregivers but the overall quality of the environment that allows caregivers to give good care. A good environment works *for* the caregiver and the child, and helps further goals. Some assumptions behind environmentally based programming include

◆ an environment set up to allow the child to independently explore, discover, and play also allows the staff to focus on PRIME TIMES, those moments of one-to-one care and learning that lie at the heart of healthy development. Rushing through diaper changing, dressing, or consoling a child in distress in order to get back to teaching or managing children is the opposite of what should happen. Those are the times to draw out, talk, listen, touch, and reassure. So, too, is the time when a baby makes an important new discovery: Alexi discovers his hand, or Marie explores consonant sounds. A rich, responsive learning environment set up to engage other children with valuable learning experiences allows one child to have the full human presence of a caregiver to encourage and share the delight of discovery.

◆ neither infants nor toddlers benefit particularly from large groups. Three is a large group for a baby. An environmentally based program allows simultaneous individual play, pair play, and small-group play and minimizes the times when all children are doing the same thing or spending time as part of a crowd.

◆ an all-day program has many hours in which to build learning experiences into the program. There is no need to rush experiences and no point in concentrating them into a limited part of the day.

An environmentally based program assumes that children learn from the entire experience the day provides. The way time and space are structured, the routines, the furnishings, the equipment and materials, and all the ways adults and children behave teach young children what the world is like, how it works, what they are capable of, and their place within it.

A good environment is planned to support all the care and learning we would like to see take place. Much of the caregivers' planning revolves around how to build learning into the environment. What furnishings will provide learning in themselves, such as a couch serving as a walking rail? What equipment will create a sensory or reaching/kicking activity center? While some adult-initiated and -led activities take place, such as a simple cooking experience or sensory play with finger paints, the program should not be activity based, that is, structured around activity times or groups. Music may take place anytime, as will some large motor experiences. Activities take place individually and in small groups within an environment rich with built-in learning. In other words, it is not that the program happens in the environment; rather, the program *is* the environment.

EXERCISES

1. List how infants and toddlers benefit developmentally from daily life in a good home.

2. Take the first and eighth characteristics for quality and apply them to your program. What characteristics support or contradict the principle?

3. Take any of the eight characteristics and add to the list of program practices that amplify it.

Part 2
Organizing the Program

Chapter 4

Understanding Infants and Toddlers

Caregiving based on knowledge of and enthusiastic appreciation for

✔ **the developmental characteristics of children under three years old.**
✔ **the wide variation in individual differences.**
✔ **the wide variation in normal development.**
✔ **the unique qualities and style of each child.**

Introduction

Quality infant and toddler care programs value children for what they can do right now, not for what they will be able to do or are in the process of becoming. They truly enjoy infants and toddlers for their strengths rather than their vulnerabilities and accept their most challenging characteristics, always viewing them in a positive way.

Getting to Know Infants and Toddlers

In a good program, caregivers know about the important skills infants and toddlers are acquiring, recognize and delight in these when they occur, and provide many opportunities for children to use them when they are ready. They know that young children rarely need to be taught skills or pushed to perform. Rather, they simply need opportunities, occasional help, and people who can enjoy their success and achievements with them.

Staff in good programs also guard against the natural tendency to overemphasize the dramatic milestones, such as the first step and the first word, at the expense of all the small, visible and invisible achievements essential to healthy development.

Development Is Not a Race

When did you take your first step? Were you a biter or a hapless victim of a biter? When did you start using words? And just for the record, when were you toilet trained?

Early childhood is a time when parents and caregivers watch development closely, caring intensely about many things. Unfortunately, often these are things that have no developmental importance. There is no future developmental advantage and rarely any significance to early achievement of most milestones. As parents, we cringe when our little Johnny's same-age cousin Tommy is saying "Mom," "Da Da," and "Pass the cookies" while Johnny is happily smiling and only infrequently producing nonsense words. Or when Jenny down the street is out for a stroll while our Alice only creeps along. But Johnny may become the orator and Alice the track star because *earlier is not better.*

Normal development assumes many different forms and proceeds at a pace appropriate to each child. Albert Einstein hardly said a word before three, and Mohammed Ali began walking at fourteen months. Yes, we should look for signs of developmental delays that possibly signify physiological problems. But that alertness does not have to create a climate of comparison, competition, and worry.

Infants and Toddlers Can Do Many Things

From birth, infants are marvelous learners, immediately investigating the sights, sounds, and feel of the world. Long before the big steps of walking and first words for infants and of true social play and first sentences for toddlers, they are exploring their own bodily powers and what this world is made of. Some of the many things an infant does include the following:

see	watch
look	inspect
hear	listen
smell	taste
feel	touch
mouth	eat
reach out	reach for
knock away	grasp
hold	squeeze
pinch	drop
pull up	shake
bang	tear
clap together	put in
take out	find
look for	kick
turn	roll
lift head up	sit up
transfer from one hand to the other	crawl to, in, out, over

creep around, in, under	swing
rock	coo
babble	react to others
imitate sounds and simple actions	solicit from others
recognize people and things	experiment endlessly

In addition to many of the above, toddlers may also do the following:

walk in, out, up, down, over, under, around, through	climb in, up, over, on top
	slide
swing	hang
jump	tumble
take apart	put together
stack	pile
nest	set up
knock over	collect
gather	fill
dump	inspect
examine	select
sort	match
order	carry
transport	rearrange
put	take out
hide	discover
investigate by trial and error	explore with each sense
imitate familiar acts	imitate adult behavior
engage in doll play	paint
smear	draw
mix	separate
pour	sift
splash	make sounds and labels
label	"read" symbols
converse	follow directions
cuddle	hug
kiss	test others
adjust their behavior to others	help themselves to wash, eat, dress

Toddlers Are not Infants (or Preschoolers, Either!)

Toddlers are child care's equivalent of young adolescents. Their behavior is uneven, often giving the appearance of more maturity than the children actually possess. The frequent result is that adults expect them to act maturely all the time. The tendency in many toddler programs is to treat the children as if they were preschoolers, only smaller and less competent. Their "collective monologues" (talking at each other but not with each other), their frequently parallel and sometimes cooperative play, their bursts of understanding and their sometimes remarkable willingness to cooperate and please mask the substantial differences between two year olds and four year olds.

Neither infants nor preschoolers, toddlers are increasingly mobile, autonomous, social, verbal, thoughtful creatures with constant urges to test and experiment. They are living contradictions: the erratic "do it myself" desire competes with the passive and completely dependent "you do it." They are prone to change their minds about what they want. These restless, mobile characters have a drive to take apart the existing order and to rearrange it, by force if necessary, to suit their own whimsically logical view of the universe. They are often charming and engaging but at times determinedly defiant or out of control with frustration or anger. Toddlers are very exciting people to work with, but their stage of development brings with it many challenges and considerable frustration for both the child and the child's caregivers.

Always Keep in Mind

Infants and toddlers are very eager, competent learners. They need less stimulation from adults and more respect, time, and materials for their learning.

> If you are concerned only with stimulation, with doing something to the baby, you ignore a vital requirement for learning and development: that babies need to discover that they can influence the people around them. Yes, they need stimulation, which they get from objects and more importantly from people. But they need to perceive their own involvement in these stimulating experiences. When stimulation is provided without regard to the baby's response, the baby is being treated as an object.
>
> . . . . Education results when, in T. Berry Brazelton's words, a baby finds 'the pleasure of being the cause'; of learning how to act in order to produce the results he wants, of learning about things that are the results of his own actions. When you respond to a child's language or gestures, or participate in her explorations of space, the child develops a sense of power (Gonzalez-Mena and Eyer, 1980, p. 45).

Infants and toddlers are sensory-motor beings. They explore the world with their developing senses and motor skills. Long before they understand a concept like "under" or "far" with their minds, their bodies are learning to move in and understand the up and down, over and under physical world. Sensory exploration expands the world that once had only a few categories, such as things to suck and not to suck, into a complex, meaningful place with textures, colors, sounds, weight, uses, and many other qualities.

Infants and toddlers are communicators. They begin with the birth cry and continually expand their range of signals and messages, both those they use and those they understand. In the first year of life, crying and gurgling rapidly become sophisticated sounds and gestures. Babies learn language by hearing lots of it in individual conversations and by having people around who listen to them and respond to their efforts to communicate.

Infants and toddlers are social beings. Their communication is directed at those they love and need, the adults who care for them, and soon the other large and small people with whom they share the world. It is the give and take of communication that connects babies to the world of other people. But they are not quite yet social in the sense that older children are, and therefore they are not very well suited to cope with group experiences.

Infants and toddlers are people with feelings. They may not understand most language or the motives of others, but they are very sensitive to tones and feelings expressed in language and body language. They experience feelings of rejection, anger, jealousy, humiliation, and hurt. They, like us, thrive on love, empathy, praise, and appreciation.

Infants and toddlers come with parents and families. All of our efforts to understand and care for children require that we view them in the context of their families—their values, culture, and circumstances.

Expectations and Responses

Creating a good place for infants and toddlers—a relaxed, nurturing, and learning environment—depends on having appropriate expectations. This means expecting infants to behave as infants and toddlers as toddlers, with all the typical variations that individuals present.

Expectations for Infants

Quality child care is based on an understanding of and appreciation for the natural behavior of children. Expect babies to

- *be different from each other.* Children will differ in interests, moods, pace, ability to signal how they feel, how they learn, how they react to change, and the care they need.
- *cry to communicate.* Crying is the way infants let us know they need our help. They don't cry just to annoy us.
- *desperately need us.* Being allowed to remain in distress is not good for infants and is likely to lead to increased crying. It works against the feeling of basic trust and security that provide the foundation for healthy development.
- *explore.* A continuous curiosity fuels the process of learning about the world.
- *test all limits.* Babies learn how the world works by testing the reactions of people and things to their actions.
- *experiment with their bodies.* They use their growing physical powers to test the properties of people, things, and space. They *need* to crawl, walk, run, kick, step up and down, move, stack, drop

and throw things, take things apart, fit themselves and things
inside of other things, and climb in and over, if they are to learn.

◆ *experiment with their senses.* The mouth, eyes, ears, and skin are
the tools babies use to learn. They *need* to touch, taste, feel, look,
and listen to the world. Babies' mouths and whole bodies are their
chief tools (for example, sucking on everything, testing the feel of
baby food or paint on the cheek or the stomach).

Additional Expectations for Toddlers

When we think of toddlers as being "in between" babies and pre-schoolers (Gonzalez-Mena and Eyer, 1986) or as resembling old babies or immature three year olds, we sell them short. We end up programming for them in ways that are either not interesting or challenging, or that are too sophisticated and that frustrate them. Either way, we may develop negative views of toddlers, defining their competence as the problem ("they are bored—they need to move up") or by defining them through what they lack: preschool skills. We need to think of the toddler stage of development as one with integrity, having its own particular characteristics, strengths, and needs.

Expect toddlers to

♦ *explore with energy.* Their new competence and curiosity often lead to sheer exuberance and bursts of energy.

♦ *explode with frustration.* Too few or too many choices, challenges, obstacles, too much or too little power can be overwhelming for toddlers. Frustration comes easily when they are blocked because internal controls and patience come slowly.

♦ *dawdle.* Whether to "smell the roses," to examine a curious object never noticed before or even a familiar, favorite one, to assert themselves, or because they have little sense of time, toddlers often dawdle.

♦ *lose control of themselves.* When the world caves in on toddlers, for whatever reason, they often desperately need reassurance, whether they are stuck in a tantrum of rage or an inconsolable pit of despair.

♦ *be contrary.* "No" is a declaration of independence. Toddlers refuse your requests, defy you, and resist your control because they are learning that they can exert some control. They are learning how to be assertive. This is an important step in learning self-control.

♦ *change moods.* So much change is happening for them, inside and out, that it is natural for toddlers to swing from being sweet and compliant to being little tyrants, from joy to rage, and from being needy babies to being seemingly mature helpers and comforters of others.

♦ *act fearful.* As their thinking develops and they move into the world, they discover that it has scary elements.

♦ *act powerful.* Toddlers begin to understand that they can cause things to happen or not happen, do things on their own, create things, go places, and get strong positive and negative reactions from people. When they discover these powers, they want to use them, and it is hard for them to learn how to use them appropriately.

♦ *experience separation intensely at times.* The pain of separating from parents may be present at times. The intensity varies from day to day and from hour to hour. It is likely to be strongest in the morning, at sleep times, and at the end of the day.

Alike and Different

The importance of expecting children to be different and of basing care on that expectation is so critical that it cannot be stressed enough. Infants new to the world not only look different: they come to us with different parents, genders, cultures, temperaments, learning styles, physiologies, physical abilities, rates of development, special needs, and on and on. Of course, children are also alike in lots of ways, so much of our caring behavior is based on our experience with other children. But that is only the starting point until we come to know the individual child.

Gonzalez-Mena and Eyer (1993) point out that understanding how children are fundamentally different

> Temperament (inborn characteristics that incline us toward specific emotional responses) can help us understand why there are differences in infants' crying, activity, cuddliness, and so on.
> . . . . The best-known work in this area was done by Thomas, Chess, and Birch (1970) in the early 1970s. They described three basic temperaments that can be observed early in life. The *easy* baby is adaptable, approachable, and positive in mood. The *slow-to-warm-up* baby is first negative in new situations but, with time and patience, eventually adapts. Such children may seem withdrawn, but, with time, they adjust just fine. The *difficult* child (approximately ten percent of babies) often is in a negative mood, is unpredictable (especially eating and sleeping habits), and has intense and irritable reactions to new settings and people (p. 160).

Gonzalez-Mena and Eyer point out that while temperament inclines babies to behave in certain ways, these characteristics may not last or predict later behavior. Our personality is shaped by continuous interaction between our temperament and our environment. The care children receive will shape their personalities. *Difficult* babies are not destined to be difficult adults, provided they receive care that adapts to their needs. Without sensitive caregiving, however, they are at risk for developing attachment problems.

Difficult babies illustrate how alike children are. They come with parents (or guardians). We cannot do well by children without always seeing them in the context of their families. A *difficult* child is not an easy child to attach to, and the child's parents will need all of our support and understanding. In fact, supporting the parent-child relationship may be more important for the child's future than anything that we do for the child at the center.

What Infants and Toddlers Need Most the First Two Years of Life

There are so many "shoulds" in caring for young children. What are those needs that stand out as critical?

A Sense of Basic Trust   The first year of life is when children need to acquire what psychologist Erik Erikson called "basic trust" (1950)—a feeling of safety and security that the world and oneself are all right. Basic trust comes from responsive, predictable care from familiar others whom one loves and to whom one is deeply attached. Without this sense, the world is far too scary a place to cope with and learn about. All self-esteem, all courage to accept challenges are founded on developing a profound, basic trust.

Bruno Bettelheim (1969, p. 63) suggested that in a group setting, security derives from the feeling that we can safely relax, that we need not worry. To "safely relax," a baby needs to feel "at home." In the words of a hypothetical young child,

> This is my place. I know these people. They know me and they like me, despite my crying and diarrhea and difficulty going to sleep. I can count on them to take care of me, to respond to me. I can be me here, with all my own quirks, and still be accepted. I will be safe here, and I can step out and explore this strange and mysterious world.

What makes a feeling of home is that sense of familiarity, acceptance, safety, of being with people you know and care about and who care about you.

Opportunities with the World of Things and People Young children need a safe world where, as Jerome Bruner (1973, p. 8) said, they are "encouraged to venture, rewarded for [their] own acts, and sustained against distraction or premature interferences in carrying them out." Children need a world rich with opportunities to see, hear, feel, touch, and move, to undertake all the actions listed earlier. They need a setting where they will feel the world at their fingertips, that this is a world to explore and enjoy.

Movement is essential. Moving around gives infants the different perspectives and vantage points that they need to move from an entirely egocentric view of space and to develop a more sophisticated sense of the relations between self, space, and other people. We know that objects are the same regardless of the angle or the distance from which we observe them, regardless of whether they are bathed by sunlight or blanketed by shadows, but infants do not.

A Sense of Autonomy Autonomy is the sense of being a separate, independent self. Infants and toddlers need to begin to feel this:

> I'm a me, a self separate from my mom and dad and my caregivers. I can have an impact on this huge world. If I can say "No" freely, I can also say "Yes" freely. I can use my powers so that I can begin to control this body and these feelings.

A Sense of Power and Competence Only when children feel a personal sense of power—"I can make things happen," "I can make a difference"—and competence—"I can do things and achieve things"—can they step out into the world as active learners and problem solvers, prepared to cope with what will come.

It is in group settings that all of us are most likely to feel powerless. Giving children choices—the freedom to move, the chance to try things, the power to get us to respond to their physical and emotional needs—tells them that they are people who make a difference. Giving

them an opportunity to do things successfully—for example, get unstuck from under a table, put on a coat, or carry a basket of bread rolls—tells them that they are capable.

What Infants and Toddlers Need Most from the Program: *Responsive, Nurturing Care*

Over twenty-five years ago, Mary Elizabeth Keister (1970) in *The "Good Life" for Infants and Toddlers* eloquently described what infants and toddlers need from us: the kind of lives they lead in good homes. Good programs occur in diverse settings and in diverse ways. Inevitably, however, they provide the sort of settings that Keister describes in which each child is prized for being a unique individual, worthy of love and personalized care; in which other people know the ways in which each child is different from every other child; in which others care about how each child feels and what he or she is learning; in which caregivers have discovered much about how to keep each child involved and comfortable; and in which they look for and respond to each child's signals and interactions.

Very young children need people who

◆ smile and talk with them or babble when they babble.
◆ retrieve toys and play peek-a-boo, hide-and-seek, and other games.
◆ feed them when they are hungry.
◆ sing to them and rock them when they are tired.
◆ hold them when they feel small or sad or loving.
◆ notice and communicate pleasure over such newfound skills as creeping, climbing, holding, dropping, or adding new sounds and words.

◆ change their position or help them discover new possibilities when they are bored.

◆ watch for the kinds of things that "turn them on," such as toys, talk, changes to explore and mess about.

◆ watch for when they need quiet and the chance to be alone.

Each infant and toddler needs an everyday setting in which diapering, easing in and out of sleep, and being helped with the mysteries and struggles of toilet learning and using a spoon are all considered precious PRIME TIMES for one-to-one nurturing and learning. Each child needs a day that fits his or her particular temperament and pace, with people who provide more encouragement than direction, more exploration and challenge than restriction, and who provide reassurance, comfort, and limits.

Children need a setting that respects their parents as the most important people in their lives, that acknowledges and uses parents' expert knowledge of their own children; that values the intense caring that parents can bring to the setting, and that encourages parents to recognize the important contributions they make to the children's learning and development.

Infants and toddlers also need a setting in which the staff who care for them are respected as important people who use their minds and bodies to do the very difficult job of providing personalized care and relaxed, happy days to babies in groups.

Infants and Toddlers with Special Needs

Of course, all children have special needs. But many programs will have young children whose conditions require consideration beyond that required for most children: developmental delays, handicapping conditions, chronic illnesses, or family situations that put them at some risk. Moreover, programs will often be concerned that particular children may have serious special needs that might benefit from early diagnosis.

This handbook takes the view that a good program always views its children as special—that is, as worthy of individual consideration and program adaptation. Any child may have a special need at one time or another, from lack of sleep, developmental spurts, or situational stress. Because of this, programs can never be "one size fits all" or mechanically follow daily routines. Children with any sort of special need require care that responds to their strengths and is shaped by the cues they provide. Often what is necessary from caregivers is more time, patience, tolerance, and willingness to learn about the child. The learning activities that help infants and toddlers with disabilities or special needs maximize their development are little or no different from those used by other children. There are, however, adaptations to the environment that may be necessary for some children with physical or sensory impairments to help them achieve autonomy and successful experiences.

Some special needs become apparent *in utero*, at birth, or during routine infant screening and exams. Many, however, do not become evident until the child's behavior offers clues to a particular problem. The result is that the question of whether something is wrong may first come up when a child is under the program's care. The dilemma for caregivers is that while their concern may turn out to be false, to not act on it would be irresponsible, given the importance of early intervention.

The first consideration in addressing the issue of infants and toddlers with special needs is understanding that the idea or reality that something may be seriously wrong with their child will be an emotional earthquake for parents. It will strike at the heart of their being, their present, future, and even their past as parents. The child's caregiver is often key in discovering whether or not a child is developing normally. As a result, she or he is likely to experience the parent's emotional gamut of fear, denial, hope, and anger. The critical importance of a strong partnership with parents, based on trust and mutual respect, becomes clear when the question of special needs arises.

Children with identified special needs who are seeing other professionals will have an Independent Educational Plan or I.E.P. This may become the centerpiece for tailoring the child's experience.

Children at risk from social circumstances have special needs. Child abuse and neglect and the effects of poverty may result in developmental delays, chronic health concerns, and behavior disorders. The major difference in serving these children may be the caregiver's relationship with their parents. The challenge caregivers face is that the partnership with parents in at-risk homes is both more challenging and even more critical than with other families having special needs.

Types of Special Needs Often Present in Child Care

Motor Delays   Often special needs are discovered in infancy through observation of the baby's reflexes and delays in motor functioning. Any number of conditions may lead to motor delays or variations from typical motor development: visual or hearing impairments, brain damage, cerebral palsy, inadequate nutrition, chronic illness, premature birth, or birth trauma. Regular exams and screening are important because early intervention is essential to maximize development.

Sensory or Perceptual Impairments   Vision and hearing problems are often discovered while a care is in child care. An infant with a hearing loss may not react to sounds and may be surprised at the presence of other people. Vocalizations may appear (like the onset of babbling) but stop, apparently because they are not as self-pleasing as they are when infants hear their own sounds and adults' responses. Parents and caregivers should be aware that untreated ear infections can lead to hearing loss. Infants with visual impairments may be uninterested in objects and fail to reach, retrieve, or search for objects past the time when object permanence should have developed.

It is important to remember that most sensory impairments are not total and that intervention builds upon the child's existing capacity as well as upon development of other senses.

Cognitive Special Needs   There are no reliable tests of infant or toddler IQ. Delays or retardation are assessed through observation and clinical testing of the child's motor behavior, reflexes, adaptive (problem-solving and predictive) responses to experience with people and things, perceptual behavior, and language. Because the infant's or toddler's motor, sensory, and cognitive function are so interrelated, pinpointing the cause of the exact condition is often difficult. Cognitive retardation may be the result of genetic conditions such as Down's syndrome, prenatal experiences (malnutrition, drugs, alcohol), or brain damage (as a result of accidents or disease [rubella]).

Chronic Illness and Special Health Needs   Children with heart monitors, AIDS, and chronic health concerns are mainstreamed in child care centers. In each case, the child may present a range of unique special needs.

Drug- and Alcohol-Affected Infants and Toddlers   Children exposed to drugs and alcohol *in utero* typically have medical and behavioral problems that vary depending on the severity of their exposure. Typically, infants are irritable and hard to calm, difficult to nurture, and require slow, deliberate interaction adapted to their cues. Swaddling, massage, and very low levels of stimulation may be necessary. Some children may be unresponsive. These are not easy children to attach to, yet that is exactly what they need. Older infants and toddlers are often likely to be easily upset, distractible, and may have difficulty adapting to new situations.

Speech and Language Special Needs   Speech and language problems are common in preschool programs and may go uncovered in infant and toddler programs. Many potential problems may be reduced with early discovery and intervention.

Communication disorders may be the result of physical, emotional, or social conditions. Nonresponsive environments may be nearly as damaging as physical impairments. Hearing problems, retardation, muscular problems, ear infections, and other illnesses may lead to problems in speech production or in processing language.

Families At Risk   Many programs serve children who are at risk of abuse, neglect, or the effects of poverty. These infants and toddlers may present several health issues and usually have parents as needy as their children. The key to serving these children is careful observation and patience, access to and coordination of social service resources, and recognition that the parents deserve the same inherent respect and support that all parents do.

A Final Word: Appreciate Them for Who They Are

Babies—infants and toddlers alike—are wonderful human beings. Understanding each child is a challenge and requires caregivers who truly appreciate and like babies for what they can do, with all the variations of abilities and temperament found in a group of them.

EXERCISES

1. Make a list of behaviors typical of children at six months, twelve months, eighteen months, twenty-four months, thirty months, and thirty-six months that are developmentally appropriate and necessary but annoying to caregivers (e.g., crying before sleep or exploring with their mouths). Circle those behaviors that drive you crazy.

2. Observe a child closely at each of the above ages for five minutes. Try to notice everything the child does to explore, cope, or master his or her environment.

REFERENCES

Bettelheim, Bruno. *The Children of the Dream.* New York: Avon, 1969.

Bruner, J. S. "Organization of Early Skilled Action." *Child Development* 44 (1973): 1–111.

Erikson, Erik. *Childhood and Society.* New York: W. W. Norton, 1950.

Gonzalez-Mena, J., and Eyer, D. *Infancy and Caregiving.* Mountain View, CA: Mayfield, 1980, 1986, 1993.

Keister, M. E. *The "Good Life" for Infants and Toddlers.* Washington, DC: NAEYC, 1970.

Chapter 5

Grouping Infants and Toddlers

excellence

Children experience the day in a small, stable group. This setting creates attachments between caregivers and children, individualized care and learning, and relaxed, happy days.

Introduction

There is no best way to organize a child care program, no inherently fixed set of assumptions free of "it depends on other factors." Staff/child ratios, group size, room size, staffing patterns, and the age range of the children are factors that affect both cost and quality of care. Each factor interacts with the others and the combination affects optimal grouping. But while there are no best ways or set-in-stone requirements, there are certainly undesirable choices that lead to low quality.

What Is an Infant? What Is a Toddler?

Is fourteen-month-old Celina an infant or a toddler? Depending on the country, state, or province that she happens to be in, she may be either. Is twenty-five-month-old Ricky still a toddler? Again, it depends on where he is. In a developmental sense, Alice is obviously a toddler and has been one since she rose and toddled across the room at eleven months. Ricky still has the oval shape and diaper-bound waddle of a toddler, whatever the state says. But each licensing jurisdiction defines what an infant or toddler is—if twos are a separate group, if a program can mix children over and under age one, or age two, or age three. From those decisions flow legally minimum staff/child ratios, group sizes, and other regulations.

Determining Groups: Who Goes with Whom?

What is the best way to determine who goes with whom? First, it is important to clarify what state regulations allow. Because regulations change and there is usually more than one option, check what the regulations say rather than make assumptions based on your usual practice. You may have more options. Consider the program's need for flexibility. Too narrow a definition of a group (for example, young infants or one year olds) may result in fewer options when you are trying to fill an opening than a wider age range would allow. Finally, of course, grouping has implications for each child's experience.

Age Range

If you were to visit programs throughout the country, you would find arrangements that range from a group that spans six weeks to five years olds spending the whole day together (often known as family grouping) to very narrow age groups, where all children's ages are within six months of each other.

The Value of Mixed Age Grouping

Many feel that there is an inherent logic to mixed age groups because they are more natural, closer to a family model. After all, human children aren't birthed and raised in litters. In group care, a natural tendency of caregivers is often to minimize individual differences. This inclination is stronger when the age range is narrow. Wider age groups result in greater awareness of children's differences. That children about the same age are very similar is something of an illusion adults maintain to keep from being overwhelmed by the variety of differences that children present. At any age, development is not uniform across developmental areas. A twenty-four-month-old child may equal this thirty-month-old child in language and perceptual development, that seventeen-month-old child in large-motor development, and this twenty-three month old in small-motor development and social development, yet all of these children are perfectly normal. Having ten children the same age says little about the developmental range of the group; a broad developmental spectrum must still be planned for.

Centers in the United States rarely use extended age grouping for children under three years old. There is rarely a span beyond a twelve- to eighteen-month range, reflecting the age grading in school and the licensing guidelines that often make mixed age grouping more costly. But there are a number of advantages in giving others the opportunity to be with children older and younger than themselves:

◆ greater continuity because a child will make fewer transitions from group to group. Children (and parents) are in the group and with the staff for a longer time and therefore are more likely to develop real relationships. Child care centers struggle with inevitable staff and child turnover as it is. To force a move every year or at even shorter intervals needlessly builds in instability, resulting in frequent changes of caregivers as well as of physical environments and peers.

◆ older children have the opportunity to be the most competent and to learn helping and caring skills through interacting with younger children.

◆ siblings may be able to be together.

◆ young children learn new skills from being with older children.

◆ routines may be easier to manage and individualize because of the wide range of needs and schedules.

◆ staff and children avoid the tension that can come when a group consists of all toddlers, all of whom have trouble sharing and coping with group life.

◆ it happens to an extent, anyway. The actual age range experienced by the children is also dependent on another factor: space available in the next age group. In a center that is usually full, children often get "stuck," unable to move until a space opens up. Or they may have to move a little sooner than anticipated to take advantage of a space.

If the age range extends beyond eighteen months, caregivers have to be more skilled to provide a program appropriate for all children in the group. It is a challenge to provide the range of materials, equipment, and experiences needed by children of diverse ages within one space. There is often a natural movement toward the lowest common denominator—that is, toward providing only materials and experiences that are safe and manageable for the youngest children and that therefore do not fully meet the needs of the oldest children—or toward aiming for the middle, which slights both older and younger children.

There may be staff members who feel uncomfortable with the younger or older children and would not work as well in a multiage group.

Are There Advantages to Grouping Children as Close to the Same Age as Possible?

Not generally for the children, but the success of whatever method of grouping is used depends to a considerable extent on the perceptions of staff and parents, who often prefer narrower age groups. Staff may feel stretched dealing with a wider age range. Parents of younger children worry about whether their children will be safe and well cared for. Parents of older children fear that their children may not be challenged, may "regress," or may slow in development.

These perceptions are important because any arrangement must have the support of both parents and staff. But many of the benefits of narrow age grouping are illusions based on the notion that same-age children are the same. It seems easier because you can provide the same equipment and schedule, do the same things, react the same ways, and de-emphasize all the ways the children are really different. It is only easier when the children are supposed to fit the program and not the reverse and when staff are supposed to do things to and for the children, such as instruct and care for them in a largely standardized fashion.

Family Grouping

A few centers have been designed specifically to accommodate "family groups" with homebase spaces fitted out for small groups of children six weeks to five years. Adjacent to the homebase are areas where the older children can be taken for activities and experiences not suitable for the younger children. The schedule includes starting and finishing the day and eating with the mixed age group in the homebase and providing some time away from "home" for the older children with children their own age. In a well-designed facility, this arrangement is close to ideal. The only drawback, however, is cost. In most licensing jurisdictions, this arrangement requires more costly staff/child ratios than age-graded arrangements.

NOTE: There are also centers where twenty to thirty children under five years spend much of their day together in "family" groupings. This is a significant misnomer. Families are not of such size and this type of grouping places particular stress on the younger children in the group.

Our Recommendations: Flexible, Moderately Wide Age Ranges

In our experience, maintaining a moderately wide age range in homebases is desirable and can receive the support of staff and parents. Assuming the approval of licensing authorities, we recommend the following ranges:

Infants
six weeks to fifteen months

Toddlers
twelve to thirty months

Intermediates (Twos)
twenty-four to thirty-six months

Our allowances for overlap provide flexibility in new enrollments, necessary move ups, and individual needs.

It is possible to include both very young babies and younger walkers in a single group as long as

◆ younger babies have some protection from older, mobile babies.

◆ the routine care of younger babies—feeding and holding, for instance—does not take up so much of the caregivers' time that they have little time for the older babies.

◆ the relative ease and enjoyment of playing and interacting with more responsive older babies does not keep caregivers from ensuring that younger babies are spending their time well.

There is a natural developmental break somewhere between twelve and eighteen months. Developmental changes include an increase in language comprehension, huge developments in mobility, greater self-assertion, and an increase in social interactions with other children. Another natural break occurs at around two years of age, when children experience a burst in language expression, increased attention span, and ability to engage in more focused and complex play. These changes have implications for the environment, the experiences offered, and the ways adults interact with the children.

If grouping is done by relatively narrow age ranges, there are other avenues to ensure mixed-age experiences. All children benefit from being with older and younger children. Shared activities, playground time, walks, and mealtimes create opportunities for infant-through-school-age children to spend time together. But infants and toddlers do not belong in large groups, and multiage experiences should take that fact into account.

Organizing for Quality: Staffing and Group Size

Staff/child ratios and group sizes have enormous impact on the cost, quality, and accessibility of child care. It is an area that everyone involved (except the children, of course) should understand. For example, if comparable quality can be achieved at a ratio of one more child to a caregiver, the cost of care is reduced and the cost savings (or additional income) can go toward increasing staff compensation and/or reducing parent tuition. If ratios needed to be decreased to improve quality, the reverse is true. If a slightly higher group size is acceptable, it can result in requiring fewer separate rooms to serve the same number of children, reducing the cost of building or renting a facility, or in creating space for something else (e.g., two toddler rooms of twelve rather than three rooms of eight children). Or it can result in more children, thus more income, which can be applied to salaries or tuition.

Staff/Child Ratios

There is widespread professional agreement that children under two years old deserve staff/child ratios of one adult to four children or fewer. Most child care authorities (including NAEYC) believe children grouped from six weeks to twelve months should have at least a one to three staff/child ratio, children grouped six weeks to fifteen months, a one to three or one to four ratio, children grouped twelve to twenty-four months or older, a one to four ratio, and children grouped fifteen to either thirty or thirty-six months, a one to five ratio.

Is quality care possible with staff/child ratios that are slightly less than desirable? This is an important question because staff/child ratios are not only a key quality factor, they are also the key factor in the cost of care and thus determine if care is affordable for parents as well as if more money is available for staff compensation. In a program with a stable, highly skilled, experienced staff and a well-designed, supportive facility, a one to four ratio for children under fifteen months, a one to five ratio for children fifteen months to twenty-four or thirty months, and a one to six ratio for around twenty-four to thirty-six months can result in good care. But it is *unlikely* that ratios higher than one to four for infants or one to five for toddlers will produce high-quality care even with other favorable conditions.

Group Size

Group size is an important factor in its own right, independent of staff/child ratios. Generally, smaller is better. Smaller groups are likely to lead to

◆ more attention to individual children.

◆ children spending time in groups of one to three children.

◆ a more relaxing, serene environment.

◆ less noise.

◆ less emphasis by adults on "crowd control."

◆ less regimentation of children.

◆ increased opportunities for staff to get to know each individual child and parent.

◆ a manageable number of adults and children, which in turn allows young children to become familiar with and to the people around them.

But it is important to note that automatically assuming that a center is better organized into homebases with small groups is a mistake. In some circumstances, a small, two-caregiver group may have drawbacks; it may not lead to the above outcomes or it may create other problems. *Group size always interacts with other factors:* the design of the facility, the space per child, the staffing patterns, the length of the day, and staff turnover.

The Number of Caregivers per Group

If smaller groups are better, it may seem like a good idea to have a homebase of one caregiver to three or four children. However, for a number of reasons, two heads are better than one, and in some circumstances a staff team of three may be the best alternative, even if it leads to a slightly larger group size. With at least two staff members in a group, one can leave the room when necessary or assist in an emergency situation that requires two adults. Having another adult to talk to and with whom to share observations, amusing moments, difficult situations, accomplishments, and frustrations is important. Infants and toddlers are charming, but they are not very good conversationalists, and the job of working with them is more rewarding when there is another adult with whom to share the experience.

A staff team of three has a number of advantages that can offset the effects of a slightly larger group size:

◆ it allows coverage of a ten- or eleven-hour day without having to combine rooms, shift children, or use part-time staff excessively.

◆ in centers with frequent staff turnover or personnel policies that include generous paid time off, staff stability is easier to maintain in three-person groups.

◆ in a two-staff group, the actual ratios, group size, and amount of individual attention experienced by the children may be worse than in a three-staff group. The children may always be together in one group, and while one caregiver is cleaning up or caring for a child, the other is with the rest of the children. In a three-staff team, it may be possible to have routines and programming that result in more one-to-one with groupings of two or three children.

◆ better use can be made of scarce expertise by spreading highly skilled staff over more children.

Three-staff caregiver groups are only desirable when staff/child ratios are superior and group size can be kept down: infant groups of three caregivers with no more than nine to twelve babies, and toddler groups of three caregivers with no more than twelve to fifteen toddlers.

Room Size and Grouping

Children need room to grow. Infants need room to crawl and creep and lurch about. Toddlers require space to climb up, over, and through; to

What about Continuity?

Ten-month-old Jesse begins her day at 7:30 A.M. with Maria. At 8:00, she moves into her homebase with Beth, her primary caregiver, who has been at the center for five months. Ginny, the lead teacher, is on maternity leave, and her replacement, Steven, arrives at 9:00. Jesse stays with Steven and Beth until Beth leaves at 4:30 and is replaced by Maita. Jesse spends the last fifteen minutes of her day with Steven and Maita. In six weeks, Ginny will be back and Steven will go to another room.

How important is continuity of caregivers? Important enough to override some of the concerns about larger group size? This is an important question. Groups based on two caregivers often result in infants and toddlers experiencing more discontinuity because of turnover of caregivers than when there are three of them. Children also experience discontinuity with the beginning- and/or end-of-the-day shuffle of caregivers, which occurs more often in two-caregiver groups. The effects of discontinuity on children are less visible in smaller groups than in larger ones, but they are no less real. Three-caregiver groups are not an answer to discontinuity. But under some circumstances, they are certainly worth considering.

push and pull wagons and strollers, and to move around without fear of trampling young colleagues. The room needs to include couch, rocker, soft spaces, changing areas, and equipment necessary to provide lots of motor and sensory experience. Regulations usually require 40 to 50 square feet per child (including crib space), but that should be taken as an absolute minimum. The smaller the group size, the more space per child is necessary. Three hundred square feet (six children x 50 square feet) is a tiny room for two adults, six children, and visiting parents to spend a lot of time together. The furniture necessary (except the number of cribs) is the same as in a 450–square–foot room for nine children. Four hundred square feet is probably the minimum size of the room that will feel tolerable with six children.

Organizing Homebases into Modules

One alternative to the dilemma of small group size leading to small rooms and a two-staff unit covering a long day is to pair two homebases into a module: for example, two groups of six to eight infants, or eight to ten toddlers, or one infant and one toddler group pairing up. Under this arrangement, the children and parents have a sense of their own homebase, caregivers, and module, and the staff are able to function as a four-person team to cover the day.

Ideally, the module consists of two separate physical spaces with shared areas and some shared functions—perhaps food preparation and napping (page 59). There is enough separation to provide a clear sense of two rooms and enough openness and access to encourage the staff to think of the space as a single unit, thus avoiding duplication of all learning centers and reducing the territorial instinct that comes with "owning" a room. All the staff in the module become familiar faces to the

Paired Homebase Modules

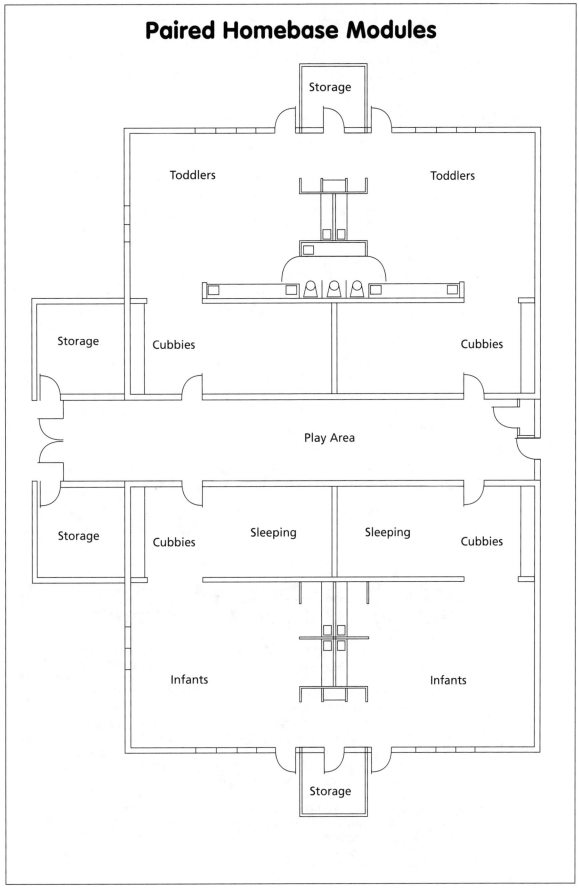

Storage

Toddlers   Toddlers

Storage   Cubbies   Cubbies

Play Area

Storage   Cubbies   Sleeping   Sleeping   Cubbies

Infants   Infants

Storage

children, thus easing the anxiety of combining rooms at the beginning and end of the day. By placing the module under the supervision of one lead teacher, staff time and talents can be maximized.

Staffing Patterns

Young children need the security that comes from being cared for by a small number of familiar adults. A center should consider continuity over time and limit the total number of people involved in the care of the children. Rotating staff through different groups in the center on a regular basis destroys continuity. A reliance on part-time staff or volunteers adds to the number of caregivers that children must become accustomed to.

Staffing patterns should reflect actual attendance patterns and not result in gaps in the caregiver/child ratio while staff await the arrival of another caregiver or the departure of children at the end of the day. Breaks, planning, and meeting time should be incorporated into the plan.

Staffing every group from opening to closing may present budget difficulties. Typically, rooms are combined and, unfortunately, children are sometimes shuffled about in a haphazard fashion to maintain ratios. Arrival and departure are times when helping children feel secure should be a priority. Staffing patterns, program practices, and room combinations should be carefully planned to minimize children's experience of unfamiliar people and locations during those sensitive times of separation.

Moving Children (and Parents) to the Next Age Group

Children cannot move up until there is space available in the next group. Sometimes children get stuck in a group while waiting for an

---

"We Care for Infants, Not Toddlers. Get Those Old Guys Out of Here!"

A common lament from infant staff: "Holly and Roger have to move up. They are bored here. At seventeen months, they are too old for the group." It is not uncommon for staff in one age group to narrowly define what the room can offer and to view the problem as the child outgrowing the room (or the opposite, being too young for the new room), rather than that the room environment and activities are failing to keep pace with the children. For any age grouping approach to be successful, the homebase staff must accept responsibility to program for the educational and caring needs of every child in the group. The programming changes with the children. Two principles are fundamental:

◆ the program has to fit the child, not the reverse.
◆ no child is ever too old or too young, too slow or too advanced for the group that he or she is in.

opening, and sometimes children get moved up a little earlier than expected to take advantage of an opening. Because it is inevitable that this will happen, each homebase needs to be able to accommodate a wide age range. While parents should get the message that their child is ready to move, they should never feel that a child has to move or cannot move because of age or development. Care must be taken to avoid giving the impression that there is something competitive about moving up—that is, that it is like graduation or some indication that the child has superior skills and abilities.

A Final Word: Circumstances Change— There May Always Be a Better Way

How children and staff are grouped lays a foundation for providing high-quality care. It is an important element determining the best use of staff and facility and a factor in determining the cost of care. But as we said earlier, there is no one right way to produce quality. Periodically, you must examine the grouping patterns that you established to make sure they still make sense and are the most cost-efficient way to achieve the vision of quality outlined in chapter 4.

EXERCISES

1. Develop a list of curriculum adaptations or equipment changes necessary to ensure that a room works for older babies waiting for an opening in a toddler group.

2. Develop two staffing plans for caring for a group of infants over an eleven-hour day: a group of seven infants with a two to seven staff/ child ratio and a group of ten infants with a three to ten staff/child ratio.

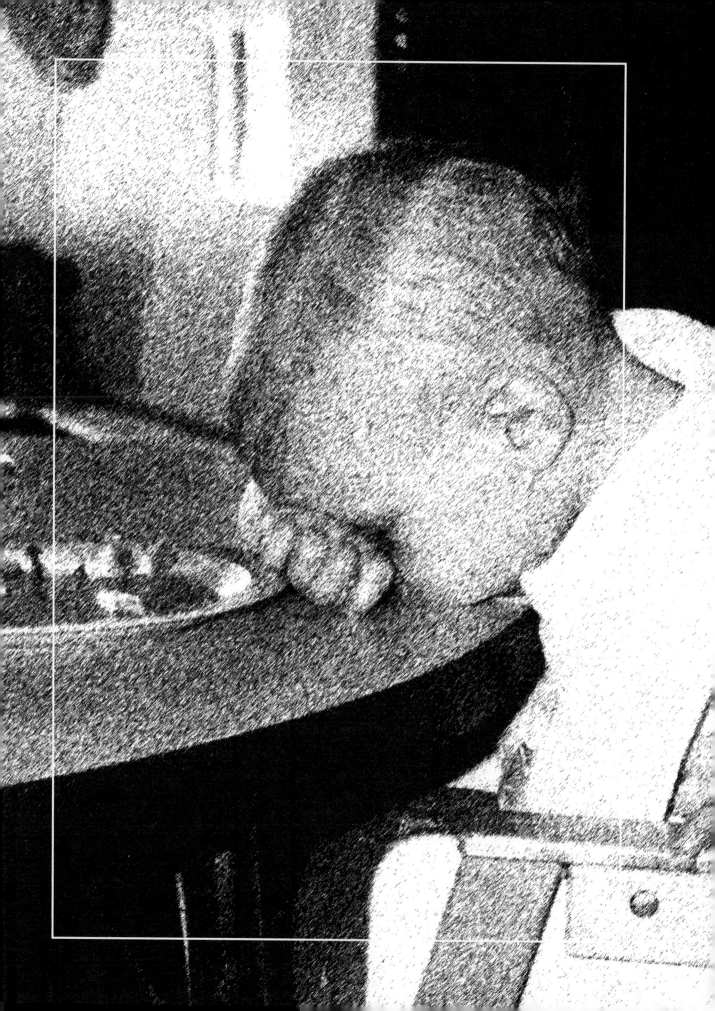

Chapter 6
Structuring Time and Space for Quality Care

excellence

Time and space are structured to accomplish the program goals of providing a safe and secure experience, relaxed and happy days, and individualized care and learning. There is a balance between familiar, predictable experience and flexible, changing experience.

Think of space and time as the framework for composing the experiences of the day. A too-compartmentalized and rigid framework will leave staff and children feeling cramped, confined, and frustrated, while one that is too loose and flexible will breed anxiety and confusion.

Structuring Time: Balancing Flexibility and Order

Planning a time schedule is always a balancing act. Child and adult security flows from familiar, predictable routines. Things happen when you expect them to: a morning group gets together at 9:00, eats at noon, and goes home at 5:30. Yet a too-fixed time clock drives us crazy with monotony. And with infants and toddlers, it is the individual rhythms of eating, sleeping, and exploring that are critical. With infants and (to a great extent) toddlers, the group schedule is built around individual schedules, not the reverse. Staff should think of the day as a whole and resist the temptation to carve it up into little bits, filling a child's day with disruptive stops and starts.

Sample Schedule

NOTE: Sleep schedules will reflect the child's rhythm and parental consultation. Bottle feeding is individualized, based on the child's needs and parental consultation.

7:00–8:30
Arrival, greeting, self-directed play, bottles, or early A.M. snack.

8:30–9:00
Breakfast or morning snack, family-style, for nonbottle-fed infants and all toddlers. Morning group ritual. Bottle feeding and sleep as individual schedules dictate throughout the day.

9:00–11:15
Self-directed play in planned learning areas indoors and out. Staff may have planned supervised activities for individuals or small groups.

11:15–11:30
Cleanup, washup, and, if waiting is unavoidable, brief finger plays or singing at table for awake, nonbottle-fed infants and all toddlers.

11:30–1:15
Lunch for nonbottle-fed infants and toddlers, staggered as morning nappers wake up.

12:30–3:00
Nap time for many toddlers; individualized wake-up.

1:15–5:00
Self-directed play in planned learning areas indoors and out. Staff have planned some supervised activities.

2:00–3:00
Snack, eating on an individual or small-group basis when children are ready.

4:30–5:30
Self-directed play in planned learning areas. Special materials or activities for those departing late. Late afternoon snack for those who need it. Good-bye, conversation with parents, departure.

5:30–7:00
Extended hours.

Notice that the day is planned in overlapping "chunks" of time that give flexibility. That is what is meant by the characteristic of wholeness—avoiding breaking the child's day up into small, discrete segments.

Any timetable or plan for the day is a guide to or a best guess about what will make sense. Adjustments are made as the children get older and their needs change. Daily adjustments may be necessary for a variety of reasons. It is easy for staff to get locked-in to a timetable because it is familiar and reduces the need for staff to make changes. But it then becomes mindless, and caregivers lose the day's rhythm and its basis in the actual needs of the children.

Remember—Go Slowly!

Good programs slow down to child time. Things are done at the child's pace, encouraging and supporting them to undertake activities themselves as they are ready developmentally, rather than rushing through routines at an efficient adult pace. Taking the time to let children take an active role in hand washing, using the toilet, eating, dressing, and undressing as their ability and interests dictate, rather than doing it for them, can make the day go more smoothly and more efficiently. But more important, these are the PRIME TIMES for each child to learn the important things in life: "I am trusted and liked" and "I can do it."

Allowing children to experience these routines one by one or in very small groups works better than trying to have the whole group participate at once. This in some ways may defy common sense, or at least common practice, for some staff seem to believe that having children do one thing at a time is the most efficient way to get through the day. However, this strategy often results in much frustration for children and staff. Children are pressured to wait, a waste of their time and something infants and toddlers are not very good at doing. In a good program, a number of different things are always going on simultaneously.

Children at this age need choices in play. It is not appropriate that there be a time, for example, when all the children are expected to engage in table activities or to sit for a group activity. Groups for singing, stories, or other activities happen spontaneously, so there is no valid reason for insisting that all older toddlers sit still at the same time. Besides, it is very hard work to make this happen!

Planning the Environment

Good programs exist in all sorts of spaces, from basements to storefronts. The space does not determine the program. However, as Elizabeth Prescott explained (1979, p.1), *the environment regulates our experience:* the physical facilities and the arrangement of space and equipment available to work for you or against you can make quality easier or more difficult to achieve.

A good setting for infants or toddlers is a comfortable space so well organized, divided, and equipped that

- ◆ the staff have a lot of time to *be with* the babies on a one-to-one basis, fully engaged, and do not have to spend all their time setting up and packing away equipment and materials or managing children.
- ◆ children experience a great part of the day in small groups of one to three or four children.
- ◆ as they show interest, children can exercise autonomy, show initiative and self-sufficiency, and do things for themselves.

What makes the homebase a great place for an infant or toddler to be in? for a caregiver to be with a baby? Think of the homebase as a place for work: The work of the staff is to care for children and to create a learning environment; the "work" of the child is to engage in developmentally appropriate play.

A Great Place to Be *and* to Be with *a Very Young Child All Day*

A comfortable place where adults can be relaxed while feeding, soothing, changing, easing children into and out of sleep, cuddling, and nurturing young children. A warm, homelike space is pleasant for staff, children, and parents. A place with couches, easy chairs, cushions, and comfortable floor space.

"Different places to be" to avoid crowding and overstimulation: semisecluded, protected from other children, small spaces, open spaces; space divided by shelving units, curtains, or pieces of fabric, behind couches or chairs, under cabinets, or on top of low cubes or furniture; spaces where a child can safely spend some time alone.

A "child-scale" place because infants and toddlers are small people, and *an adult-scale* place because caregivers are not (small people, relatively). The environment needs to be scaled down for children. Chairs should allow young feet to touch the floor, tables should be a comfortable height (just above waist-high when sitting), and objects or pictures on the wall should be easily visible to babies who are on the floor, walking, and being carried by adults.

A spacious, bright, and cheerful place with good lighting and low windows so that children can look out. Windows that open add air and interest and should be made of shatterproof (tempered) glass or provided with other kinds of protection, such as wide ledges or screens, to prevent children from banging them with toys or climbing into them. Abundant natural light should be available, complemented by artifi-

cial light that allows for a range of lighting conditions much like a living room. Staff should avoid the tendency to overuse artificial lighting, which creates an institutional feel.

A place of beauty and tasteful aesthetics that reflects a concern for light, color, texture, and pattern. Avoid primary colors on the walls and floors and permanent murals because so much of the equipment and play materials are likely to be brightly colored. Children's art and teacher displays, mobiles and brightly clad, moving bodies in the room add much color. *The challenge in creative programs is to not overstimulate* by creating rooms that make children feel as if they are inside a kaleidoscope. It is safest to use subdued, somewhat neutral colors on walls and floors, much like those used in living rooms. Nap rooms and bathrooms should also have a pleasant aesthetic.

A well-heated, cooled, and ventilated place from the floor on up.

A quiet place that tolerates noise. Intrusive, unpleasant, or overwhelming noise discourages attempts by babies to communicate. Divided space, acoustical ceiling tile, ceiling fans, carpeting, soft furnishings, limited group size, and zoning of activities reduce noise.

A nice place to touch with a variety of textures, responsive materials and lots of softness in the environment: soft furniture, water, grass, swings, rugs, pillows, fingerpaints, playdough, clay, and laps.

A Great Place to Work

A room arrangement that regulates behavior. A divided space with clear boundaries, traffic patterns, spaces of different sizes and with different functions will regulate crowding and wandering. Children will spread out if the room is arranged and activities are planned to draw their attention to different areas and if adults spread out. Bounded and contained spaces will help control the flow of all the smaller materials and equipment pieces that may wander. Portable (movable) dividers as low as 18 inches high enable areas to be changed in size, shape, number, and arrangement and still allow caregivers to keep an eye on what is going on. The alternative—big open spaces strewn with play materials —is like a mine field: unattractive, unsafe, unworkable, and requiring caregivers to function mostly as traffic cops.

A variety of floor coverings that are easy to clean. Carpeting and tile or linoleum that can be cleaned easily. Even floor surfaces help babies to learn about the world: for example, they discover that a ball goes a long way with a little push on a tile floor but not on the carpet. On the other hand, crawling may be easier on the less slippery carpet.

An "I can do it" place that allows autonomy. For the child, equipment such as towels, sinks, clothing, as well as books and play materials placed at their level encourages autonomy and choice. For the adult, adult height sinks and storage in the room.

A learning place where learning is built into the environment. Sensory learning through different textures, lighting, colors, temperatures or breezes, views or angles of vision: carpeting, rugs, fabric, and materials that have different feels to them or that respond differently to light; mirrors, reflective glass and metal; open windows, lights on

and off, use of fans to provide air currents. *Motor learning* with furniture and equipment that encourage or allow climbing up or over, moving around, through, over, under: couches, pillows, stairs, ramps, planks and crates, small platforms, and cubes.

A place with ample, convenient, labeled storage for children and adults. Wall storage, cabinets, open and closed shelves, duffel bags, toy boxes, all have their place, as do individual cubbies or bins and hooks for the belongings of individual children. These should be accessible to both parents and staff. Note a fundamental law of storage: the closer materials and equipment are to the point of use, the more they will be used.

A place with ample, easy-to-use communication space and equipment such as clipboards, chalk, and white boards, Post-It notes on a wall, and writing implements accessible to both parents and staff.

A place of order. Not compulsive tidiness but an arrangement that encourages children to clearly focus and distinguish the properties of things (toys, food, materials). A tasteful, organized, orderly environment can tolerate the considerable creative disorder that comes with valuable messy play and toddler dumping. In a room with covered storage, attractive walls, carpets, and basic furnishings, the creative use of cardboard boxes, rags, rocks, old clothes, and other "junk" often appears inventive and enriching. In a drab room, the use of the same materials may result in a "junky" effect. Money spent on basic furnishings is money well spent.

A place with sufficient space. Sometimes centers assume that the youngest and smallest children need the least amount of space. Actually, infants and toddlers need more space per child: in order to accommodate a greater number of adults in the room, furniture (couches, cribs, changing counters), the fact that they do not always cope well with each other in close proximity and that one of their favorite activities is moving around in space. Overcrowding leads inevitably to frustration, bad tempers, and an increase in unpleasant interactions, especially biting.

A place for parents that attends to their needs when they bring and pick up their children: child cubbies, communication space, places to sit and watch, places for visitors' purses and coats, and signage that provides all the information they need to function in the space and the message that this is also a place for them.

Other Important Environmental Considerations

Crowding and Bunching Up When the children spend the day in groups, they experience more stimulation, more distractions, more distress, more stress, more risk of harming each other, less constructive play, and less personal attention from staff.

Bunching up is common in infant and toddler programs: the majority of adults and babies end up close together, using only a limited amount of the available space, whatever the overall size of the space. There are two reasons for this. Infants, especially, often seem to stay within close proximity to their caregiver. A second tendency is for the adults to position themselves close to each other and often facing each other, thus increasing the number of children in the bunch. Layout of furniture often encourages this, as the adults draw from their experience of homelike settings in arranging the furniture. The couch and chair arrangement illustrated on the left—

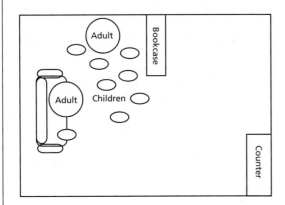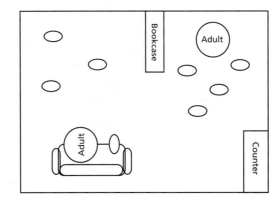

—seems comfortably homey, but it often results in two or more adults sitting on the couch and chairs and five to ten children crowded into a tiny area; a decidedly nonhomey condition.

In living rooms and lounges, we use furniture to draw adults together to socialize. In classrooms, we often plan space to accommodate group activities. But in settings for infants and toddlers, we want the opposite: *to separate them and spread the children throughout the available space,* thereby increasing the field of action and reducing the chances of conflict and collision. No good comes from babies being kept together in small, even groups.

Unfortunately, achieving this is easier said than done. First, our adult instinct is to face each other and to face the action. It feels strange to turn our backs and focus away from centers of activity and other adults. We also want to talk to other human beings like ourselves when we are amid charming but nonverbal crowds of small people.

Supervision Is Not Simply Surveillance

"We need to see every child every second to supervise them." This adage sounds sensible and is often built into state regulations. This thinking often leads to very open spaces lacking seclusion. Even "behind" spaces like couches are pushed up against the wall, little or no separation is created between cribs and play space, and caregivers are constantly scanning the room, never focusing on the child in front of them. Everyone is together, children are always in a group unless restrained in a seat or swing, visible and audible to each other, and the likelihood of overstimulation is high. In these settings, accidents and incidents of infants exploring each other unpleasantly or of acting up aggressively will be high.

Good supervision is not simply a matter of the caregiver acting as police officer, as accident and crime stopper. Good supervision creates a well-planned, safe, engaging, "yes" environment, a relaxed, orderly day; children understanding the expectations adults have for them; and caregivers knowing the children. In a wide-open environment, there are likely to be more problems; the only virtue is that caregivers can see them as they happen (unless, of course, their backs are turned or they are filling bottles or performing other necessary tasks). With low dividers, couches, counters, and shelving as dividers, children are only momentarily out of view, much as they are at home. But the reduction in stimulation and group size can greatly increase safety and security in the room.

Avoiding bunching up requires a room arrangement and daily planning that consciously draw staff and children toward the far reaches of the room, to secondary rooms, or outside; in other words, that encourage spreading out. Self-monitoring and supervision that recognize the tendency to bunch up and the need to spread out are always essential.

Use All Your Space Get outside! Infants benefit in terms of health and learning by having opportunities to go outside. Use the playground, sidewalks, strollers, carts.

Use *all* the inside space: common spaces as well as corridors. Visit other parts of the center, checking first for potential hazards.

Separate Crib Rooms? The issue of whether or not children will sleep and play in the same room is often determined by the space available. Ideally, with infants, there is at least a crib area, if not a separate room. While most infants are amazingly flexible and will adjust much more easily than adults to resting or sleeping with activity going on around them, staff often restrict the play of active children when other children are asleep and move toward trying to have all children sleep at the same time.

Whether a separate area or room, the space should be spacious enough so that cribs or cots are separated by about 24 inches. Carpet will help to absorb noise. If there is little ventilation, a wall-mounted fan will increase air circulation and provide some masking noise. Windows need to be curtained to regulate light. A rocking chair within the space can be used by caregivers to help babies go to sleep and as a quiet spot for breast-feeding mothers.

Cots and mats should be comfortable, safe, and easily cleaned and stored.

Soft music is calming for some babies, so a cassette player in the sleeping area can be helpful.

Accessibility and Special Needs Infant and toddler spaces have to work for all children and adults, including those with differing motor and sensory abilities. Unfortunately, one of the keys to accessibility is space, which is almost always in short supply. Pathways and turning radiuses large enough to accommodate child and adult wheelchairs or walkers are important.

Accommodating children and adults with sensory impairments is largely a matter of designing an environment with clear sensory cues that is not a jumble of sight, sound, smell, and texture. Individuals with hearing or visual impairments try to maximize their abilities. Hearing and touch take on special significance when sight is limited, as do recognizable visual cues that work with limited sight. Visual cues, touch, and vibration are important for maximizing the experience of children with hearing impairments. The concept of landmarks and sensory markers that orient the individual visually or auditorially is useful. For a toddler who is blind, the sound of the fish tank, the breeze from the fan, the eucalyptus in the science area, the dividing line between the carpet and tile, and the red felt name tag on his cubby are important cues. For a child with a hearing impairment, good room acoustics and a relatively orderly acoustical environment (e.g., not a three-ring circus atmosphere) are important to help maximize the hearing the child does have.

All infants and toddlers benefit from environments that are clear and manageable, but these are particularly important for children with impairments or delays: clear displays and a manageable number of learning choices, clear pathways and delineation of areas, and designs that allow them to accomplish basic care tasks with a maximum amount of independence.

Learning Centers

In a program based on setting, rather than activities, space is planned and children can function relatively autonomously. An environmentally based program includes activity areas for routine activities, for example, diapering or feeding areas, and others for learning, often called interest areas or activity/learning centers. We will use the term *learning centers* to describe a part of the space to be used for specific purposes. In these learning centers, materials are stored and used to facilitate child-directed play. In a learning center-based program, learning centers are the basic units of planning. Note the difference between an activity-based curriculum where nearly all planning is thought of mostly in terms of activities in time blocks (e.g., an activity from 9:30 to 10:00).

Learning centers not only help adults to organize materials and equipment in a sensible way; they also encourage children to spread out, to see possibilities for play more easily, and to play and explore more constructively and with more focus.

What areas to have depend on the amount of space available, the age range of the children, and staff expertise. The small size of babies makes a number of learning centers possible in even a small space, and centers often assume a number of functions. In limited space for toddlers and twos, a "wet" or "messy" area may encompass play with art and craft materials, sensory play, and projects. Quiet areas become multipurpose sites for quiet activities. A table area becomes the site for table toys and projects (as well as lunch). With more space, areas can develop more specialized functions.

One drawback to learning centers is that when an area is defined by content, dramatic play for instance, it is easy to lose sight of the reality that dramatic play exists everywhere and in many activities. Sometimes a tendency develops to become inflexible about where activities may take place—for example, thinking that hats should stay in the dramatic play area. Caregivers need to recognize that some learning centers are really "take-out areas," whose materials are available for transporting to other areas. In fact, with infants and toddlers, many areas become "take-out" areas without physical boundaries, for a favorite activity is transporting objects from one place to another, just for the sake of moving, carrying, pushing, or pulling them.

Infants and toddlers may not appreciate the logic behind adult definitions of areas. Especially when planning for younger, mobile babies, staff need to keep in mind that moving things around in space, fitting things inside other things, and generally altering the set up will be a priority and that these interests take precedence over whatever logical grouping of materials makes sense to adults. Staff need to be very flexible when children mix materials from different areas.

Characteristics of Learning Centers *Learning centers have size, shape, and height.* The size of the area should be tailored to the number and size of the users and to the activities within. If it is too big, a larger group than is desirable may congregate in the area. If too small, the area is likely to become cluttered, crowded, or simply may not work.

Areas may be as small as a window or a rug. When it comes to shape, adults typically square off corners. However, round and oddly angled areas are appealing to children. Areas of varying height created through the use of hanging fabric, canopies, platforms, overhangs, or raising or lowering the floor add character, charm, and clear definition.

Learning centers have different surfaces. Floor space, table or countertops, and walls or dividers for mounting materials or for use as easels allow a variety of learning/play opportunities.

Learning centers can have personality and ambiance. A mood can be produced by the combined effects of all the elements: businesslike, cozy, chaotic, cheery, noisy, bland, serene, even perhaps melancholy (a womblike place where children can go to feel sad). The mood is created by the activities, the sounds and smells, the colors and textures, and the feel of the place. Artwork, furnishings, ritual behaviors—all the things that create an ambiance in our own personal spaces can be used in the homebase.

Learning centers can communicate and signal behavior. An easy message is open/closed, signaled by a gate, a sign, a sound, or a light. There are other signals that engage children, such as a new picture or object that catches their eye and gives the message "Check me out," or a smell that sets off a stampede to the sensory area.

Learning centers can have understood rules and expectations of behavior. How shall tasks get done? How must the inhabitants interact? The more these expectations are built into the space through arrangements of furnishings, materials, and symbolic instructions in the area, the less need there is for adult indoctrination and supervision. All of us, but children especially, pay more attention to what actually happens than what is supposed to happen (witness how little highway speed limits are observed). If the rule is no throwing things, but it is only enforced intermittently, children understand that it is not really a rule.

Keys to Effective Learning Centers   The right size and scale. Think "baby-scale." Learning centers can be as small as a two-foot-square space on the wall or a four-foot-square rug or as large as a whole room. The size of the area should depend on what is to happen there. The shortness of under-three year olds must be kept in mind in planning the heights of surfaces and chairs. Work spaces should reflect the fact that many times toddlers do their work sitting or lying on the floor or standing up at tables rather than sitting in chairs.

Open storage. Have sufficient open shelving accessible to children to clearly and discretely displays materials; provide picture labels to encourage older children to return materials. With infants and toddlers, clear displays mean only a few items per shelf, clearly separated from each other. Clear plastic containers or other containers that allow visibility reduce the amount of dumping or tipping out. Collections of objects in containers are just begging to be dumped out for inspection, so if that is not the idea, it is better to display items individually on shelves.

Adult storage. Props and other materials not in use should be conveniently located close to their eventual point of use.

Good boundaries. Boundaries define for children where actions will take place. A pit (depression), rug, low dividers, shelves, boards, or boxes can serve as defining boundaries. The more materials a learning center offers, the more useful are physical boundaries to contain them.

Boundaries that require children to make a physical decision to enter or exit—for example, to open a gate, step up, over, or down—result in children spending longer times in that area. More symbolic boundaries —for example taped lines, rope, and stop signs—can be useful with older toddlers and twos.

The right amount of seclusion. Creating some visual and auditory seclusion is important because wandering and succumbing to distractions are primary problems for children in group care. Using furniture or low dividers to separate spaces helps.

Clear expectations for child and staff behavior. Clarity about how materials can be used and how staff are expected to behave (for example, get down on the floor, closely supervise the use of particular materials, keep the material in the area) assist in creating a relaxed atmosphere. A poster with pictures of what is expected is very effective.

Zoning. Planning the overall relation of different areas and their impact on each other can minimize problems. For example, messy areas should be placed away from carpets and active areas away from quiet areas.

Sufficient number of areas and choices. Building in choices, some novel, some familiar, is important in engaging children's interest. There is no simple formula for deciding how many learning centers and what choices should be made; however, keep in mind that the aim is for children to be alone or in groups of two or three and to be actively engaged. Too many choices can be overwhelming; too few can be boring.

Rotation. Change, even small changes, helps to keep up children's interests. The rotation of play materials within learning centers, the alteration of the arrangement of areas, even changes in their location within the space may be enough to stimulate renewed interest when children show signs of boredom.

Developing a Room Layout

It helps to set aside preconceptions and knowledge of how the room has been used in the past and to start with an empty room, either in fact or in mind.

Start by thinking about the fixed space: doorways, windows, bathrooms, sinks. Try to get a picture of the several kinds of primary flows: people traffic, food and supplies and ensuing equipment, noise, dirt, and cool and warm air. Think about how these affect the program and the children.

Think about what is going to take place in the room: eating, large motor activities, messy play, and quiet play. List absolutely everything, including events such as children undressing for water play, children and parents arriving and putting away their belongings, and parent and staff talking together.

Now ask what other possible spaces are available, such as the hallways and outside, to supplement or replace activities in the room.

What are the essential activity settings, and what are the learning centers needed? Which areas need to be multipurpose? For example, table areas are typically used for eating, table toys, as well as messy play. Which areas are generally permanent—for example, dramatic play and the book corner?

Given all of the above,

◆ what flow of communication and materials is necessary?

◆ what transformations are necessary during the day to create an eating space, a nap space?

◆ what features exist in the setting that lend themselves to locating one area in a particular part of the space? These may include the placement of windows, sinks, electrical outlets, doorways that lead to other parts of the center or to the outdoors, floor coverings, storage, heat.

Anita Olds suggests thinking of a neighborhood, a warmer concept than that of zones, "defined both by the fixtures they require and by their personalities. All the areas which need water should be grouped near the sink. But it is probably better to put painting, rather than water play, close to the reading corner. The movement and talk that occurs around a water table are distracting. In creating areas, think about separating messy and neat, quiet and noisy, expansive and contained activities"(Olds, 1984, p. 14).

The next step is to consider what minor physical alterations would greatly enhance the space, for example, more wall storage, display space, or bench tops (see figure page 76).

Keep in mind:

◆ all children (and most adults) give credence to the maxim, *"Materials placed close together will be used together."* Thus, for example, unless the guinea pig can swim, keep animals away from the water play area.

◆ young children, like bowlers, need their whole bodies in order to perform a task. They need room; they are always getting used to rapidly changing bodies that don't seem to respond quite as competently as they imagined they would. Children not only need the freedom to move about the space but to use their whole body when engaged in activities, whether it be stacking blocks or grasping a toy. When allocating space to a learning center, we need to visualize children lying extended while focusing on toys. Conflict, accidents, and messes follow upon cramped space.

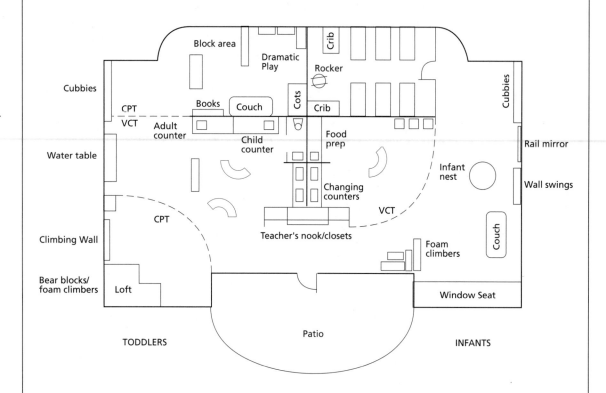

Furnishing the Environment

This handbook looks at appropriate furniture and equipment in our discussions of care and learning and considers equipment issues of environmental health and safety in chapter 11. Here, we want to note some important concerns with selecting furnishings and equipment and to provide some observations on common equipment.

There are no best furnishings for infant or toddler programs. Many decisions are a matter of taste and opinion; either there are few developmental implications or professionals do not agree on the issues. In those cases—when to switch from cribs to cots, cots versus mats, what age to introduce computers, the need for lofts or particular equipment and so on—knowing both prevailing practices in the community and parent and staff perceptions will result in better purchasing.

General Criteria for Selections of Furnishings

1. *Durability*—how long will it hold up? Center use is at least ten times as hard as home use.

2. *Safety*—sharp edges or corners? parts to swallow? toxic finishes? Will the item be pulled or tipped over? Will it wear or break in a manner that then makes it dangerous?

3. *Health*—does it allow for easy cleaning and disinfecting?

4. *Size/scale*—is it the right size and scale for projected and unanticipated use by all children or all adults—including those with special needs?

5. Is it consistent with the program goals, i.e., developmentally appropriate experience, autonomy, authenticity?

6. Does it facilitate the caregiver's task?

7. Does it add to the child/parent's sense of security?

8. *Aesthetics*—is the design attractive? Do the color, size, and shape add or detract from the overall aesthetic (e.g., will there be too much primary-colored, plastic equipment)?

Some Thoughts on Common Furnishings

Equipment for Food Preparation and Feeding   *Refrigerators:* essential in the infant room (even in programs with kitchens) for food preparation and medications; highly desirable in toddler rooms.

Bottle warmers or *Crock Pots:* essential in the room. NOTE: *Microwaves are not recommended* because uneven heating creates the danger of internal burns to the throat and esophagus.

Infant feeding: specific factors guiding the choice of high chairs, low chair trays, "sassy seats" that attach under a table, or very small "me do it" chairs and tables are the program space that is available for equipment when not in use and the caregiver's preference for sitting, standing, or sitting on the floor (with low chairs).

Toddler feeding: developmentally, once the child can sit up, tables and chairs are much preferable to high and low chairs with trays that restrain the child unless they lead to replacing individualized mealtimes with group meals. Group tables with built-in seats are not recommended because they confine children and place them very close together.

Equipment for Sleeping   *Cribs:* the important specific criteria for selecting a crib include small size, safety criteria (including less than 2⅜ inches between slats), and adjustable mattress height or drop side.

Cots: storage is a key criterion in choosing between folding mats and cots, as well as cleanability and durability of stitching and fabric.

Equipment for Comfort and General Function   *Couches, easy chairs, and futons:* great for sitting, climbing up and on. Flexibility of futons and "flip" chairs and couches is a huge plus. Specific criteria to pay attention to: size and stain resistance (NOTE: using throws extends fabric life).

Bean bag chairs: useful for age fifteen months and over, *but not safe for infants due to threat of Sudden Infant Death Syndrome.* Specific criteria: durability of seams, washable covers.

Rocking chairs and glider chairs: nearly essential, even though potential for pinched fingers requires supervision. Specific criteria: spacing of slats and safety of rocker mechanism for inquiring fingers.

Infant bounce seats (air chairs): these are useful but subject to overuse. Particularly for younger infants, more holding and use of infant carriers (Snuglis) and less use of these chairs is desirable.

Chairs: criteria for choosing chairs should include space requirements, stacking, aesthetics, size, weight, and support. Armchairs, light enough for toddlers to move around, and educubes that have multiple play uses are desirable.

Tables: tables have limited use for play, so it is not desirable to add tables beyond those used for meals except for small tables with rims for loose-part play, tub or water tables, and nesting tables.

Play pens, play lofts: useful programmable play space for non-mobile babies. Specific criteria: portability and size relative to space.

Equipment for Toileting, Washing, and Drinking   *Changing counters:* changing counters should have *at least* 36 inches of space for the infant, 48 inches for toddlers, and a 3-inch lip to help prevent rolling off. Straps are not desirable both because they are unpleasant for the child and because they give caregivers a false sense of security. Counters should be in the room or in an alcove that provides visibility and easy access to the room. Steps up to a changing counter are preferred by some, but many (including the authors) are concerned about the risk of allowing children to climb up 36 inches over a nonresilient surface, even under adult supervision. It is highly desirable to have the

Single Diaper Changing Area

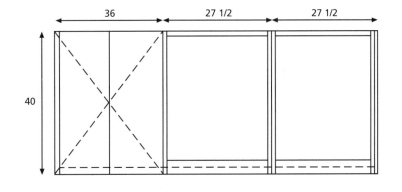

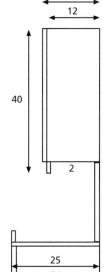

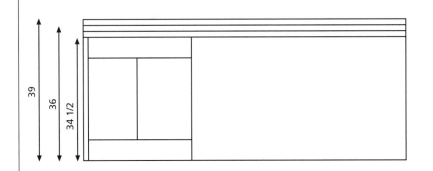

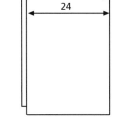

sink included in the counter (add another 18 to 24 inches to the length). See figure above.

Toilets: child-height toilets or potty chairs should be available to children around eighteen months old.

Sinks: child-access sinks should be 16 to 18 inches off the floor with easy-to-grip and -use handles (levers preferable), aerated, with low water flow and a basin at least 8 inches deep to reduce splashing. Hot water should be kept under 110 degrees.

Drinking fountains: it is desirable for toddlers to have access to a lever-operated fountain with mouth guard protection or to individual cups for independent use.

Equipment for Transporting Children   Four- and six-passenger carts, single and double strollers, and car seats for field trips in cars or vans are all very desirable to get children out and about (but not to replace "toddling walks").

Equipment to *not* use *Wind-up swing:* these swings are justified for use only when programs endure such poor conditions that they have few means to cope with children's distress. They are nearly always overused to pacify infants. They are also not very durable.

Walkers and jump ups: walkers and jump ups are not recommended because they have no positive developmental effects (and may slightly retard motor development) and can be dangerous, particularly walkers.

Evaluating the Space

As the children get older, the composition of the group changes, and just as the daily timetable needs to be looked at critically every now and then, so does the arrangement of space. There may be bottlenecks, spaces that are underused or not used at all, places that are constantly messy and disorganized, and places where the play is not as constructive as it could be.

◆ Watch how the children and adults use the space. Wandering, illegal climbing, using each other as playthings, or seeking tiny spaces all indicate what is missing in the space for children. Staff leave similar clues. Items left on changing tables indicate a need for storage surfaces. Fumbling around for tissues points to a need for greater accessibility. Constantly walking through play areas and interrupting activities there or stepping over babies says something about pathways.

◆ Take a child's eye view of the space. What does a baby see and feel?

Periodically, not just in times of crisis, it can be very helpful to have someone outside the room observe. They may notice concerns, as well as the effects of good arrangements.

A Quick and Simple Evaluation

Look at your space when all the adults and children are gone. Ask yourself the following three questions:

◆ Does this seem like a great place to be a baby?
◆ Does this seem like a great place to be with a baby?
◆ Does this seem like a good place to work?

If the answer to any of those questions is no, then the more daily magic adults must provide to make things work. The more *use* and *education* built into the setting, the better it will work.

Changing the Space

Because a familiar place is an important source of security, change should be thoughtful and major familiar landmarks should stay constant. Involving the older children and having all the children witness change makes alterations in space less stressful.

It takes time to tell whether a change in environment will have the desired results. Staff need to give most changes a few weeks for staff, children, and parents to adjust before deciding whether they are helpful or not helpful improvements.

A Final Word: Preventing Overstimulation

We often put so much energy into making our programs rich and inviting that we forget about guarding against a human and physical environment and a daily schedule that result in children feeling bombarded with stimulation. The result is sensory overload. How much is too much? Too much causes distress or prevents children from getting involved.

It is fairly easy to judge when a child does not have enough to do. It is considerably more difficult to judge at what point a baby has too much to react to or interact with. The best guide is the child's involvement and mood. A child who is unhappy or distracted, who only interacts very briefly and superficially with toys and people, may have too many things to react to.

While younger children sometimes have the capacity to turn off or ignore things around them, overstimulation is still an ever-present concern. A child who frequently has to turn off excess noise, confusion, and activity in the room uses up energy and is also very likely to turn off meaningful experiences. This is particularly true of children with special needs.

Overstimulation is different for each child. Young babies, for example, may be startled and upset by loud or unexpected noises that a toddler would find entertaining. Some children are adept at filtering out irrelevant stimuli and pursuing their own activities, while others are more apt to notice everything and to try to respond to it. The latter group of babies needs more protection, more quiet time, for it tends to be excitable and overwhelmed by the need to respond to everything and everybody. Knowing each baby's characteristics will affect the way a sensitive caregiver interacts with each of them.

Also keep in mind that mobile babies have more control over the kind and amount of input they are exposed to than do younger babies. Nonmobile babies often have too much or too little to react to.

EXERCISES

1. Chart the paths of major traffic flow in a baby room. Do they cut across learning centers? What can you do about it?

2. What are the pressure points during the day—the times that are difficult for staff and children? Why is this so? What can be done to improve them?

3. Look at the arrangement of time and space in a center you know. What messages do they give about the qualities that staff value in children?

REFERENCES

Olds, Anita. Quoted in "Fine Details: Organizing and Displaying Materials," *Beginnings* (Summer 1984): 13–16.

Prescott, Elizabeth. "The Physical Environment—A Powerful Regulator of Experience." *Child Care Information Exchange* [vol.7] (April 1979): 1–5.

Part 3

Quality Caregiving

Chapter 7
Good Care for Infants and Toddlers

Each child has a primary caregiver who develops a special relationship of mutual trust and respect with that child and his or her parents and works with all the program staff to ensure a positive child care experience for the child and parents. Each child is cared for in a warm and affectionate manner that best suits his or her particular nature. Every child learns that

✔ **no matter how young**
✔ **no matter how old**
✔ **no matter how messy**
✔ **no matter how fussy**
✔ **no matter how angry**
✔ **no matter how active**

no matter what, he or she will be loved and well-cared for.

Introduction

Human interactions are the heart and soul of a good program for babies. Nothing is more important than creating a place that is fueled by adults' simple enjoyment in caring for babies.

Essential Qualities of the Child's Experience

Good care happens when caregivers constantly stay focused on the important elements of the child's experience. Caregivers are always jugglers, with many priorities to balance like balls in the air as they plan curriculum, routines, and parent connections. Which are the balls made out of glass they cannot afford to drop?

Warmth and Affection

Babies need to be cared for in a way that lets them know they are special, individuals with their own needs, preferences, and moods. Pleasurable experiences shared with caregivers over time will foster the development of positive relationships.

Time Alone with the Primary Caregiver

Each child should have the opportunity for some time each day alone and truly engaged with the primary caregiver. What the two do together is not nearly as important as how they do it: The child should be treated as an important person who can bring pleasure to others. This helps to develop the child's positive sense of self.

◆ *Beng waddles over with a forbidden paper clip. His caregiver smiles and accepts the paper clip and together she and Beng put the paper clip out of reach on the counter, all the while talking together.*

◆ *Alexander is desperately sad and afraid after a bout of being wholeheartedly angry. Bobbie, his caregiver, accepts his outreached hands and holds him; their physical contact and her soft words help him understand that the storm inside him is gone.*

◆ *Eight-week-old Talia spent a good deal of the morning nestled against her primary caregiver Maiya's chest. Maiya went about various tasks, continually responding to Talia's sounds and movements with rubbing, cooing, and smiling.*

In each case, because the caregiver responded appropriately to the child's social overtures and indications of need, the child had an opportunity to initiate pleasurable social interactions.

It Isn't What You Give, It's What They Get

Have you ever had someone who loved you try to show you love and care, *but you didn't feel loved or well cared for?* It is the love and care *the child feels* that counts, not our giving. This is a much harder standard of quality to achieve; it means that we have to be in tune with the child's reactions, not simply to evaluate what we did.

Individual Care

Every infant or toddler deserves caregiving practices especially tailored for him or her rather than practices that expect the child to fit the program. Yes, the developmental goals for each infant or toddler in a group will be similar, but the ways of achieving them will vary, depending on a particular child's needs and characteristics.

◆ *Jacob hates to be hurried, while Anna is always in a hurry and gets fussy when diapering goes on too long. Ramon is always wary (and weary) late in the day and Keisha is still raring to go.*

There will be children with a range of temperaments (e.g., easygoing, slow-to-warm-up, and difficult); energy levels and parent preferences for caregiving practices.

Continuity and Consistency of People and Practices

Only a small number of people should be regularly involved in the care of each child. Why? Consistency of warm, responsive, individualized care teaches the child that the caregiver can be trusted and that the world is a somewhat predictable place. Being able to anticipate experience gives the child feelings of power and control.

Responsive Care

Infants and toddlers need to make things happen, to learn that they can exercise some control over the social and physical world. It is how they test and make sense of the world. A caregiver's job is to understand each child's capabilities and provide him or her with opportunities to do something interesting to the world instead of always being done to and for.

Probably most important is caring for children in a way that helps them to learn they can have an effect on other people and that overtures on their part will usually lead to predictable responses. Responsiveness of caregiving applies to every aspect of care, from providing toys geared to children's developmental capabilities to providing food when they signal that they are hungry to responding with a smile and vocalization to the children's smiles and sounds. Of course, the appropriateness of the response is as important as its dependence on the children's behavior.

Learning from Everything

Every experience is potentially a learning experience, and babies should be cared for in a way that optimizes their opportunities for learning and social interaction during routine daily activities. Babies learn attitudes and feelings about people as well as information about the world and ways of solving problems from the way they are cared for. Since routine activities occupy a large part of the child's day, caregivers should see these not as chores to be done as quickly as possible but as PRIME TIMES for being together, talking, and learning.

Protection from Overstimulation

How much stimulation is too much? It varies from child to child. If babies have too many things around them to play with, touch, listen to, and look at, they may be overwhelmed. They need a balance of sameness and variability in order to engage experiences and learn effectively. Babies need time to absorb new information and consolidate new skills, and this cannot be done under the constant bombardment of new experiences. The caregiver, by being aware of the atmosphere and staying calm, quiet, and gentle during even the busiest times, can influence the atmosphere of the room to a large extent.

Protection from Prolonged or Excessive Distress

Distress indicates need. Very young babies may need help in quieting themselves, and all babies need help and warm support in learning to manage their distress. When adults respond to distress promptly and appropriately, babies learn to manage their own distress instead of crying excessively to get what they want. Does this mean that distress should always lead to a baby's getting what it wants? No. It means that crying is a legitimate way to communicate and that a baby should not be allowed to cry for a long time or to become hysterical.

Respect for Each Child's Disposition to Learn

Babies are born with a disposition toward learning as a pleasurable activity. How can you maintain and enhance this disposition? Probably most powerful is a caregiver's own enjoyment of caregiving and her own capacity to show pleasure in learning. Caregivers should be aware of what is pleasurable to the child and encourage the child's reactions. If learning is a pleasurable experience, more learning and exploration will take place. Also, learning to learn with pleasure involves a special kind of social interaction with the caregiver.

Pleasure in Other Babies

Babies enjoy and learn a great deal from interacting with other babies. For very young babies (noncrawlers) this means frequently placing them near one another. At the same time, babies must be protected from each other as they begin the difficult task of learning how to interact. Caregivers must help older babies who have little self-control and no understanding of or ability to share. It is also important to give babies opportunities to be alone. Spending all of their time as part of a group might encourage an excessive dependence on others for entertainment and help. Children under three need some protection from each other and some places where they cannot be intruded upon by other children.

It Feels like Home: Links between Home and Child Care

In a good child care program, there is consistency between the ways the child is cared for at home and in care. Caregivers must respect the

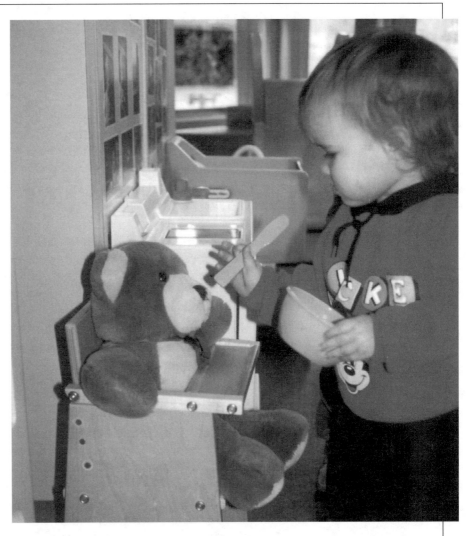

parents' right to make decisions about the care of their child and try to follow the parents' practices. Arrangements should be set up to ensure that parents and caregivers can talk with each other daily about the child.

Guidelines for Quality Interactions

In their wonderful book, *Infants, Toddlers, and Caregivers* (1992), Janet Gonzalez-Mena and Diane Eyer developed guidelines for caring for children that emphasize respect for children and primacy of caregiving moments as the bases for interactions and developing trust. The following is an adaptation of their principles (pp. 9–24):

◆ *Involve babies in things that concern them. Respond to their interests.* Involve children in feeding, diapering, dressing, searching for toys; use language and respond to their efforts to communicate: "Here's your spoon," "Let's reach for the cup," "Hold your boot," "OOPS, you dropped your boot." Encourage children's fascination with zippers, buttons, shoelaces. Don't work around them or distract them to get the job done faster.

◆ *Invest in quality time, when you can give them your full human presence. Don't settle for being together but only "half there."* Be on the floor, the grass, the furniture, *with* them. Good caregiving is not about overseeing children but rather about being with them.

◆ The most powerful moments are true give and takes, reciprocal actions, or communications in which we connect: singing a child to sleep, playing "hide-and-find," setting up for lunch together.

◆ *Learn the child's unique way of communicating (cries, words, gestures, movements, facial expressions, body positions), and teach them yours.*

◆ *Don't underestimate or ignore their ability to communicate.* Examples: Maria's enthusiasm is clear when she arches her body and waves her chubby fist, while Arthur demonstrates his by puffing his cheeks and grunting. When Matilda is tired, her sunny disposition sours and she clings and whines.

◆ *Invest in time and energy to build a total person. Don't strive just to make the child "smart" or "nice."* Better babies are not babies who walk or talk first, who do tricks or are quick to respond to activities. Better babies are babies allowed the range of active experiences with people, things, and their own bodies to motivate them to keep exploring and experimenting.

◆ *Respect the child as an individual person. Don't treat him as a cute doll or object to be manipulated.* Tell children what is happening or what will happen: "I'm going to check your pants now," "Let's look for some dry clothes," "We have to wait for a cracker now, I know you're hungry."

◆ *Be honest about your feelings, and authentic in your interactions. Don't pretend to feel or not to feel something.* It is okay to tell children that their actions are annoying you or making you angry. Your body language clearly lets them know it, anyway, and to try and hide it in your voice is only confusing. "I know you are only experimenting with gravity by dropping your spoon, but it's annoying me. Stop, please, or we are finished!"

Obviously, caregivers need to control their anger in interacting with children. But it is appropriate to use words to tell them how we feel. It is *not* appropriate to act out strong negative feelings of anger, frustration, and impatience.

◆ *Model the behavior you want to teach, and use words to describe what is happening.*

◆ *Don't preach or scold.* Fourteen-month-old Jason is exploring ten-month-old Emily fairly roughly. "Gently, Jason," says the teacher as she gently strokes both Jason and Emily. "Feel how smooth your arms are."

◆ *Let children learn to solve their own problems when appropriate. Don't take away valuable learning opportunities.* Don't step in right away as Elena meets George on a narrow ramp or Stevie tries to pull the toy out from under the couch and cries out in frustration. When you decide that you need to step in, look for a way to provide the least amount of support that might resolve the situation.

◆ *Build security by teaching trust.*

◆ *Don't teach distrust by being undependable or incomprehensible. Keep promises.* "I can't pick you up right now, but I'll do it as soon as I finish changing Marina's diaper." "I'm leaving now, but I'll be back." "We are going to go inside in a minute." "I'm making your bottle right now." Predictability and communication teach trust.

◆ *Be concerned about the quality of development in each stage. Don't rush babies toward developmental milestones.* Who was the first to walk, talk, or learn to use the toilet in your social circle? Does it matter to you now? Better isn't faster, better is fuller and richer experiences and appreciation for all the milestones, whenever they occur.

Infants and Toddlers in Distress

The sensitivity of your caregiving practices may be instrumental in influencing the skills a child develops for expressing needs, getting attention from adults, and coping with frustration. In life in general and in group settings in particular, periods of distress are a given. However, good planning and sensitive caregiving will greatly reduce the stress that babies experience.

Causes of Distress: The First Few Months

Babies cry for many reasons, and the reasons change as babies get older. There is typically more crying from younger babies. As babies get older, instances of crying may become fewer but more sustained and intense and the reasons for crying become more obvious.

Very young babies often cry because of

◆ hunger

◆ tiredness

◆ wet or soiled diapers

◆ pain (e.g., gas, teething, colic)

◆ other discomfort (e.g., clothing that is too tight, too warm, too cold; an uncomfortable position; removal of clothing)

◆ boredom

◆ overstimulation

◆ sudden change (e.g., a loud noise, sudden loss of support, bright lights, being placed in water, being picked up abruptly).

Sometimes an infant's reason for crying is not obvious, and the caregiver will have to respond in a trial-and-error manner, even with a baby she knows well. The caregiver's manner should be gentle and soothing, for both she and the baby are likely to be feeling impatient with each other and themselves at the time.

Causes of Distress as Infants Grow

After the first couple of months of life, new causes of distress emerge.

Early Frustration As babies become increasingly aware of the world around them, they seem to develop some awareness of their limited repertoire of skills. A good example of this occurs in the early stages of reaching, when the baby's aim is not accurate and any efforts are fumbling. After several unsuccessful attempts to obtain an object, some infants and toddlers seem to become very annoyed with their own ineptness and may cry vigorously. Some babies become markedly less irritable as competencies increase. However, as infants become more mobile and take more active, assertive, adventuresome approaches to the world, they are certain to attempt many things they cannot do safely and get themselves into problem situations. New frustration and some scratches and bruises are inevitable.

Often infants become more impatient and easily upset during a time when they are attaining a new skill such as learning to walk. Their tolerance for frustration in most areas seems to drop as they direct their efforts toward developing new competencies.

Infants also become distressed when something pleasurable is terminated, such as when an adult withdraws attention or an interesting toy. Crying sometimes indicates impatience because needs are not being met fast enough.

So what do you do? There needs to be a balance between helping the child by making the situation easier to cope with, rescuing the child, and letting the child work things out. For example, a nonmobile baby who is upset because a toy is out of reach and who cannot move to retrieve it should, of course, have it placed nearer. On the other hand, always accommodating a child who does not like being put down after being held or who loudly protests the end of the applesauce at lunch may encourage excessive crying to get his own way. A better response to this kind of crying is to engage the child with something else.

Distress at Nap Time Crying or less intense fussiness and whimpering may be the major cues a baby gives to indicate readiness for a nap. If the child is not asleep when put down in the cot, he or she may cry. The child may be irritated at having been taken away from the action. If the caregiver is fairly certain that the child is sleepy, she should leave the child for a while. What is a while? It depends on the child and the level of distress. The caregiver who knows a child well can tell when a point has been reached at which the child will not be likely to quiet himself or herself and therefore needs help.

When babies are around nine to twelve months old, they get used to the routine and seem to accept napping or resting when tired, so the job of getting them to sleep may become easier. Because of their new motor skills, they may also become more physically tired. On the other hand, some babies at this age become less willing to miss what is going on in the room, and stopping to nap may prove difficult. Firm, affectionate, consistent handling is especially necessary with infants and toddlers who resist nap time.

Unpleasant Encounters with Other Children As babies begin to move around, opportunities to interact with other babies increase. Many pleasurable play situations occur as babies discover each other. However, there will inevitably be occasions when infants and toddlers upset other babies by exploring them too roughly or by taking a toy. The caregiver should view these situations as times to help babies begin to learn how to interact, not occasions for moral judgment and discipline. Both babies in such a situation need support and help. Sometimes separating them is the best solution. A duplicate toy may be introduced.

Fearful Response to Strangers Sometime during the last half of the first year, many babies go through a period of showing negative reactions to strangers. This period should be respected and babies' feelings considered. When a stranger is present, stay close to a baby who is reacting to the stranger with concern or hold the baby, and let the stranger know about the child's concern. Unfamiliar people viewed from a caregiver's lap are less threatening than those seen from the floor. Of course, caregivers have to be careful not to be overly protective of babies who are distressed by strangers. If a caregiver runs to hold a baby protectively whenever a stranger approaches, and encourages the stranger to stay at a distance or to leave the room, the baby may be learning that new people are to be feared. Instead, using her relationship of trust, the caregiver is in an excellent position to help the child begin to react positively to new people.

Excessive Confusion and Change Crying both contributes to and reflects the atmosphere of the room; for example, the noise level, the amount of activity, how crowded it is, the calmness or confusion. Some babies are much more adept than others at filtering out stimulation. Obviously, if there are staffing changes, a number of new children, or distress, this may cause distress.

Kids Move in Mysterious Ways

"Why is Joey crying now?" We don't always know the source of distress, but we usually come up with a reason that satisfies our need for explanation: change of routine, something at home, the weather, a cold. Sometimes the cause becomes apparent a few days later when the child develops a cold, ear infection, or some other illness; often it does not. Parents and caregivers can be helpful to each other in looking for explanations and seeking to alleviate the child's distress.

The Caregiver's Role

Crying always has meaning for the child—infants and toddlers don't just cry "for no reason." Therefore, sensitive caregivers always respond to crying by noticing it, considering its meaning, how to react to it, and then by reacting. This does not mean that a good caregiver always intervenes immediately when a infant or toddler cries. On the contrary, the caregiver may decide to wait for a time to give the child an opportunity to quiet himself or herself. A child may cry not because anything is wrong physically but because he or she wants to be held close or played with. Respect these needs and attend to them as you do needs for food, rest, or dry diapers. *When infants and toddlers feel hungry, tired, confused, frightened, or insecure, they* need *to be nurtured.* They need reassurance, holding, laps, hugs, smiles, and touches. A child in distress doesn't benefit from indifference or slow responses. If a child is crying and you can pick him or her up, do it!

Are there exceptions to this? Yes, some babies seem to need to wind down by crying themselves to sleep. In this case, crying isn't vigorous and does not go on for a long time.

You may not always be able to solve the child's concern, but you can at least acknowledge the feelings and respond sympathetically. For example, you can say something like, "I know that you are having trouble waiting for your bottle," while rubbing the child's stomach. Making eye contact and physical contact reassures the child that at least the world cares.

How you respond to distress is critically important. Your sensitive response helps the child learn to trust other people, to trust that needs will be met and help given when requested. At the same time, you are helping the child to develop resources for coping with some unpleasant situations and relieving his or her own distress.

Individual Differences in Response to Distress

There are wide individual differences among babies in the frequency, intensity, and causes of distress episodes. While it can be said that all normal babies cry sometimes and under some circumstances, there are not specific cries for particular situations that are typical of all babies. But you can become sensitized to the meaning of particular kinds and intensities of cries in individual babies, that is, whether they indicate hunger, pain, tiredness, or a rather half-hearted attempt to protest.

There are vast differences in the ways babies show distress, just as there is great variability in the way they show pleasure (of course, this is true for adults as well). For example, a fairly mild cry by Thea, who seldom gets upset, would be more cause for concern than that same cry by Damien, who is often irritable.

Babies also differ widely in their ability to quiet themselves when upset and therefore differ in the kind of consolation they require from caregivers when they are upset. Some young infants (less than three to four months old) become excited easily and are generally very "fussy." They may need much direct help in quieting themselves by being picked up, carried, rocked, or, more indirectly, by being cared for in a serene, consistent, predictable setting. Some infants, even if they become very distressed, seem to be able to calm themselves relatively easily, while others seem to have to "cry themselves out" and require adult intervention in order to stop. For some infants, this intervention may mean a few comforting words at a distance while for another child in the same situation, the caregiver will know that she has to pick up the child.

Do not worry about spoiling a young infant by responding quickly to crying, for this responsiveness and help will aid in the development of later skills for self-quieting. Some infants can quiet themselves and should be given the opportunity to do this; some cannot. Your response depends on understanding the individual baby and the cause of its distress. From the beginning, the way you react to the baby's crying builds the relationship.

Response to Distress and Cultural Differences

As in almost everything, cultural practices differ in adult response to crying and other signs of distress. Some cultures typically attend to distress quickly and consistently, while others respond to some crying and ignore others. Some cultures believe that some crying is a sign of good health and exercises the lungs, and others that it is a sign of parental inattention. Every center should have a good understanding of the practices of the babies' families, some of which will be based on cultural background. While it is useful to have some information about cultural practices, a little information can be dangerous. It is important not to overgeneralize and assume that child-rearing practices of all parents will be based on cultural background—or worse, to generalize from apparently similar cultures (e.g., Vietnamese and Chinese) when we do not understand the many differences. We know that practices within our own culture vary quite a bit but often tend to generalize about other cultures.

At a workshop on cultural differences, caregivers from a variety of cultures highlighted some of the issues that arise in relation to crying and distress. Some cultures keep babies close: the baby is held or strapped to the mother's back or front (usually the mother, but often grandmother, sister, aunt), fed on demand, and toileted by anticipating their need to urination or have a bowel movement. Mothers in those cultures become particularly tuned in to their babies' needs and anticipate them before children become distressed. These babies seldom cry at home. When they experience the very different reality of group care, they may have trouble adjusting unless the program accommodates their expectations by holding and using infant carriers.

Caregivers also pointed out that when and where babies cry may be significant and elicit different responses. For some Chinese, it is especially bad luck if a baby cries on New Year's Day, as it is thought to bring bad luck to the family for the entire year, so a lot of care is taken on that day to prevent distress. Other caregivers mentioned that crying in public is considered inappropriate and that crying in the crowded family living conditions of many new immigrants results in great care taken to prevent distress.

While centers cannot always accommodate what babies are familiar with, it is important that staff be sensitive and understand that it will be hard for some infants and toddlers to adjust to being on their own, to experience new levels of distress, and to calm themselves initially.

Discouraging the Crying of Toddlers

There are times when it is appropriate to withhold attention from toddlers briefly to avoid reinforcing negative behavior or to give them chances to solve their concerns, such as frustration with a toy or peer. But it is important that this controlled noninterference doesn't become less responsive nurturing.

Caregivers have a lot of demands on their time and energy, and it is not unusual to see programs where infants get attention only when they cry, act out, or the caregiver finds it convenient. Guard against this! As babies get older and develop other ways to communicate, you don't want toddlers to learn that the most effective way of getting attention is to cry. If a child does not receive consistently positive responses to such communications (e.g., being picked up when holding out arms, being smiled at when smiling), then he or she may learn to rely primarily on crying as a means of getting attention.

There are times when a child wants more attention than a caregiver can possibly give. If you feel the needs of this child have been met and the child is receiving a lot of quality individual time, you may decide to ignore distress and see if its frequency decreases over time. But cooperation between parents and child care staff is essential if changes in the child's behavior are to be expected.

Young children need to learn to work out minor irritations on their own, but they need our support to do so. It is difficult but wise for a caregiver to respond by saying something encouraging and doing nothing when a child complains over a small problem that the caregiver believes the child has the competence to work out on his own. Allowing the child to do this is one way a caregiver provides appropriate challenges that lead young children to develop new competencies and skills.

Prevention of Distress

Obviously the prevention of distress is important, in part because distress is contagious. The best strategies for preventing distress and keeping it at a minimal level are to anticipate needs before they occur. Some methods of doing this include the following:

- ◆ knowing children's schedules.
- ◆ being alert to early signs of hunger, sleepiness, or irritability.
- ◆ providing a safe, interesting environment that is neither overly stimulating nor overly restricting.
- ◆ helping children learn to have pleasurable interactions with each other by protecting them from hurting each other.
- ◆ providing many opportunities for success.
- ◆ giving children encouragement and help.

Many potentially distressing situations can be avoided by knowing a child's limitations. What gets in the way is seeing the child's distress as a deliberate test or as making unreasonable demands. For instance, a child who in the caregiver's judgment should not be hungry may get upset if he has to stand by while another child gets fed. Rather than ignoring the problem or punishing the child for being unreasonable, make the situation easier to tolerate by helping him to get interested in another activity or allowing him to participate by eating a biscuit or piece of fruit while the other child is being fed.

Coping with a child's distress is a major source of caregiver distress. A child's crying tends to affect everyone negatively who can hear it and brings out a gamut of adult feelings—sympathy, anger, frustration, and even embarrassment ("How come my babies are always crying?" lamented one caregiver). A period of prolonged fussiness and crying will wear down even the most patient and understanding caregiver. Punishing (including ignoring) a child for crying is not acceptable. A caregiver working with an irritable or distressed child who will not be quieted needs support and relief from other caregivers, for these are perhaps the most difficult times of caregiving.

Primary Caregiving

The primary-caregiver system ensures that every child has a "special" person and that each parent has a primary contact. How is the primary caregiver "special"? She becomes an expert on the child, an advocate, and a coordinator of the child-and-parent experience. NOTE: *The primary caregiver-parent relationship is as important as the primary caregiver-child relationship.*

A primary caregiver's relationship with the child and parent should begin on the child's first day or even earlier, at the intake. While a child is adjusting to being in care, it is easier to get to know one new person well initially rather than several.

"Primary" does not mean exclusive. The child should not become totally dependent on the presence of one person in order to have a good day. Primary care is not the same as a small group structure, and children do not spend the day at their caregiver's side, like chicks with a mother hen. Other staff develop a warm relationship with the child and have caring and learning interactions as the child explores the learning environment.

The caregiving is primary in two senses. First, much but not all of the caring and nurturing and communicating with parents is provided by the primary caregiver. Second, the care is primary in the sense that PRIME TIMES, the most intimate and personal of care, are the major responsibility of the primary caregiver, although not to the exclusion of others.

The Role of Primary Caregivers

Primary Caregivers

- *Communicate.* You are the essential link in the communication chain between parent and program and child and program. You ensure that each day the child's experience is communicated to the parents—not just what you witnessed, but what others observed or enacted. You relay parents' concerns and suggestions to other staff.

- *Advocate.* You empower parents and children by translating their individual concerns and needs into action through the efforts of all program staff. You are the vehicle that ensures that the program "wraps around" the child and family rather than the one who insists that he child and parent fit the program.

◆ *Nurture.* You tune in to the child and develop a special bond that ensures all needs are met. You ensure that PRIME TIMES are carried out in a manner that both empowers the child and establishes a sense of security and basic trust.

◆ *Teach.* You care for each child in a manner that maximizes language experiences and the learning potential of all interactions. You ensure that the learning environment works for that child: a balance of developmentally appropriate experiences and neither too much nor too little stimulation.

◆ *Observe, monitor, and evaluate.* You make sure that the child's experience in the program is positive and that parents' concerns are addressed by continually assessing the child-and-family experience. Methods include observation, discussions with other staff, talks with parents, and assessments of the actual experience of the child and family: the care actually received rather than the presumed experience or the intended care.

Primary Caregiver's Basic Responsibilities

For each of your children, you are the "expert." You should know
◆ each child's age
◆ daily schedule
◆ developmental skills, abilities, and special needs
◆ individual personality traits, moods, interests
◆ parent and child food preferences and food sensitivities
◆ diapering and toileting needs
◆ sleeping needs
◆ preferred play and learning experiences
◆ guidance and socialization patterns

For each of your parents, you should know
◆ parents' names and schedules
◆ concerns and sensitive issues
◆ desired daily information

Important Tasks
◆ each day make each child feel special and help his or her day go well.
◆ each day make parents feel special and positive about their children.
◆ keep co-workers caring for each child up to date on all of the above.
◆ write up Daily Experience Sheets.
◆ meet with lead teacher to discuss each child's development and program experience and the parents' experience.
◆ plan appropriate individual experiences for each child.
◆ develop a positive relationship and effective communications with the parents.
◆ introduce parents to other staff.
◆ participate in parent conferences.
◆ advocate on behalf of the child and parents.

Avoiding Ownership   *"Would you change Marcel's diaper? He's your primary."*

Primary caregivers do not "own" the children. All staff have some responsibility for all children and collective responsibility for maintaining the learning environment.

An overzealous or rigid system of primary caregiving can work against the children's best interests by creating excessive delays in attention or by encouraging children to become so dependent on one caregiver that they find it difficult to function without them. Also, staff may become so attached to children that they resist caring for other children or allowing their "primaries" to move to another group.

The best way to avoid exclusive ownership is to openly acknowledge the issue as a natural tendency and to frequently discuss it when it seems to be a problem.

Assigning Primary Caregivers   Children can be assigned to a primary caregiver by the lead teacher based on compatibility with their parents' schedules and a combination of the following factors, listed in order of importance:

◆ compatibility of parents' and caregiver's schedules.

◆ roughly balanced number of children for each caregiver; this probably works best if the children are of varied ages.

◆ likely demands on caregiver (if some children are likely to be particularly demanding for an extended time, they should be distributed among the caregivers).

◆ compatibility of parent, staff, or child characteristics—"a good match."

Once assigned, children should not be reassigned while they are in the group unless staff changes or other pressing reasons make it absolutely necessary. The goal of the system is to promote security through continuity, and reassignment results in the opposite.

Issues in Assigning Caregivers   *The "Match."* How important is "the match" between the caregiver and the child, or the caregiver and the parents? Clearly, the eventual relationships are critical, but "matchmaking" is difficult logistically and doesn't guarantee results. It might be useful to think of the arrangement as more similar to an arranged marriage or an adoption than to a "love match." Caregivers and parents have a huge interest in trying to make the relationship work (as do the babies, although they, of course, may not know this), and most often it is successful. If there are characteristics that suggest a particular match, and *if* schedules and the number of primaries per caregiver work out, matchmaking is probably a good thing. Compatibility of culture and values are particularly relevant characteristics.

Competition for "the best" Primary Caregiver. Will all parents want the "most qualified primary caregiver"—the one with the most training or the highest position? Will parents feel the teachers or lead teachers are the best primary caregivers? Maybe, but not if they

understand that the primary care system is just one system that promotes quality care. The primary caregiver is not supposed to determine the child's learning experience. The educational experience of *all* of the children is the major responsibility of the person most qualified by training and experience to provide it, presumably the lead teacher. That is, planning the learning environment, activities, and guidelines for adult-child interactions is her job. The qualifications for a good primary caregiver are those we would expect from any caregiver: sensitivity, skill, and understanding of the program philosophy and practices.

Primary Caregivers Aren't Perfect. Many of us have an image in our head of the ideal caregiver. She may look like a grandmother, or a sister, or some idealized image. It may not be a "he" or someone who speaks with an accent, someone with few literacy skills, or someone who is nineteen or sixty-two years old. But if we look beyond that image, high-quality caregivers come in all shapes and sizes, speak different languages, and possess the usual assortment of human imperfections. Programs need to help parents recognize the qualities that justify each caregiver's place in the program.

Consider these comments by parents:

She could barely write. Her daily experience sheets were pretty atrocious —sparse, poor grammar, and worse spelling. When she spoke, her syntax was scrambled, and sometimes I had trouble understanding her. But I was so glad that she was Mikey's primary caregiver. I knew that Shirley would love him to death and watch out for Mikey (and John and me) as if he was her own. I cried when Mikey moved up."

Lamar was opposed to having Ben care for Tamara, and I wasn't sure myself. But we reluctantly decided to try it out. Ben was wonderful—very gentle and thoughtful—and I actually came to really appreciate that Tamara had a male caregiver. He was different: more exuberant, more physical, and he encouraged Tamara to be adventurous as she became a toddler. He even won Lamar over.

Primary Care is a Good System—Most of the Time

My baby was assigned to Wah, and we really liked her. But she went on maternity leave six weeks later and we got Vicki, who went on vacation for two weeks within a few weeks of her assignment. This is continuity?

The primary-caregiver system is designed to ensure that every parent and every child feel secure. But used mindlessly, it can make everything worse. Some examples from experience:

1. Assigning a child to a caregiver who is about to go on vacation or worse, on maternity leave. A few weeks may not feel like a long time to the staff, but to a baby or a new parent, it's a huge chunk of their child care experience.

2. So close a relationship develops that the child has a horrible day when the caregiver is not present.

3. All communication breaks down with parents when the primary caregiver is not present—no daily experience sheets, no casual conversation.

4. Assigning a child to a caregiver whose schedule is such that parents never come into contact with her—e.g., the caregiver works 8:00 to 4:30, and the child is there from 7:30 to 5:00.

All of the above are common mistakes. They happen because trying to solve one problem—staff schedules, for instance—may create another for primary caregivers.

The moral of the story: Any system requires thoughtful use. Keep your eye on what the system is supposed to accomplish and if it doesn't accomplish the goal of more continuity and better care, adapt or discard the system.

Caring Well for Children with Special Needs

Identifying Children with Special Needs

Many special needs are not evident when infants or toddlers enter the program. Because the typical range of development is quite wide, it is not easy to know when to become concerned about a child. If you have a concern that a child may have a condition beyond what is typical and that he or she may benefit from early recognition and intervention,

◆ observe the child closely and identify the behavior (or absence of behavior) and when it occurs.

◆ compare the child's behavior to developmental norms.

◆ consult with the lead teacher or director, at the same time respecting the child and family by limiting discussion of your concern with other staff.

◆ carefully discuss the concern with parents, recognizing the potential for their emotional reactions. If necessary, rehearse the conversation with the lead teacher or director.

◆ develop a plan for more observation, consultation with an outside resource, or screening with the parents. *Always* consult with the parent before bringing in resources external to the program.

Caring for Children with Special Needs

It is important to remember that your responsibility is to provide quality child care to a child with special needs, not therapeutic services. In other words, it is the caring that allows the child to succeed in your center, not professional services that his or her condition may require. When caring for children with special needs, keep in mind the following:

Recognize and Understand Your Own Feelings   Caregivers' thoughts and feelings about children with special needs are usually complicated, often a mixture of positives and negatives. A group of teachers at a workshop generated a list of the emotions they felt when they began working with children with special needs:

◆ sadness: *I almost cry when I think of the life she will lead with cerebral palsy.*

◆ pity: *I felt so sorry for Billy and his parents that it got in the way of seeing him as a complete child instead of just the blind kid.*

◆ anger: *Sometimes I find myself tired and mad. Why is this kid here if he can't control biting other children? And I get really mad at his mother—it was her drinking when she was pregnant that caused the problem.*

◆ disgust: *I hate myself, but sometimes I am revolted by the drooling and crying.*

◆ denial: *She's really okay. I just want to fix her, work really hard, and give her everything she needs, and then she will be better. She will be normal.*

◆ ignorance: *I really had a lot of misconceptions about babies with heart monitors and I was scared to death all the time.*

◆ vulnerability, incompetence, and fear: *Why me? I can't manage this child and my other babies. The parents are going to blame me if something goes wrong.*

It is natural for caregivers to struggle with a variety of feelings on their way to acceptance and appreciation of the child with special needs, particularly before actual experience with the child. Being able to acknowledge and share feelings with other staff is usually helpful, as is understanding that acceptance and a more relaxed attitude may take time.

Learn about the Special Need and Use the Parents as a Primary Resource   There is a lot of information about children with special needs available from local and national resource centers, schools, and advocacy organizations (see *Healthy Young Children*, pp. 186–187, and subscribe to *Exceptional Parent*). For physical handicaps and health conditions, often the best places to start are with the information obtained by the child's parents from other professionals and with the information the parents have gained from caring for their child.

Adapt the Program to Fit the Child   Whether the need is special or not, serving individual children requires adapting the program to them: the environment, routines, and caregiving practices. Adapting the program does not mean overprotecting children. Children with disabilities need opportunities to be challenged and to undertake manageable risks, to learn to get along with other children, to manage limits, and to experience both success and failure. Realistic expectations are important. If goals are too high, they invite failure; if too low, they diminish children's potential.

Develop an Individual Care Plan for the Child   Just as with any other child, infants and toddlers with special needs should have individual plans developed in partnership with their parents in order to have successful experiences at the center. The special-care plan should include any special medical, diet, or other care requirements.

Work as a Team   Teamwork with parents, other staff, and other professionals is essential but may be a challenge. There is more to communicate about, more emotions, more of a tendency for primary caregivers to become possessive and own a child, and more of a tendency for other staff to cede care to the primary caregiver. Often complications of both logistics and status occur when working with other health and human service professionals. Child care staff often feel (usually correctly) that their knowledge of the child is not accorded enough respect. It is important to reach an understanding of the value of all of those who support and care for the child.

The Importance of Beauty and the Child with Special Needs

"It took a long time for me to admit that I used to look at Sophia and feel disgust sometimes. I saw her as ugly and clumsy and embarrassing. She wasn't like the other twos—she couldn't walk , she slobbered, she couldn't do much, and she cried easily. And she was mine. Where was the beautiful baby I was sure that I would have? I felt sorry for myself.

"It's funny. When she moved out of the church basement center and got to go the new center and I saw her every day in a beautiful place, with big windows, trees and flowers, pretty pictures, and people who told me what a doll she was and what she could do, I had those feelings less and less. She was beautiful , and yeah, she was mine."

Children with disabilities and children from at-risk homes need and deserve to be in physically attractive settings among people who think they are wonderful. It helps everyone to see them in a different light.

A Final Word: The Challenge of Good Care for Every Child, Every Day

Providing every child with consistently good care every day and every parent with feelings of satisfaction is a challenge. Success depends on continually focusing on the characteristics and experience of individual children and their families with sensitivity and patience. Living in this world demands that we cope with a wide range of circumstances and no small amount of stress. Helping infants and toddlers develop the self-esteem and skills that fit their unique personalities and that enable them to manage daily life provides them with the foundation for social competence and well-being.

EXERCISES

1. When do you feel poorly cared for or loved? What is missing in the care you receive? Can you find parallels between those instances and some of the care received by the babies in group care?

2. When and where is overstimulation likely in your program? List all the contributing factors.

3. When are children most likely to be in distress in your program? What changes might alleviate the causes?

4. List a number of examples of how primary caregivers can make a child feel special.

5. List a number of examples of how primary caregivers can make a parent feel special.

REFERENCE

Gonzalez-Mena, J., and Eyer, D. *Infants, Toddlers, and Caregivers.* Mountain View, CA: Mayfield Press, 1993.

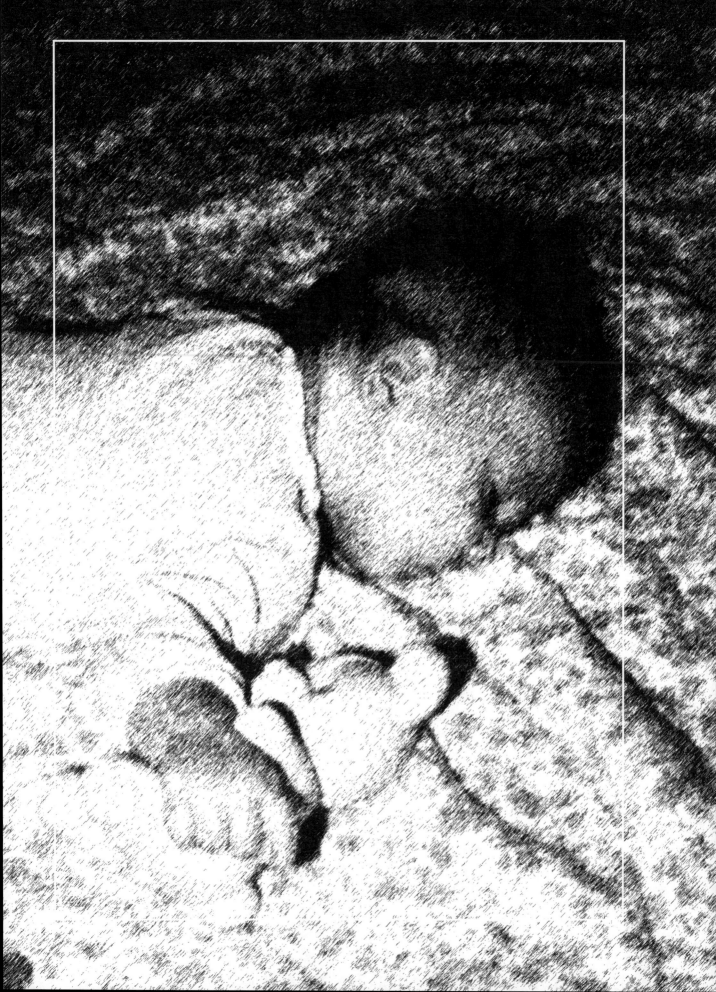

Chapter 8
Prime Times: Caring Routines

excellence

Caring times are individualized, relaxed, gentle, full of conversation and self-help. They are neither impersonal nor institutional. Caring times are recognized as prime times for developing a sense of well-being and personal worth and PRIME TIMES for learning. In the process, each child derives a sense of individual importance and well-being.

PRIME TIMES and Caregivers

We use the term *caregivers* throughout the book because giving care is the most valuable and most difficult aspect of the adult role. Education is a critical aspect of care but only one aspect. Designing caring routines that actually empower children and enhance their development is a huge challenge in group care.

The term *PRIME TIMES* signifies the critical importance of care in the child's life in the program. Caring times are PRIME TIMES. These are the times when the child's primary human needs of food, sleep, disposal of bodily waste, bathing, clothing, and nurturing from others are addressed. These times occupy a large part of both the child's and the caregiver's day in care. With a relaxed pace and gentle one-to-one contact between caregiver and child full of language, interactions, and real give and take, these are PRIME TIMES for developing a strong sense of personal worth and power, language, and a basic trust in the world as a good place. If the child is actively involved, respected as a person, and has personal needs met, these become PRIME TIMES for developing a sense of autonomy.

It makes no sense to rush through caring times to "get to the curriculum." The often-heard complaint of some caregivers, "All we do is care for the kids, we never get to the teaching," fails to recognize that those caring times are also prime teaching times: the times that children have their caregivers alone and learn through responsive care that "I am somebody, I am important."

In fact, the major goal of the rich, built-in learning environment is to engage children in independent play that allows caregivers relaxed time to diaper or nurture them: to touch, to talk, to listen, to play all the call-response games that children set in motion.

Some General Guidelines

When caring for a child,

- go as slowly as circumstances permit. These are the one-to-one times that count most.
- talk to and physically handle the child with respect when checking diapers, undressing, feeding, and nurturing. Approach the child as a person and tell the child what you are doing and why: "Alfonso, I think I should check your diaper, okay? You'll feel much drier when we're finished. Let's find a dry one."
- in carrying out these routine activities, try to keep uppermost in your mind the importance to children of developing positive self-concepts, their need to have some autonomy and to do some things for themselves, the importance of offering them choices, and the potential of these experiences to foster their sense of mastery.
- avoid talking about children across the room to other staff as if the children are dolls or are not there, saying, for example: "Alfonso's wet—would you change him while I check Alicia?" Part of being a person is not being discussed as if one were invisible or incapable of hearing.
- know yourself. Be aware of your personal feelings toward PRIME TIMES and how those may have been shaped by your own past experiences.
- adults bring strong feelings, opinions, and attitudes to PRIME TIMES from their own family experiences. Group care often means submerging some personal feelings and preferences in order to care for children in a consistent fashion.
- don't let your attitudes toward food, bodily wastes, or dirt and grime make PRIME TIMES a negative experience. "Why don't we clean you up?" is much better than "Oh, you are stinky," or "What a messy boy." Especially in relation to elimination, avoid using words like "dirty" or "smelly."
- pay attention to your body language, for children will take in its messages as much as they will your words. For example, do you wrinkle your nose, grimace, or handle children roughly during some routines?
- focus on the child's experience of discomfort, fear, or whatever causes the need to be nurtured rather than on your feelings of sympathy, disgust, fear, or overwork.

Respect for Parents' Views

Routine activities related to eating, sleeping, using the toilet, washing, and dressing are also areas where parents, because of cultural, religious, or personal preference, are likely to have strong views and to want to participate in decision making. While this makes caregiving more challenging, it is critically important for a variety of reasons that parents play a major role in decision making in these areas about their child's care. (See chapter 14, Partnerships with Parents.)

Planning Caring Routines

The goal of the daily schedule is to allow individualized care and learning within a smoothly running, predictable day. *Feeding, diapering, and sleeping should follow the child's schedule.* Not all toddlers can go all morning without a nap. For infants and young toddlers, there should be some flexibility around breakfast and lunch to synchronize with their sleeping schedules. Post each child's typical daily schedule for eating and sleeping as a guide and reminder, but don't let this get in the way of reading cues from the children about their needs.

Such flexibility relies on being organized, communicating with other staff, and operating with a sense of teamwork. Individualizing is not as simple as just sitting back and being responsive. It requires that tasks for staff be allocated. A checklist of jobs for staff to do on a daily, weekly, and as-needed basis will help. Equipment and supplies must be accessible and plentiful.

An obsession with order and neatness will interfere with providing good quality care, but continuous tidying and restoring of order are important to make the environment attractive and functional for both children and staff. The quality of play deteriorates in a disorganized environment.

Separation and Reunion: Arrivals and Departures

Children's arrivals and departures are not always included in lists of routines, but they are an important aspect of every child's day. Actually, how children start the day in the program and reunite with their parents may determine the quality of their day.

Arrivals and departures may also determine the quality of the parents' day. The difficulty or ease of separation may set the tone for the parents' day. Since arrival and departure times provide the parent with the majority of their contact with staff and with their primary glimpse of the program, these times play major roles in the parents' feelings about using care, the program, and the staff.

Helping children and parents arrive and separate should be PRIME TIMES. But these are often hectic times in a program, ones in which the full complement of staff needed may not be present or may be very busy. Consequently, parents may be overlooked in staff planning. When children come and go is up to their parents; staff cannot control "rush hours." But if parents have flexibility, they can be encouraged to come at the "off" or less busy times, when they are likely to receive better attention from the staff. Programs should also consider staffing patterns that favor such times with more people.

Separation and reunion need to be thought of as family affairs, that is, as involving the feelings and well-being of both parents and children.

The value of talking with parents when they drop their children off, however briefly on some days, cannot be overstressed. A system of exchanging written information between staff and parents on a daily basis is valuable as long as it supplements but does not substitute for face-to-face communication.

It is sometimes true that separating at the beginning of the day can be painful and/or difficult for the parent but not for the child. This needs to be acknowledged with respect for and empathy with the parent and may be a challenge for the caregiver, who may perceive that the parent's behavior and feelings are making separation more difficult for the child and life more difficult for the caregiver.

Loving Good-Byes

"I can't believe it. Allison's mom saw I had my hands full but wouldn't just put Allison on the couch or the rug—she had to hand her to me. Parents are so irrational!"

This caregiver is right—they sure are. But so are we. Love is not rational. How do you feel about parting and separating from loved ones? When you travel by airplane, even for just a few days or weeks, do you let your spouse/lover/parent just drop you off and pick you up at the curb, which is eminently practical? Or do you want them there at the gate when you go in and out of that umbilical-like tunnel to the plane? A physical exchange of the baby is important to many parents; their level of concern is a wonderful thing. Caregivers need the staffing and resources to accommodate this exchange.

Separation on a Daily Basis

Separation distress recurs throughout children's (and parents') experience, often unexpectedly and for no apparent reason. That is, nothing can be identified at home or at the center that would cause distress. The likely explanation is that the cognitive or intellectual powers of infants and toddlers are developing so quickly that their perception and understanding of even a regularly occurring familiar situation in their daily experience can seemingly change overnight. Separation takes on new meanings or children develop new understandings of it, and these can cause distress. Of course, this is true of adults as well (for example, in new love relationships, people begin to develop new perceptions, understandings, and new hopes—"What did he mean by that look?").

Good-Byes Are *Painful*

The pain that comes from separating is real, for both parents and children, and staff need to acknowledge that. Especially after a child has been coming to day care for some time and is apparently settled in and then becomes distressed, it may be tempting for caregivers and parents to deny the reality of the pain. Even when a child knows the caregiver, knows the place, and enjoys it, and at some level knows that the parent will return at the end of the day, the act of parting can still be painful. It is tempting to dismiss the child as just making us jump through hoops because the distress stops soon after the parent has departed.

It is our job to help parents and child separate, even when there is no distress or ambivalence. Greeting and welcoming both parent and child make it easier for the child to make the transition from home to care and reassures the parent. For the child, saying good-bye to a loved one is much easier while in the arms of another special person.

Parents Struggle with Separation (and Getting to Work on Time)

Saying good-bye is easier for the child if the parent does not race in and race out, although there will be days when parents are running late and this is what happens. Saying good-bye is also easier when parents do not express uncertainty or ambivalence, for example, by saying, perhaps several times, that they are going to leave but not doing so, or by actually leaving and then reappearing.

Parents do want to do what is best for their children but often are uncertain about how and when to leave. When their child is distressed, parents may feel as though they should not leave until the child is happy. Sometimes parents are reluctant to leave because they are uncertain about leaving their child in your or any care. Others may

view the child's distress as a sign that they are the most special person to the child.

When parents are the ones who appear to be having more difficulty separating, they require sympathetic assistance from staff, not criticism. Some will need gentle (and direct) advice from staff about leaving if they are clearly floundering and having difficulty knowing when and how to do it. This does not mean that staff should make the decision and tell parents the procedure to be followed.

Parents should be encouraged to phone in during the day to find out how their child is, and staff should see this as an important aspect of building a trusting relationship with them. Reports to parents at these times should be positive and optimistic but honest. That is, if the child is still upset, say so, but couch this in terms of it being normal and assure the parents that things will get better.

Parents may be tempted to sneak away without saying good-bye, thinking that this will either be best for the child or, knowing that the child will be distressed at separation, that doing so they may avoid the pain that leaving caused their child. While showing sympathy for parents' pain, staff should help them understand that it is never best to leave without saying good-bye, for this diminishes a child's feelings of trust and security and may in fact cause the child to become even more "clingy."

No Surprises

As with all other potential sources of parent stress or unhappiness, the best time to begin to help parents work through the issue is *before* they are in the midst of it. Talk about separation and other painful issues at the parent intake and prepare them for what might happen. Have a handout available, even if the same material is in the parent handbook.

Support the Child by Acknowledging Feelings

Caregivers should help each child through hard times by acknowledging feelings, giving them words, and comforting the child. One of the many things children learn from adults in the early years is what feelings are appropriate in different situations and how to recognize and acknowledge their feelings. Children need to have their feelings validated, not ignored or denied. Simply distracting the child to stop the distress is inappropriate unless it is preceded by communicating your acceptance of the child's feelings. (Think about how you would feel if, when you are sad or worried, someone tries to distract you without acknowledging your feeling first.) Say to the child who is sad something like, "I know you miss Mama. Are you very sad? Mama's working, and you'll see her after snack. Should we go look for a truck to play with?" instead of, "You're okay. Let's go play with the truck." The child is unhappy and therefore not okay.

Use Rituals and Special Objects

A special ritual or routine for the child who is settling in can be comforting, for it gives the child a feeling of control, a feeling that "I know what is going to happen now—when Dad leaves, my caregiver Mary and I always go over and feed the fish, and then we find a good toy to play with." Letting the child play an active rather than a passive role in the separation often helps. For example, the child is in the caregiver's arms and together they open the door for the parent to leave, wave good-bye, and look out of the window at the departing parent.

It is natural for children to miss their parents during the day. Children for whom the experience of being in care is new may feel comforted by having an object that belongs to the parent accessible to them, a jacket or handbag, for example. For some children, this seems to serve as an indication that the parent will definitely come back. This is a good example of how the minds of young children can work differently from those of adults. We adults know that the parent will definitely come back because their child is there, whereas for the child it makes sense that Mom will return to get her handbag! Having a photo of the family in a place accessible to the child can also be reassuring. Caregivers should talk during the day in a natural way about the parents with the child. Parents should be encouraged to visit during the day, even if the child becomes distressed at the second separation.

let's take a nap

by Nikki Giovanni

almost every day
after my lunch
after my milk
after I go to the potty
and teddy and piggy, my green turtles
have been fed
and i can't think of anything to do quick enough
mommy says "come on chocolate drop"
cause she thinks I don't remember what she wants
"lets take a nap"
just cause I'm a little feller don't mean I'm dumb!
then she takes off my shoes and pants and
hops me into her big bed
and i have to:
    climb on her chest
    be tossed in the air
    get tickled under my chin
    hear this little piggy three times
    and get the bottom of my feet kissed
        at least twice
before i put her
to sleep

"Soon" to Whom?

It is tempting to comfort children by saying that Mom or Dad will be back soon. *Soon* is a word that has many interpretations, depending on the context in which it is used. "Your birthday will come soon" may mean in two weeks; "Lunch will be here soon" may mean within thirty minutes; and when the caregiver says, "We'll have to go inside soon," she may have in mind within five minutes. Consequently, saying to a child whose parent is due an hour from now, "Daddy will be here soon" can easily be misinterpreted and result in frustration and disappointment. For an older toddler, it may help to list all the events that will take place before the parent arrives. Saying, for example, "We will have a sleep, then some afternoon tea, go outside, and when you have had a little play outside, your daddy will come," gives a more accurate sense of time to that child than "soon." The safest thing is to avoid the use of the term.

Reunions

While it is more likely that attention will be given to separations at the beginning of the day, reunions at the end of the day can be just as challenging. At the end of the day, staff, parents, and children are all likely to be tired. Babies have usually had enough of being in a group, and as other children start going home, they begin to anticipate the arrival of their own parent. It may be difficult to be one of the last to leave. It is important to provide interesting things to do, as well as extra cuddles and attention, for those children who do not go home first. Saving some special books or play materials for the end of the day can make the time special. In fact, the end of the day, if the staffing is adequate and tasks are organized, can be a pleasant time, with fewer children and therefore more opportunity for PRIME TIMES.

They Do Love Parents Best

At the end of the day, parents no doubt want an enthusiastic welcome from their child and a smooth and pleasant exit from the center. Unfortunately, for a variety of reasons, it doesn't always turn out this way. Instead, on some days, several other possibilities await parents:

◆ the children may look up briefly from what they are doing when the parents greet them and return to the activity.

◆ the children may see their parents and become distressed.

◆ the children may "act up" and engage in taboo behavior.

◆ the children, even those who did not want to stay in the morning, may actively resist going home.

None of these is what parents have in mind! They may think, "Well, it's happened—she likes these people better than she likes me; she'd rather be here than at home." The caregiver may be thinking the same thing. The parents may be embarrassed, sad, or annoyed. Of course, it is not always possible to say what children's behavior means, but the least likely interpretation is that they actually would prefer staying with the caregivers. Parents need to know that. Other possibilities:

◆ ignoring the parents or giving them only cursory greetings may actually be a sign that children have adjusted well, feel secure at the center, and knew all along that their parents would return. In other words, this behavior could just mean, "I'm glad to see you, but it's no big deal. I knew you'd come back, and so I'll just continue with what I was doing." This is not unlike the way older children respond to being reunited with their parents or the way adults respond to short-term separations from people they are close to.

◆ "falling to pieces" may be a natural reaction to the sight of the person a child is closest to. It takes a lot of internal strength and stamina for young children to cope in a group all day, and by the end of the day most of them are tired and their resistance is low. Seeing that "most special person," the one they know will love them no matter how awful they act, may just serve as a cue to act the way they feel, and the way they feel is miserable. Again, this is not unlike the way we adults cope with difficult days. We maintain a professional demeanor with colleagues, are on our best behavior, but when we get home with the people we are closest to and feel the most comfortable with, we "let it all hang out" and act the way we feel. Parents need to be reminded that children consistently behave better with caregivers than with them; they save their worst behavior for their parents. It's like the old song lyrics—"You always hurt the ones you love, the ones you shouldn't hurt at all."

◆ acting out, behaving in unacceptable ways, breaking rules, and defying limits may be the young child's way of testing an interesting situation. There are two people, the caregiver and the parent, who sometimes set limits and enforce the rules. "So, who's in charge?" Unable to articulate the question with words, the toddler asks the question through behavior. In fact, unless this is talked through with parents and expectations are made clear, parents will be uncertain and may think that while the child is at the center, the staff are in charge. The staff, thinking parents are responsible when they are present, may be looking critically at parents and wondering why they don't give their child some much-needed discipline.

◆ resisting going home may mean one of several things: the child may be expressing a wish for the parent to just stay a while in this place that is special, to just be there. The child may be resisting an engrossing activity being forcibly suddenly ended. The child may be saying something like, "I didn't like it when you dropped me off here rather abruptly this morning, so I'm not going to go easily tonight." The toddler, anticipating the hustle and bustle that may characterize his world until bed time, may even be voting with his feet to stay in this child-centered place!

◆ it is important that staff share these possible explanations with parents so that they understand their children are complex little social scientists who use their behavior to experiment with how the world of people works and their place in it.

Clear and Real *Communication*

Making clear in daily communication with parents that you enjoy caring for their children and reporting the positives in their children's day make both separation and reunion easier. A report to the parents that is honest but sensitive to their perspective is important. All parents like to hear "good news" about and indications that the staff like their children. Share all good news, but be more tactful about "not so good" news. Report the children's struggles in sympathetic and admiring tones. Most important, leave your own struggles out. Difficult parent-child separations may make our days hard, but that is our job.

Bottles, Meals, and Snacks

For children (and for many adults), what is more primal and important than eating? Meal and snack times are two of the most telling times in terms of quality in a program for babies. The pace, atmosphere, and extent to which they are actually used as PRIME TIMES are good indicators of the overall quality of the program.

For a young baby, in addition to satisfying nutritional needs, these times offer an opportunity to have the caregiver all to himself or herself, to be talked to, to be close. The nature of the feeding experience changes greatly over the first year of life. The close, peaceful time when a caregiver holds a drowsy infant and gives a bottle soon changes into a much less serene, more exciting scene when the infant is being given solids. Eventually, the child takes over much of the responsibility for self-feeding, sometimes acting with more enthusiasm than skill.

For an older infant, feeding also becomes a time to find out about new tastes, textures, and colors, to begin to learn names of common objects, to master the difficult job of holding a spoon, to maneuver it into the dish, to balance it all the way from the dish to that elusive target, the mouth, and then to savor the wonderful feeling of having mastered a new skill. Learning to hold one's own bottle and eventually to manage a spoon and cup represent early and important achievements in the baby's increasing efforts to master his or her world.

For older infants and toddlers, eating becomes a much more social situation that involves peers. Meals and snacks for older babies and toddlers are times for eating, learning, and practicing small motor skills, developing a sense of independence and autonomy, and having conversations. Caregivers need to be relaxed and flexible if eating times are to be pleasant.

Involving Parents in Decision Making

Parents are likely to have definite views about feeding their child. It is expected that parents will be involved in almost all decisions around feeding infants, such as timing, type of formula used, and all aspects involving the introduction of foods. (See *Infant/Toddler Needs and Services Plan* on page 118.)

Knowing what the practices and patterns are at home is particularly important. Having information about when and how much an infant ate before coming to care each day allows the caregiver to anticipate cues of hunger. It is essential with young babies to keep an up-to-date record of foods introduced and any special information, such as food allergies. Written records of daily food intake should be provided for parents. The introduction of new foods should occur at home, or, if at the center, following discussion with and permission from the parents. Parents need to let staff know when a new food has been introduced at home. Foods should be introduced one at a time, in case there is an allergic reaction.

Parents may have special food requests because of cultural or religious background, the child's medical condition, and personal preference; these should be respected. Parents may be asked to provide requested special foods for their infant when these cannot be provided by the center.

Breast-feeding should always be encouraged, and the parent should be made to feel welcome and provided with the degree of privacy requested.

Planning for and Managing Mealtimes

Mealtimes are one of the most complex times of the day. In many groups, depending on the age range, there may be young infants who are being bottle fed or who must be fed solids, infants in high chairs, and some older infants or toddlers at tables. Without planning and preparation, mealtimes can be chaotic, disordered, and no fun for anyone. If possible, feeding should occur in small groups and in a relatively

Infant/Toddler Needs and Services Plan

Date: _____

Child's Name: _____ Birth Date/Age of Child _____ _____

Parent(s) Name: _____ _____

Primary Caregiver: _____

Homebase: _____

Sleeping Routine

Pre-nap routines/rituals: _____

_____

How many naps per day (typical): a.m. _____to _____ p.m._____to_____

Length of nap: _____

What position does your child prefer: _____

Waking behavior/routine:_____

Special concerns: _____

Eating Routine

Solid Food: _____ Time of day you want given:_____

Special meals to be served in homebase: _____

Allergies: _____

Food dislikes or eating problems: _____

Food likes and eating preferences: _____

Special diet/requests: _____

Special concerns: _____

Bottle/Cup Routine

Circle: Bottle   Cup

Formula: Brand _____   Amount _____

Time of day you want given _____

Juice: Type _____   Amount _____

Time of day you want given _____

Milk: _____   Amount _____

Time of day you want given _____

Breast Milk: _____   Amount _____

Time of day you want given _____

Introducing Solid Foods

We recommend introducing infant cereal at 4-6 months, vegetables, fruits, and their juices at 5-7 months, protein such as cheese, yogurt, cooked beans, meat, fish, chicken, and egg yolk at 6-8 months, whole egg at 10-12 months, and milk at 12 months. We also can introduce the use of a cup and spoon at 8-10 months.

If you do not wish to follow our recommendations, please sign:

_____

Comforting/Distress

Does you child have a security object?   Name?_____

Does your child use a pacifier?   When?_____

Other information? _____

Diapering Routine

Please circle which type of diaper to use: Disposable   Cloth

If the child needs lotion or ointment, please specify which brand: _____

Does you child have any services that are different from those provided by the center's routine program? i.e., special exercises, special materials, accommodation of special services.

_____

_____

_____

Other Information

_____

_____

_____

The Needs and Services Plan will be updated every three months or sooner if requested by parent/guardian.

Parent Signature _____Date _____

Staff Signature _____Date _____

Date of change _____   Parent Initials _____   Staff Initials_____

Date of change _____   Parent Initials _____   Staff Initials_____

Date of change _____   Parent Initials _____   Staff Initials_____ quiet place, especially for those babies who are easily distracted by what is going on in the room. Remember that whenever possible, meals should be attended to by the infant's primary caregiver.

Individualized Schedules

Information from parents, combined with cues given by the infant and knowledge of the typical schedule, determines when an infant gets fed. Cues may include crying or fussiness, finger sucking, or making sucking movements. It is likely that young babies' schedules will be different enough that everyone will not be hungry at the same time. This should be encouraged rather than discouraged.

Individualizing schedules may extend mealtimes, but it also reduces the number of babies eating at one time and allows for more personal attention. Meal routines depend on careful planning, and each staff member should know what his or her role is. Post all information on routines, including individual children's eating habits, so that nothing essential is locked away in an absent staff member's head.

Competing Priorities: Individualized versus Group Times?

Many programs believe in individualized schedules in theory but do not individualize in practice. (Most often this is due to the need to maintain staff/child ratios, accomplish staff chores, or desire to have the children be able to go on walks or participate in activities instead of sleeping through them.)

But occasionally individualizing is put aside to promote the positive group experience of mealtimes. In most instances, except with older twos, this makes little sense. There is more value in the individual pacing of sleep schedules and feeding than in group engagement. Yes, older infants and toddlers often enjoy the sociability of mealtimes, but they have similar experiences during the day.

Toddler Mealtimes

Toddlers may find it difficult to move from active play to sitting down and eating. It will help if the transition from playing to eating is peaceful and proceeds at a gentle pace so that the children can relax. Calming music, minimal waiting time, and a calm manner on the part of the adults will help the children relax.

Mealtimes are one of the few necessary toddler group times. Ideally, waiting at the table is kept to a minimum and children can sit down when the food is ready to be served. However, when waiting is necessary, finger plays, singing, or storytelling can occur rather than creating unnecessary group times to offer these experiences.

Children should be allowed to leave the table when they have finished. To require them to wait until everyone has finished only creates frustration for the adults and the children who have finished and often results in pressure on those children who need more time.

The Physical Setup at Mealtimes

Children (and adults) respond better to pleasant and comfortable atmospheres for eating. The goal for mealtimes is competent, developmentally appropriate self-help. To support children's competence, table heights should be slightly above waist height, and chairs should allow feet to touch the floor. Having one's feet dangling in midair is very uncomfortable. (If you need convincing, try sitting on a bar stool with no rungs, let your legs dangle, and you will find that very soon you start to squirm, wrap your legs around the legs of the stool, and generally feel uncomfortable.) Toddlers are not very good at sitting still at the best of times, and uncomfortable furniture only makes doing so harder.

Chairs with solid sides give young toddlers support and help them remain seated. Individual feeding tables that surround the child with a rimmed tray work well for older infants and young toddlers. Putting old infants or young toddlers at tables with other children too soon may require more mastery than they possess. Feeding oneself, staying balanced in a chair, and relating to others close by may be too much to ask of a one year old! If toddlers must eat on carpet, a sheet of plastic or linoleum under the eating area makes cleaning up easier.

Putting toddlers in small groups, several to a table, with plenty of space between them, helps them avoid interfering with each other, and smoothes the activity. Although what is on someone else's plate may be identical to what is on theirs, toddlers may not be able to resist another person's food if it is within arms' reach.

Toddlers should learn to hold cups and spoons and to serve themselves. Spoons should have short handles and rounded bowls. Cups should be sturdy, wide-bottomed, and wide enough in circumference to require two hands to hold. Dishes with sloping sides rather than flat plates make self-feeding easier because they confine the food better. When toddlers decide they want to use cutlery, it helps to be able to push the food against the side to get it onto the spoon. Very small pitchers give toddlers the chance to practice pouring. At the end of the meal, they can take their dishes to a cart.

Spoons should be provided, but caregivers should be relaxed about whether fingers or spoons are used. Eventually all toddlers become interested in the fine motor activity of getting food on a spoon and maneuvering it to their mouth, so they don't need any pressure to "eat properly"; they initiate taking control of this important activity by feeding themselves.

Food

Food should be kept simple but attractive, nutritional, familiar, varied, and tasty. Foods should reflect the cultural backgrounds of the families in the center and those in the local community. Familiar foods can be very comforting to a child who is coping with a very different environment.

The amount children eat will of course vary, but a general rule of thumb is one serving spoonful for each year of age. Initially, small servings, with the possibility of seconds if they are wanted, work best.

Offering some finger foods on a plate—for example, pieces of fruit or biscuits—gives older toddlers the chance to make their own choices rather than having the food placed in their dish. Desserts should be treated as normal parts of meals and should be nutritious. This does not necessarily mean that they have to be offered along with the main course, but staff should avoid giving messages that somehow the last course is the most special.

Holding Bottle-Fed Infants

Bottle-fed babies should be held while they are drinking, as this is an important time to be close. A child being given a bottle deserves the same sort of one-to-one attention and physical closeness that a breast-fed child receives. It is a time when babies and caregiver attach.

When children choose to hold their own bottles or more than one child is being fed at a time, some physical contact and eye contact are particularly important. For example, place the infant holding her own bottle next to you on the floor while you feed another child. Propping bottles is not acceptable. However, helping a child who is holding her own bottle into a more upright position is important because drinking in a reclining position is bad for the baby's health.

NOTE: The difficulty of feeding more than one infant at a time is one reason to value individualized schedules.

Assisting Infants with Self-Help

If a child rejects a food one day, make a mental note of it and perhaps reintroduce the food in a week or two at a time when the child is hungry. To the extent possible, let the infant determine the pace of feeding. Some babies eat and drink very quickly and efficiently, while others are slower and may lose interest or become tired before they have had enough to drink. Babies should not be rushed, and caregivers should respect differences.

Some young babies like to "assist" the caregiver with feeding by putting hands into their mouths when they are full of solids or by grabbing or batting the spoon. Feeding solids is no job for the fastidious, especially when babies are learning to feed themselves. Often by the end of the meal, the child, the chair, and probably the caregiver will need to be wiped clean. Feedings must be free from unreasonable demands on the child for neatness, attention to the job, and persistence. As in other areas, caregivers should take their cues from the child's interest in grabbing the spoon or from signs that the child is ready to learn to self-feed. Obviously, finger foods are easier to manage than spoons.

Of course, some ability to self-feed does not mean that the baby is ready to manage the entire job. Some children will need help in feeding, as they may tire of the challenging task before they are full. Also remember that signs of interest in self-feeding are not signals for adults to withdraw their attention from the child.

Toddler Self-Help

Toddlers require our patience, good humor, and appreciation of their emerging skills and drive to experiment. The behavior that drives us crazy—dropping, flinging, smearing, imitating each other—is a result of their drive to learn. Allowing some messiness—which, after all, is really experimentation, exploration, and sensory play—is essential if they are to move beyond this stage to a more businesslike approach to eating.

While toddlers do begin to learn some conventions about eating, a focus on learning table manners is inappropriate for under threes. Caregivers can gently discourage excessive messiness and playing with food with wild abandon, but the need to explore textures and the mess that inevitably results from efforts at self-feeding should be accepted. Caregivers may need to remind children who are distracted by the activity going on around them that they need to eat, for they may forget that they are hungry and that the business at hand is eating. Excessive playing with food is usually a sign that the child is not hungry or has had enough to eat. Table manners or eating conventions (which vary tremendously with cultures) get learned eventually through modeling. Trying to teach them too rigidly and too early will only result in frustration for the adult and the child. Spills and inadvertent messes should be responded to in a very matter-of-fact way, and a wet cloth and sponge should be kept nearby.

Children should be encouraged to try new foods but should never be forced to eat or to try any food that they vigorously resist. Ultimately, the right of refusal must be honored. Giving children choices is important, for it builds autonomy and reduces power struggles. Care should be taken not to use food to appease, to occupy time, or to reward a child for behaving well ("Eat your squash or no dessert").

Out of consideration for hygiene and safety, it makes sense for toddlers to be required to sit down to eat. They will need regular reminders, for toddlers get irresistible urges to wander while they are eating, but most of them will eventually get the idea if they are reminded.

A well-planned routine and reliable timing should allow caregivers to stay seated and to eat with the children. Adults should avoid hovering over children as they eat or assisting from above or behind their heads. As toddlers finish, individuals or small groups can get cleaned up rather than make everyone wait at the table. Once again, the key is individualization.

Snack Times

All of the suggestions about mealtimes apply to snack times except that in some programs snacks are served (to older infants and toddlers) more informally than meals. Instead of having a particular time of day when all activity stops and all children sit down together, snacks can be brought out and children invited one by one or in small groups to come over and have some.

Diapering, Toileting, and Washing Up

Assembly line diapering and toileting are never good practices. Check regularly to see if a change is needed, for some babies seem not to be bothered by wet or soiled diapers and will not indicate that they need changing. As a reminder for staff, it may make sense to specify on the daily timetable several times at which caregivers will ensure that each child has been checked. These should only be reminders, *not* diapering schedules.

Waiting is not something toddlers do well. In addition to planning routines to allow for individualization, use the environment to engage children who have to wait. Create a space near the bathroom or changing counter for a small interest area—perhaps a water table, paper attached to the wall for coloring with markers, or a music center with tape-recorded songs.

Diapering

It takes organization for the routine to proceed smoothly for both child and adult and to actually be a successful PRIME TIME.

Typical diapering of a responsive six-month-old infant could easily involve the following learning experiences:

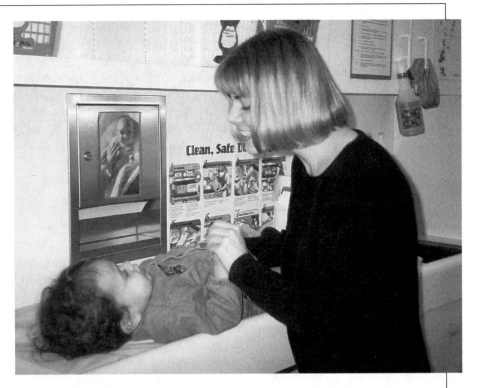

- ◆ motor activity: kicking vigorously while the caregiver removes confining clothes.
- ◆ cognitive activity: the caregiver's face disappears behind the diaper and reappears.
- ◆ language activity: caregiver and baby talk, coo, and laugh together.
- ◆ social activity: caregiver talks to the baby, laughs with him, touches him gently, and responds to smiles and babbles.
- ◆ sensory experience: the feel of being free of clothes, the soft, fresh, dry feeling of a new diaper replacing the cold, wet one.

Most important, the gentle manner of the adult and a need met without undue delay increase the baby's trust in people.

As described in chapter 6, p. 78, an ideal changing area supports relaxed, focused, and sanitary diapering. There should be ample counter space with a 3-inch, recessed lip; a sink with a spray large enough to bath a child; ample, compartmentalized storage an arm's length away. The changing routine should be posted at the changing area. Proper sanitation is critical, including following universal precautions for blood-borne pathogens. Chapter 12 on health and safety details the changing routine.

Toilet Learning

Caregivers have to work together to avoid making toilet learning a dominant focus of the toddler program. There may be pressure to get toddlers to reach this developmental milestone as early as possible (admittedly, changing the diapers of toddlers who enjoy a wide range of foods is not exactly the highlight of anyone's day!). However, the process should be undertaken with a minimum of fuss and treated as just one aspect of a varied program.

When to begin helping a child learn to use the toilet should be a decision made largely by parents and based on signs of readiness from the child, with caregiver's advice, if desired. Cultural expectations often vary, and it is important for staff to know about these. Often beginning too early leads to frustration and power struggles between child and adults.

There are a number of plans or gimmicks promoted in books for parents and day care staff, and adults can become confused by this conflicting advice. As is true with many aspects of helping children to grow and develop, a heavy dose of common sense and insights gained from sensitive observation will help.

The importance of individualizing the age at which children learn to use the toilet cannot be overstressed. Parents and caregivers should respond to individual children's cues and signs of readiness. Between eighteen and twenty-four months, children can be prepared for learning to use the toilet by helping them to understand about elimination and by giving them words for urination and defecation. Learning to pull their own pants down and to sit on a toilet or potty chair are the other important developmental steps. Toddlers show readiness by staying dry longer and showing an interest in the process of using a toilet. They will tell you they are urinating or defecating while they are doing it. Somewhere between two and one half and three years old, the average child learns to stay dry most of the day. Before this age, there is wide variation in children's interests and abilities in toileting, and these should be respected.

A relaxed pace and nonjudgmental approach are essential. Because the child is struggling for self-control and with all the complicated emotions of power, shame, failure, and accomplishment, our job is to be calm and supportive and to reduce the pressure that the child feels. As children show readiness, adults can respond with help and encouragement.

If a child is truly ready and the adults are relaxed about it, then training is not really necessary. Adults need only provide some assistance and support, and learning will happen. This process is enhanced for toddlers by being in a group, where they learn much from each other. They may develop an interest in sitting on the toilet when they see others doing this.

Children can learn on potty chairs, child-sized toilets, or, less preferably because of their size in relation to the child's size, standard toilets. What is important about the equipment is that it be accessible, comfortable, and easy to sanitize. Similarly, clothing that is easy to pull up and down provides greater autonomy for the child.

Washing Up

This is another time when children sometimes are treated as things rather than people. Helping a child clean up is a time for talk about body parts and sensations. It is also a time when toddlers learn important self-help skills if they are allowed to get and use soap, paper towels, and washcloths independently. Be sure to use a clean washcloth or paper towel for each child. Child-height sinks with soap dispensers and faucets, easily manipulated by small hands and mounted 16 to 18 inches off the floor, make both the caregiver's and child's job easier. If a stool or platform is necessary, make sure it will not slip and can be easily cleaned underneath.

Bathing can be a wonderful time for many infants, although some seem to find it uncomfortable. A slow, gentle bath, during which the child is told what is coming and is allowed to anticipate and help ("Do you want to hold the sponge?") is as educational and positive an experience as a child can have in group care.

Tooth Brushing

Children aged two and older can begin to learn tooth brushing. While tooth brushing at the center is not something of critical importance for toddlers, programs that can incorporate it into mealtime routines in a relaxed and sanitary way should do so. Not only does the ritual of tooth brushing build up the habit of good dental hygiene, it also gives children a sense of accomplishment.

Sleeping and Resting

Moving into and out of sleep are times when most human beings are very vulnerable. If there is ever a time to be relaxed and gentle with children and to treat them as individuals, it is while helping them to move into and out of sleep. It is a time for individualized schedules and patience, which give toddlers some leeway in settling down and waking up while they make the transition to a group nap schedule.

If sleep times are based on the needs and styles of each child and variations are expected from day to day, napping becomes a natural, even pleasant activity rather than an arena for confrontation. Some babies go to sleep easily and predictably, while others resist sleep from a very early age and have difficulty making the transition from one state to the other. Even with babies of the same age, there is great variation in the amount of sleep they require and when they require it. Sometimes knowing that a child needs a nap determines what the caregiver does more than how the child acts. Some babies need a wind-down period of quiet play before they can relax and go to sleep. Cues that a child is sleepy include rubbing eyes, showing disinterest in play, clinging to an adult, sucking a thumb, putting his or her head down, getting clumsy, slowing the pace of activity, becoming very easily frustrated, and becoming fussy for no apparent reason. Tension, excitement, or change may affect a child's ability to sleep.

Like us, toddlers vary in their energy levels and paces. Some children need to crash in late morning while others will not sleep for more than an hour in midafternoon. The program's space and schedule need to take into account children who don't fit the 1:00 to 3:00 nap time.

Gently into Sleep

When possible, put the infant down to sleep the way his or her parents do at home—rocking, patting, and so on. Such gestures not only reassure the child but help parents have a sense of control and continuity. Even as adults, we have our own individual going-to-sleep rituals. Of course, it is not possible for staff to engage in a one-on-one extended ritual with each child, so they should avoid locking themselves into lengthy rituals with each child while other children become restless and impatient awaiting their turns. For toddlers on cots, nap time is often a time for rubbing backs and temples and later helping children slowly rejoin the world.

It is common for some babies to react to being put down for a nap by crying vigorously. Babies differ a great deal in their ability to quiet themselves after this kind of upset. Consistent, predictable handling and allowing the child to work things out with appropriate support will help the child develop the ability to put himself or herself to sleep. No set rule can be stated for how long a child should be allowed to cry before being picked up again. A caregiver who knows a child knows when he or she is past the point of self-quieting.

Sometimes a child who will not sleep will rest quietly on the cot for a while with a few toys or a book as quiet entertainment. Some babies want a special comforting object, for example, a blanket, when they are going to sleep. Others find music calming. Darkening the room will also help.

Some babies wake up slowly and need a gradual introduction to the brightness and activity of the playroom.

Cribs and Cots

The move from cribs to cots should be made when the child shows signs of being able to stay on the cot and not fall off or get up to roam around. Sleeping arrangements at home will influence what the child is comfortable with at the center, so once again, communication between parents and staff will contribute to a better decision.

Young children should view sleep and rest times as relaxed, comforting times of day. Cribs or cots should never be used as places where children are put for misbehavior. The use of sleep or rest as a kind of punishment teaches children that it is something unpleasant and therefore to be avoided or resisted.

Transition Times

To the extent possible, good child care programs eliminate the need for extended group transition times, in which activity ceases and the group moves from one segment of the day to another. Individualization of the program means that there will be few times when everyone is doing the same thing, when children are waiting or roaming around aimlessly, or when play abruptly stops to prepare for some other activity. There is no place in a good program for lining up.

When materials or equipment has to be put away, children should be warned ahead of time that they are about to be interrupted. Enlisting the help of toddlers should be done in a gentle and inviting way, with sensitivity to the limitations of their interest in tasks and without expectation that they will have the same interest in restoring order that adults do! With an individualized program, there should be few times when everyone has to stop their play and either help or sit idly by while a major cleanup takes place.

Toddlers can be encouraged to help put things away, but there is no point in forcing it. Ongoing tidying up by caregivers minimizes the need for massive cleanup.

Moving Into and Out of the Homebase

Initial Settling In

The first few days and weeks in care set the tone for the total child care experience. Beginning group care for the first time or even coming to a new place after experiencing another center is unsettling, at the least, and can be very frightening for children (and parents). The routines for children described in this chapter and the approach suggested for working with parents in chapter 4 are designed to build relationships that help children, parents, and caregivers withstand the wear and tear of group living. It is very important to make clear to parents from the beginning that the staff want to form partnerships with them on behalf of their children. Parents will not know what is expected of them in such areas as providing information, asking questions, being in the centers, helping out, and making requests. Therefore they will be very much guided by what they are told initially and, more important, by what they experience on a daily basis. Let parents know what to expect of their children as they settle in and let them know the value of a smooth transition from home to care each day, even after their children have participated for some time.

Children Adapt to Change Differently

Some children show obvious discomfort when new to the group. Others show very little. Staff and parents need to remind themselves that it is perfectly normal and expected that babies who are over about six or seven months of age may react negatively to new people. There are great individual differences among babies, just as there are among adults, and some adapt more easily and quickly than others to change, new people, and strange places. Some just need time to adjust, while others actively resist and protest any significant changes. Even when a child shows no obvious signs of discomfort or fear, a young infant notices everything that is different—the sights, sounds, and handling. This can be stressful.

Some children seem at home right away and become involved in activities, while others want to observe from the sidelines for a time until the place becomes familiar. Caregivers should not necessarily interpret lack of involvement as a sign that children are unhappy and need to be pushed to participate. Staff should continue to interact with them and to invite participation without pressuring, allowing each child to adjust at his or her individual pace.

Encourage Parent Time in the Room

Parents should always be strongly encouraged to spend some time in the room with their child during the first few days, gradually tapering off as the child's stay is extended. Ideally, when parents first leave the child, they will leave for a short time, several hours perhaps, rather than for a whole day. The interval that they are away should be long enough that the child has a chance to get over being distressed and to become settled. While this is not always possible due to parents' commitments, parents should understand that it is very important for both the child and the parent and is strongly recommended. Staying around for a few moments in the morning not only helps the child settle in but makes the parent feel more of a sense of belonging to the center and builds a closer partnership between parents and staff:

◆ it gives the parent an opportunity to become familiar with the staff, how they work and care for children, and generally how the day goes in the room so that when the parent is not present, he or she has more of an idea about what is happening than the tiny slice of life of greeting and departure.

◆ it gives the staff the chance to chat with the parent and extend the discussion begun at the intake on the child's likes and dislikes and to observe how he or she actually cares for the child in areas such as feeding, helping to go to sleep, comforting when distressed, and disciplining. In short, it helps staff to become knowledgeable about the child much sooner than they would without that contact and more aware of the care that the child is familiar with.

◆ having someone familiar and loved around makes it much easier for the child to adjust to new people and a new place. A child will be less fearful of a strange person if that person is observed relating in a friendly way to the parent.

There is no best plan for settling in all children. The important thing is to have a plan developed by the parent and caregiver that takes into account the needs of both parent and child. Everyone should understand that despite a plan, there may well be ups and downs and that it may be a matter of days for some babies and weeks for others before it all feels smooth.

Occasionally parents and even some staff may support the notion that the best way to orient a child to care is to "throw them into the deep end and let them sink or swim," meaning give them no gradual introduction but rather just bring them to care, leave them, and get it over with. While it is true that it is possible to drag the process out too long so that it becomes counterproductive, a process that takes into account the perspective of the child and the need to help him or her feel comfortable and secure with the situation in the long run benefits not only the child but the parents and staff as well.

Understanding the Parents' Perspective

Putting a child in care, especially a baby, and especially on a full-time basis, is a big decision for parents. Even when they are very sure that this is the best decision, they may have some doubts and uncertainties. Staff need to remember that while they may know that they are competent and worthy of parents' trust, parents have no reason to believe that until their first child has been in the program for a time and until they have experienced for themselves how good the caregivers are. They have no reason to trust the staff until they get to know them, and this may take a long time. Because infants and young toddlers cannot report on their day or on how they are feeling about care, parents may be anxious.

Some parents will come to care certain that they are doing the right thing; some will be ambivalent. It is important to remember that some who use care would much rather stay home with their child, but they do not have that option. Some parents in all categories are subjected to criticism about their use of care and may feel that by using care, they are not being good parents. To make things more complex, while some parents are aware of their feelings and may communicate them to staff, others are not comfortable doing so, and some are not even aware of their feelings.

Parents may feel ambivalent about the fact that their child separates happily. It is easy for professionals to see that separating easily is a good thing and to be critical of parents who, as caregivers often see it, "seem to want to make their child cry when they leave." Parents may believe that a no-tears, happy separation actually means that the child is more attached to the caregiver than to the parent. Staff need to help these parents to see that this is not the case and to reinforce constantly the notion that the staff will not and do not want to replace the parent in the child's affections.

Some centers find that it is helpful for new parents to talk not only to the director and staff but also to be oriented by parents who have used the center for a time and are familiar with it. Other parents may give a different perspective on the center from that given by the staff. New parents may feel more comfortable asking other parents some of their questions rather than asking staff. In addition, new parents can meet other parents who already use the center this way.

All of the above means that settling in and separating is a "big deal" for parents and children and should be treated as such by staff. Staff should make clear through written policies, initial, and ongoing communication with parents that, although they will aim to form a special relationship with the child, they do not see themselves as taking the parents' place. Discussed in much greater detail in chapter 14, the partnership with parents is critical and depends on parents understanding that staff believe that parents are the most special people to the children and that there is no evidence that their children's being in care changes this.

Welcoming New Families

Once enrolled, each new family needs a relaxed and warm, reassuring welcome. The first few weeks are critical in establishing a partnership between parents and staff, but staff must take the lead. While staff may sometimes feel intimidated by parents and new staff may not feel totally confident about their own skills, they need to remember that parents may be equally intimidated by staff and the newness of the situation.

The lead teacher or primary caregiver assumes responsibility for introducing the parents to all homebase staff; homebase staff need to make an effort to put parents at ease. The primary caregiver should be assigned and all necessary preparations carried out before the child's arrival:

◆ assign and label cubby, crib, or mat.

◆ put a picture of the child and parents on the cubby.

◆ make a welcome sign with child's and parents' first names and post it prominently.

◆ post all information necessary to individualize the child's care.

◆ prepare congratulations note for parents described on p. 280.

The First Six Weeks

In the first few weeks, the primary caregiver should make extra efforts to ask parents how things are going for them and their child. At the third or fourth week, the director should write a handwritten note asking the parents how things are going and extending an invitation to talk. At the end of six weeks, the primary caregiver should give the parents a six-week questionnaire, read the response, and pass the form on to the director.

Transitioning Children (and Parents) to the Next Age Group

Sooner or later, children move to the next age group. For some children and parents (and attached primary caregivers), this is a time of anxiety. For others, it is a time eagerly anticipated, and there are few tearful looks backward.

Successful transitions depend on good planning and recognizing and understanding the perspective of children and parents. Some things to keep in mind:

◆ children cannot move up until there is a space in the next group. Sometimes children get "stuck" in a group waiting for an opening, and sometimes children get moved up a little earlier than expected to take advantage of an opening. Because of this, it is important to make sure the group works for children at both ends of the age spectrum.

- ◆ care must be taken to avoid giving the impression that there is something competitive about moving up, that it is like graduation or some indication that the child has superior skills and abilities.
- ◆ most children need more than a few days of visiting a new group to feel comfortable. Preparing for transitions is an ongoing process that begins a long time before the actual move.
- ◆ Parents should get the message that while the child is ready to move, if the child doesn't have to move or cannot move because of age or development caregivers will adapt the room to "fit" the child.

Ongoing Relationships between Rooms

Ideally, even in large centers, there is a sense of community and relationship between different age groups and different rooms. A child in an infant room comes to know the toddler staff and the toddler rooms through visiting, shared activities, and shared common space. The same is true of toddlers and preschoolers. Through the newsletter and other communication, parents come to know the people and aspects of life that their children will soon become a part of.

The Ready List

Once a child is actually ready to move, regardless of whether or not space is available, or a few months before a move is anticipated, staff in the two rooms or modules should make a concerted effort to begin the transition. This involves having the child visit, accompanied by the primary caregiver, sharing activities, and making other efforts to gradually familiarize the child with the new room. At the same time, parents should be made aware of the approaching transition and be given information on the child's soon-to-be new homebase.

The Last Few Weeks

When a move date is known, the current primary caregiver and the newly assigned primary caregiver should get together and map out a plan for daily visiting in the new group and make sure that parents have all the information necessary to feel secure about the move. Each child's and parent's needs are different.

The New Group

The first week in the new room should follow the lines of the first week for any new child and family: picture on the cubby, welcome sign, first-day note to parents, and a reassuring phone call if necessary. It is also important for many children to keep in contact with the old room. "Cold turkey" transitions are not a good idea.

Maintaining Parent-Caregiver Partnerships

The core of the parent-caregiver relationship lies in the daily moments of arrival and departure. The partnership hinges on those few moments of interaction. Some hints for successful daily contacts, in addition to those discussed under arrivals and departures:

◆ greet *both* the parent and the child as they arrive.

◆ if you are busy when a parent and child arrive, greet them and let them know that you will be with them as soon as you can.

◆ be sensitive to cues from the parent about whether they are in a hurry. If they look as though they are and there is nothing urgent to talk about, don't keep them.

◆ try to have the room set up in an inviting way so that there is something attractive to engage the child upon arrival. This helps the child make the transition from home to child care.

◆ if the parent has a concern and you are very busy, explain this and make a definite appointment to talk about it. Remember you may use the telephone during slow times. If the arrival time for a parent who always wants to talk is hectic, suggest how a slight change in arrival may allow you more time to talk.

◆ communicate a tone of openness. Displaying the menu and the daily program, letting parents know when students or other visitors will be present, informing them of staff changes—all of these communicate the message, "What happens here is your business, too."

◆ invite parents in and be ready for them. Encourage them to breast-feed, play with their child, or simply observe. Help them to feel comfortable.

Leaving the Program

Just as it is important to be sensitive in helping children and parents to settle into the center, caregivers should work with parents when a child is going to leave the program to ensure a smooth transition. For some infants and toddlers, gradually decreasing the amount of time spent at the center may be helpful if parents' schedules allow it. It is important to acknowledge the feelings of the caregiver and parent as well as the child; these often include a sense of loss, and, in the case of parents, anxiety about the future.

A Final Word: Thoughtful Routines—Every Child, Every Day

Routines are essential if all the tasks associated with good care are to be accomplished. Good routines can institutionalize "noninstitutional" care when caregivers focus on the goal of the routines: consistent, high-quality, personalized care. When routines become mechanical and mindless, the tasks may get done, but the essential quality gets lost.

Exercises

1. List what a child learns while being bottle-fed by a primary care-giver.

2. Observe the nap time routines at a center. How are individual differences acknowledged and accommodated?

3. Describe a transition you have made in your life (e.g., to senior high school, college, or camp) and consider its parallels to child care transitions. Discuss this with another adult who went through the same transition to discover individual differences between the two of you.

Reference

Giovanni, Nikki. "lets take a nap," in *Spin a Soft Black Song*. New York: Farrar, Straus & Giroux, Inc., 1985.

Chapter 9

·····················

Guiding the Behavior of Infants and Toddlers

excellence

Children are helped to learn self-control and how the world works in a relaxed, positive atmosphere of support and understanding that recognizes the child's struggle. Discipline is viewed by adults as an important aspect of teaching and learning. Children are accepted as they are, not as immature creatures whose deficits and weaknesses need to be fixed up right now. Development is viewed as a process of growing, with each age and stage having its own characteristics, its own challenges and needs.

···

Learning to Live

Young children's job is to try to learn to behave in the mysterious world while trying to make sense of it. This is a tremendous challenge, full of complexities and confusing messages. Young children strive for understanding, independence, and self-control. Children learn by exploring, experimenting, and testing the limits of their environment and experiencing the consequences of their *behavior*. In this way, they begin to understand how the world works, their own limits, and appropriate assertiveness. In this drive to understand, they need adults to set limits in order to

◆ keep from harming themselves, other people, and the physical environment.

◆ feel safe and secure, for they can find their own lack of control frightening and they need to know that an adult will stop them if they can't stop themselves.

◆ begin to get an idea of what behavior is expected of them; that is, read the expectations of other people.

◆ protect their caregivers' sanity!

This learning is a pretty tall order, not mastered even by some adults, and so by the age of three, children will have only begun the journey.

What Is Discipline?

Discipline, guiding children's behavior, or *setting limits* are all concerned with helping children learn how to take care of themselves, other people, and the world around them.

Guidance and Discipline Are Learning and Teaching

Discipline is simply one of the many kinds of teaching that adults do with young children, so we can apply what we know about teaching in other areas. *Discipline is not punishment.* Punishment is an unpleasant reaction by adults after children do something that is not acceptable. While discipline helps children identify unacceptable behavior and reduces the chance of it occurring again, it is much more than that. It teaches children what *to do* by letting them know when they do something we approve of, such as showing care for others, self-control, or cooperation.

The Goals of Guidance and Discipline: Self-Control and a Positive Group Environment

The program's goals are to promote independence, autonomy, self-esteem, and caring toward others and the physical environment. The basis for these is a secure, orderly, developmentally appropriate caregiving environment; a positive, "yes" environment that allows children to experiment and test their *behavior* within clearly defined limits. The environment is geared to their competencies and interests. This approach is based on respect for very young children and an appreciation of how hard it is for them to begin to learn to guide their own behavior. Caregivers often have to provide the self-control that babies lack.

What Do I Do?

Imagine driving in a world without traffic lights and signs, where parking lots lack lanes or marked parking stalls. You are expected to comply with complicated rules by police who often issue directives you don't fully understand. When you foul up, you are punished and issued new directives.

Children must feel like this as they navigate the complex world of child care. When they misbehave, often our first inclination is to see them as the problem and try to change them through guidance or punishment. But often it makes more sense to change the environment (provide duplicate toys) or the situation (spread the children out to either reduce the chances of the *behavior* or to regulate the behavior). Yes, it will be imperfect. But just as some motorists run stop signs and park illegally, environmental planning can certainly cut down the chaos.

The long-term aim of this approach to discipline is to have each child capable of self-discipline and to motivate behavior by understanding, concern for others, and a desire to do the right thing, rather than by a desire to escape the painful consequences of doing what is not allowed.

Discipline involves a mix of gentleness, understanding, and firmness. Relationships with young children will have unpleasant moments, times of tension and disagreement, times when they may drive you crazy. Those are the times that you, as a caregiver, have to keep in mind that *you are on the same side as the children—allies, not adversaries.* Toddlers in particular have a way of engaging adults in struggles and confrontations, and caregivers can easily become invested in winning or teaching them a lesson. Yes, discipline involves firmness. But it also involves empathy, negotiation, and sometimes compromise. When there is a struggle, look for a solution where neither the adult nor the child loses face but where the child learns something that makes it less likely that the *behavior* will occur again.

Two-year-old Amy had worked for thirty minutes making a large, gooey mud cake decorated with leaves, sticks, and stones. She insisted on bringing it inside and playing on the table where the toddlers were having lunch. She became upset when her caregiver Ming told her she could not. Resisting the urge just to take the precariously perched "cake" away from her and leave it outside, Ming explained that it wouldn't fit on the table with the food. She quickly took a cardboard box and created a lunch table for dolls to share the picnic "cake" together outside.

What Creates Discipline Problems?

Settings with the following characteristics are guaranteed to produce "discipline problems," no matter who the children or adults in the program happen to be:

◆ too high expectations for self-control.

◆ too little space or too much open space.

◆ too few materials or too little equipment.

◆ materials or equipment that is too challenging or too simple.

◆ a lot of waiting time.

◆ inflexible routines, spaces, schedules, and people.

◆ too little order or predictability.

◆ too much change.

◆ too many temptations, that is, objects and places that are forbidden.

◆ too much noise.

◆ excessive requirements for sharing.

◆ long or frequent periods of sitting still.

◆ lots of times when children are expected to just look or listen instead of getting directly involved.

Not only will children have trouble coping, but constantly being unable to meet expectations may also itself lead to defiant, difficult *behavior.*

Infant Discipline?

Is it surprising that discipline is an appropriate topic to consider in relation to infants? (No one is surprised that it is a major topic of interest in relation to toddlers!) If we accept that early interactions with people and inanimate objects help children to learn about themselves and the world and that the basis of learning to control one's own *behavior* is feeling secure that one's own needs will be met, then discipline begins at birth. It begins when adults interact with babies in ways that teach them to feel secure that their needs will be met. That, in fact, lays the basis for a capacity that will come later to wait, give, trust, love, and care for others. A concern for infant (or toddler) discipline is likely to arise over three issues:

◆ *Encounters with others.* Group care offers children very early opportunities to begin learning the give-and-take nature of relationships with other children and adults.
◆ *Learning to wait and to control impulses.* A challenge for young children is learning to stop doing something interesting that is also unacceptable.
◆ *Protection.* Young children need adults who intervene to keep them safe and to protect others and the physical environment around them.

Positive learning can come from these experiences if caregivers understand the limitations of babies' abilities to guide their own *behavior* and encourage them to be active, curious explorers rather than "well-behaved" children.

The Importance of Consistency

Discipline is an aspect of care about which adults often have strong views borne of our experience both as children and as caregivers. At almost every center, there will be differing views about appropriate behavior and effective methods of discipline. These views will vary greatly depending on cultural preferences, socioeconomic background, and individual beliefs. Some caregivers and parents value assertiveness and an active approach to the world, while others value acceptance and cooperation. Some adults have different standards for boys and girls. How we behave, even more than what we profess to believe, is often based on how we were raised.

How important is consistency in guidance? Between adults at the center, consistency is critical; the program needs a consistent philosophy and approach. It is destructive not only to children but to the whole idea of a program culture to allow a number of individual approaches to child guidance. It is important for staff who work together to discuss discipline and air their differences in order to reach agreement about ways of responding to the children in their care.

Consistency of responses to important behaviors requires that caregivers recognize that children are different. For example, responses to a child's smearing on the table with pumpkin at lunch should differ when done by one-year-old Jimmy and two-and-a-half-year-old Gloria. Another dimension of consistency is follow-through in response to a child. It is not helpful to say to a baby who is tipping her juice on the table, "If you keep doing that, I will take the cup away" and then to ignore her as she continues to do it.

Consistency between what is done at home and in the day care setting is desirable because it simplifies the children's task of learning appropriate *behavior*. But consistency between home and program is often limited and children do learn that different settings have different expectations (however, caregivers and parents need to understand and tolerate children's confusion as they learn the rules). When there are differences, mutual respect is essential in avoiding parent-staff conflict because damage resulting to the parent-staff relationship is even more harmful to the child than inconsistency.

Discipline and Culture

In her invaluable book, *Multicultural Issues in Child Care* (1993), Janet Gonzalez-Mena discusses the fact that "good discipline" is an inherently culture-bound idea. It is clear that the ideas presented in our book reflect a predominantly white northern European/English/American/Australian point of view. Gonzalez-Mena writes:

Good early childhood practice, much of which is influenced by the value systems of white Americans with northern European background, dictates that any discipline measure has behind it the goal of self-discipline. . . . Though the adult starts with externalized controls, the idea is that they will lead to "inner controls," a term often used by early childhood practitioners.

In some cultures, however, externalized controls are not expected to lead to inner controls. Children are always watched—not just by parents, but by the whole community. A misbehaving child away from home will be guided and directed by whoever is around. . . .

According to Lonnie R. Snowden (1984),
The Black Community invests effective responsibility for the control of children's behavior in an extensive network of adults. . . . Because of the extended parenting, children's behavior receives proper monitoring and more immediate sanctions than is the norm in American society. Children need to be expected to develop more extensive exploratory tendencies and assertive styles, since respected external agencies can be counted on to reliably check excess. The school, however, exercises less direct and legitimate control, while expecting a relatively docile, immobile pattern of behavior. The cultural conflict is clearly drawn (p.188).

How difficult is it when adults expect children to behave as if the locus of control lies within them. . . . Not many adults expect this of infant and toddlers but they expect this of preschoolers. If they discipline with the idea of eventual inner controls in mind, the methods they use may be quite different from the adults who see the locus of control as something external to the child. Gone is the kind of consistency that empowers the child (p. 70).

Sandoval and De La Roza (1986, p.71) describe the way extended family and interdependent network orientation work to provide external controls in the Hispanic community:

In grocery stores and other public places the mother is not inhibited from shouting directives to the young children to constantly remind them—even when engaged in no mischief—that her inquiring but protective eyes are on them. . . . By loudly verbalizing their directives they also mean to engage others in the social control of their children, seeking sort of consensus protection (quoted in Gonzelez-Mena, 1993, p. 71).

Gonzelez-Mena points out many other examples, including differences in how the Japanese and Chinese approach discipline and conflict resolution. She quotes a Japanese teacher: "As the year progresses we put fewer and fewer toys out during free-play time to give the children additional opportunities to learn to share and to deal with conflicts as they arise." Then the teacher stays back and lets the children work out problems. In fact, one child who continually provoked fights and hurt children was considered to "serve the function of giving other children a chance to experience a range of emotions and to rehearse a variety of strategies both for resolving their own disagreements as for mediating conflicts among others" (Tobin, Wu, and Davidson, 1989, p. 33). Chinese teachers, on the other hand, usually see children as "unlikely to come to know correct behavior through unsupervised play with peers or through a process of self-discovery and self-actualization. . . .Teachers bear the responsibility of teaching students self-restraint and correct behavior" (Tobin *et. al.*, p. 33).

What does the material that Gonzelez-Mena presents mean for your program? Do you have to completely socialize and discipline based on a number of different cultures? Not really—that would be impossible. It does mean, however, that above all else, good caregivers must recognize that cultures are different and worthy of respect, and that these differences may result in difficulties for children and parents from other cultures struggling to make sense of program practices. The practices we outline here in this book are not the "right way"—ordained by God or experts. This book (and NAEYC accreditation) is culture bound. When children and parents behave in ways consistent with their culture, it may present problems for us. That does not make them (or us) wrong. It means that if we respect the child and parents, we will strive to work through problems without judgment or condescension. In a very multicultural program, we may have to modify our practices considerably. In a program that serves predominantly one culture, the least we can do is respect and understand the legitimacy of the minority culture.

A Question of Balance

Imposing restrictions, setting limits, and helping infants and toddlers learn controls must be balanced with encouraging an active, curious, exploratory attitude toward the world. Too much emphasis on control and too many restrictions will tend to discourage them from exploring. An adult working with young children should not be overly concerned with teaching them to behave properly, although older toddlers are certainly ready to learn some controls.

Caregivers need to be sure that they are not encouraging or rewarding undesirable behavior. Young children need attention, and they may learn in group care that the best way, in fact about the only way, to get attention is to do something that will be disapproved of. It is often not possible to ignore undesirable behavior, but the caregiver needs to be astute enough to see when it is being used to obtain attention and to ensure that sufficient attention is given at other times for doing the right thing.

Appropriate Expectations

Behaviors that may be considered inappropriate in older children are natural ways for infants and toddlers to explore and express curiosity.

Infants

When younger babies first begin to move around, they seem to relate to each other not as people but as interesting objects to explore. Don't react on the assumption that babies intentionally hurt other babies. Gentle redirection is called for. Similarly, infants have no sense of property rights and are not born with the notion of sharing; therefore, they may take toys from others. The notion that "this toy belongs to all of us" is meaningless to them. When younger babies (less than approximately ten to twelve months) do this and the "victim" does not mind, it is probably best for the caregiver not to intervene. As babies get older and become more aware of others or when the victim protests, the caregiver should intervene to direct energy and attention so that babies can learn ways of interacting that will be pleasant for everyone. Also remember that mouthing is the major way infants explore the world around them, and when they chew crayons, eat more dough than they manipulate, or suck paint brushes, they are not yet developmentally ready for materials not designed to be explored orally.

Older infants (over six to eight months) can begin to learn some controls. The caregiver may, for instance, show an eleven month old some ways of interacting with another baby that are likely to be received more positively than hair pulling. Around the age of ten to twelve months, babies become more sensitive to reactions of approval and disapproval from adults.

No longer exploring others as objects, older babies begin to explore each other as social scientists: "If I do this, what will happen?" The casual push, smack, and poke may be motivated by the simple desire to see what will happen.

Toddlers Are Not Preschoolers

Some of the characteristics of toddlers—for example, their need to assert their autonomy—contribute to the difficult situations they find themselves in. When toddlers are uncooperative, even defiant, they need adults who are gently firm, enforce reasonable limits, but understand the difficulty the toddlers are having.

Active, curious toddlers are often labeled as aggressive because they frequently interact with other children in unpleasant and sometimes hurtful ways. Much as infants explore people as objects, toddlers now explore others as social scientists: "If I do this, what will he do?" The "aggressive" label is inappropriate because toddlers have little understanding of the impact of their behavior on others and, while they may set out to achieve a certain aim (for example, get the toy back), they do not willfully aim to hurt another person. Most of the hurtful things toddlers do to others are the result of characteristics of the developmental period:

◆ *egocentrism.* Toddlers mostly believe they are the center of the world. They learn gradually as they get older that this is not quite true (albeit a lesson many individuals and humanity in general never seem to quite grasp). This egocentrism makes life in groups hard. It is often like the frontier, ruled by the idea that if you want something, you take it; if someone is in your way, you move them; if you find the reaction you get interesting when you push or hit someone, then you do it again. They have a very hard time putting themselves in someone else's place. Toddlers are beginning to develop empathy and apparent understanding of others' feelings; however, this is unpredictable and should not be expected on a regular basis.

◆ *lack of understanding.* In the process of exploring other people, infants and toddlers hurt them. In some cases, this is simply because they do not understand that it hurts because they are unable to take another point of view and in others, they do not attend to the cause and effect: their actions caused the other child's distress.

◆ *good intentions, bad implementation.* Toddlers may often do annoying or unhelpful things with good intentions. That is, they may mean to help, to show affection, to investigate or find out, and their lack of understanding or clumsiness means that their execution of good intentions is not so good! A poke in the eye may be a clumsy greeting, a spilled cup may be inept self-help. In these situations, show encouragement and appreciation of the good intention while at the same time trying to teach a better way to carry out the good intentions.

◆ *lack of self-control.* Often, even when toddlers have some idea that what they are doing will not be approved of, they simply cannot stop themselves. There is a difference between knowing what you should do and having the willpower or self-control to do it. Young children are like hungry dieters confronted with heaps of their favorite foods. This is why they often require adults to supply the willpower they lack.

Good Caregivers Pick Their Battles

Toddler caregivers should decide which issues matter and which ones can wait. Similarly, your reactions should tell the child something about the seriousness of the offense. For example, hurting another person is much more serious than knocking toys off a shelf, and the reaction should be much sterner. Minor infractions and acts designed deliberately to test limits usually require a bit of humor and lightness on the part of the caregiver. Working with toddlers will be very heavy going if every misdeed is treated as an occasion when the child must be "taught a lesson."

Minimizing Conflict

If the facility and routines have been designed with very young children in mind, most limits and prohibitions will have to do with interactions with other people, not with harm to materials and furnishings.

Caregivers can minimize the number of occasions that call for repeated no's and restrictions. Some examples of ways to do this follow.

◆ a ten month old is obsessed with trying to climb onto the rocking chair. His desire to do this far exceeds his ability to do it safely. The caregiver, who is busy feeding another baby, cannot be with him to assist his efforts. She moves him to another part of the room while telling him that he cannot climb on the chair, places him near some safe, low climbing equipment, and removes the rocking chair temporarily from the room. She also makes a note of his particular interest in climbing.

◆ an eight month old notices that another baby is playing very busily with a toy that happens to be her favorite. She cannot sit by and watch this and crawls over to take it away. The caregiver, understanding that the situation is very frustrating for her, sees this as a good time to involve her in a game.

◆ two babies are together on the floor. One little girl is very irritable and reaches out to pull the other's hair over and over at the slightest frustration. The caregiver understands that she needs some time alone and puts her in a semisecluded, quiet corner playpen with some toys.

◆ two toddlers are losing interest waiting for their turn to stir the gelatin. The caregiver gives each of them a small bowl to stir, noting that in the future she should restructure the activity for simultaneous stirring.

◆ Two-year-old Kira and Roberto are always dumping everything. Caregivers create a dumping pit with lots of containers and loose materials like blocks. They also note that many of the items Kira and Roberto have dumped are not readily recognizable in their containers on the shelf. They buy some clear plastic containers that reduce the dumping (but toddlers still love to dump).

In all these situations, the caregiver, sensitive to the child's limitations, changed the situation to make it more tolerable rather than expecting the baby's *behavior* to change.

Children with Special Needs

Some children may be more of a challenge in a child care setting because of a special need that results in difficult behavior: inability to calm themselves, distractibility, aggressive behavior, or hyperactivity. The principles for helping them succeed in the setting are the same as for any other child: understanding the child, partnering with the parents to determine what works best, adapting the setting, and keeping the special need in perspective—it is only one aspect of the child. It is easy to lose perspective. Whether the special need is based on a physical condition like the prenatal effects of alcohol or drugs, the results of abuse and neglect, or other atypical conditions, the child is more than the special need and caregivers have to avoid the inappropriate but understandable "he doesn't belong in my class" attitude. Most infants and toddlers with special needs can be successfully mainstreamed in good centers because their problematic behavior is similar to what most children exhibit, just more frequent or more intense.

Principles for Effective Guidance and Discipline

Effective guidance is based on an ideology that guides every interaction:

- discipline is a matter of planning, setting clear limits and expectations, redirection and logical consequences, not punishment.
- discipline is also a matter of prevention—anticipating situations and "heading them off at the pass."
- our job is to gently encourage and support self-control, to protect children, and to help them learn how to behave reasonably.
- it is natural, not naughty, for babies to poke, push, hit, even bite each other, especially if there is nothing more interesting to do. It is natural for babies to experiment with food and materials—to drop, tear apart, smash. It is natural for toddlers to test limits, to assert themselves in order to find out about their own power.
- our job is to keep the children interested and the room arranged to prevent children from bunching up, since the more bunching there is, the more unpleasant incidents there will be. Try to resolve incidents calmly and patiently as they happen.
- each child has to be respected as a special individual who even at his/her worst is not a "little criminal" but a very young person struggling to achieve self-control. It is not appropriate, accurate, or fair to characterize children as bad, mean, nasty, or to use other terms we apply to adults.
- labels stick. Avoid labeling children, as this tends to create a self-fulfilling prophecy because children believe what we tell them about themselves.
- catch children when they are behaving well. Let them know with your attention and approval when they are behaving in acceptable ways—showing caring, self-control, and other characteristics you would like to see more of.
- model appropriate behavior. Children learn by identifying with and imitating our behaviors. Shouting at children to keep the noise down does not make sense, nor does abrupt handling of a child teach her to be gentle with others. When very young children are treated fairly, shared with, comforted when they are upset, reasoned with, and in general cared for sensitively, they learn important and lasting lessons about how to treat other people.
- when there is little risk of harm, let babies try to work things out for themselves.
- overuse of the word "No" renders it ineffective.
- a child learns what is acceptable more quickly if all adults react in the same way to the same *behavior*.

The Do's and Don'ts of Good Guidance and Discipline

When a young child is hurting another child, damaging the physical environment, or about to hurt himself, *we*

◆ tell the child to stop in a firm but friendly voice (at close range to that child whenever possible, not from across the room). An adult's tone of voice can communicate approval or disapproval effectively before a baby can actually understand the words.

◆ give brief reasons why the behavior is unacceptable keeping in mind the limits of young children's understanding of their own behavior. Explaining both helps us stay calm and builds children's understanding so that they can gradually make those judgments themselves and guide their own behavior. Reasons may be obvious to us but not to children. Why can the ball be thrown but not the wooden block? What is the difference between dropping and throwing? Why can they run outside but not inside, and what is running anyway as opposed to fast lurching? Why can they pour water at the water table, but not pour out juice at lunch? (A very good question.) What is wrong with trying to pick up the baby? The answers to those questions may be obvious to adults but not to toddlers.

◆ state and model the acceptable behavior: "Be gentle with John," while stroking John's arm. Find an acceptable alternative when appropriate. If you are stopping children from doing something, don't just tell them what they cannot do, tell them what they can do as well.

◆ help children stop doing the unacceptable behavior, for example, by redirecting to a new activity or physically removing them, the object, or the victim, if necessary. Often, words are not enough. Even when children understand the directive to stop, they may not have the willpower to stop. Giving a number of verbal warnings is not helpful, and in fact, can almost provide children with an incentive to continue doing what they are doing.

◆ offer children reasonable choices wherever you can accept the them. Examples: "Do you want to finish your drink or get down and play?" "Would you like to go outside and throw the ball or play with the blocks?"

◆ avoid implying a choice when there is none. "Would you like to give Joey a turn on the swing now?" is not appropriate unless a resounding "No" on the happily swinging toddler is acceptable. When there is no choice, be prepared to help the child go along with the decision you have made.

◆ always recognize and acknowledge the child's feeling of anger, confusion, or hurt as legitimate.

◆ seek help if you are about to lose control or too angry to handle the situation.

When a young child is hurting another child, damaging the physical environment, or about to hurt himself, *we do not*

◆ shame or humiliate the child.

- shake, jerk, squeeze, or physically indicate our disapproval.
- say, "Bad girl or boy" or otherwise imply that the child is the problem, instead of the behavior. Also avoid the use of the terms "good boy" and "good girl" for acceptable behavior.
- moralize or let too much of our anger come through. Caregivers may tell a child they are angry, but they should never react in anger to a baby, as this will make a baby fearful and anxious.
- use "No" too often. Use the positive "Hold onto the cup," and other words like "Stop" or "Please don't" instead of "No."
- use bribes, false threats, or false choices.
- use food or scheduled activities (outside, field trips) as reinforcers or denial of such as punishments.
- retaliate—that is, do to the child what he or she did to someone else. Remember, children learn the most from us through modeling.
- make children say they are sorry. Uttering the words is an empty and meaningless gesture unless the words reflect true sentiment. Until toddlers fully understand what they have done, they are not likely to actually feel sorry. Requiring "Sorry" as a standard response to unacceptable behavior can be interpreted by the child as a way of magically undoing the thing he or she has done. Thus some two year olds utter "Sorry" just before the wrongdoing.

When a young child hurts another child, damages the physical environment, or is about to hurt himself, *we always:*

- make clear that it is the child's behavior and not the child that is unacceptable.
- help the child with appropriate language to understand the problems with his or her behavior.
- use redirection, logical consequences, or Cool-down Time, depending on the age of the child, the misbehavior, and the child's state.
- assist and encourage children to use language to express their strong feelings.
- try our best to appear confident (even when we are not), knowing that our manner will affect the child's decision to cooperate.

Logical Consequences

When a child behaves in an inappropriate manner, the most effective discipline is for the child to experience the specific logical consequences of his or her behavior. For example, if Ahmad can't play at the water table without splashing other kids, he should be directed to other play until he can play with water without creating a mess. If twenty-two-month-old Marie can't use the markers without drawing on the wall, she can't use markers and will have to play elsewhere.

Young toddlers may not have the ability to make the link between their behavior and the consequences every time. It is important that the consequences be enforced in a matter-of-fact way, not in a punitive, "I told you so" manner that serves mainly to fuel the adult's feelings of power and control over the child.

A logical consequence helps to teach, while generalized punishment—for example, sitting in a chair for a period of time—teaches little or nothing. If an older toddler refuses to accept the consequences, he or she may need some quiet, relaxing time to pull himself together.

Cool-Down Time (formerly Time-Outs for Older Toddlers)

There will be probably always be times when a child is not capable of self-control and redirection and needs some time to settle down. Cool-down Time is *not* punishment. It is not the same as sitting a child down or isolating him for a rule violation. (We decided not to use the term *time-out* because many programs now use a time-out as punishment: "Go sit in the time-out chair and take a ten-minute time-out!") Instead, Cool-down Time is just what it sounds like: a quiet, relaxed, neutral break; a cooling-off period for the child to regain self-control. Cool-down Time is used when a child is losing control and refuses redirection—for example, acting aggressively, throwing a tantrum, complete defiance. If a child has violated a rule without losing control or has regained control, he should experience the consequence of his behavior, not be compelled into Cool-down Time.

Cool-down Time should occur in soft, cozy places—perhaps an easy chair or a corner with pillows. While a child may have to be compelled to take Cool-down Time, the ultimate goal is for the child to achieve the control to take the time by herself when it is needed. Often the adult will need to help the child regain control. If the adult approaches Cool-down Time with an adversarial stance, the child will see it as something negative and unpleasant, and the time-out simply becomes ineffective punishment. If the adult maintains an attitude of alliance and understanding, even though the child may resist, he or she will eventually get the message that "This is something I need right now, and since I don't have the self-control to do it myself, my caregiver is helping me."

NOTE: Cool-down Time is not appropriate for infants and young toddlers. It is appropriate only after the children begin to have some sense of how they can help themselves, usually around age two. If a child is unable to relax and calm himself down, Cool-down Time should always occur with a nurturing adult.

Cool-down Time Procedure

- ◆ After a child's repeated refusal to cooperate or inappropriate behavior, the adult says gently, but firmly, "You need some Cool-down Time."
- ◆ Without implying any moral overtones, place the child in a comfortable Cool-down Time area (at the edge of the room with some materials or books to occupy the child). "I know you are really angry, but you need to cool down on the couch here before we can play some more. Tell me when you are ready to talk." Pay the minimum attention necessary for the child to remain in the Cool-down Time area while regaining control. If you need to hold the child, try and do so in a neutral manner, neither warmly nor angrily.

◆ When the child regains control, say something like, "Are you feeling okay? Are you ready to come and be with us?" If you left the Cool-down Time area, the child should be told to come to you when he or she feels okay.

◆ Help the child to express the feelings leading to the Cool-down Time by putting words to emotions and behavior: "You got very angry when you couldn't get a trike, didn't you? You really wanted that trike." Give the child the physical nurturing he needs.

◆ Explain your position: "I know how upset you are, but I won't let you hurt people and I won't let people hurt you. Next time if you get really angry, you can take some quiet time and I'll spend some time with you."

◆ If the child regained control quickly, acknowledge it.

After Cool-Down Time

◆ Adjust the environment to avoid the situation the child had trouble with.

◆ Praise the child for every instance of self-control.

◆ Be prepared to catch situations before the child loses all control and encourage the child to take self-initiated, quiet relaxing time.

Remember, Cool-down Time is not *punishment.* This is so important that it bears repeating (we had to throw out a perfectly good term—time out—because it became synonymous with a punishment chair: *Cool-down Time is* not *punishment.* It is simply allows the child (and sometimes the caregiver) time to settle down.

When a Child Is Struggling

What do we do when a child is really struggling and her actions cause harm to other children or herself? Parents are upset: "Why is that child still in the program?" We have to do something. It is important to approach the situation systematically:

Step 1: Observation

A. Observe the child in the environment:

1. the child's approach to activities.

2. attention span and interest in activities.

3. amount of energy the child uses.

4. child's mood and general demeanor.

5. how well the child gets along with others.

6. how the child begins and ends an activity.

7. what the child's relationship is with you, the teachers.

B. Observe how the environment affects the child. As with biting, note and chart everything about the specific homebase situation that the child experiences:

1. activities going on.
2. other children's activities or interactions are doing.
3. general atmosphere of the room.
4. how often activities change.
5. how the child functions during transitions in daily routine.
6. time of the day.
7. are group or individual activities problematic?

Step 2: Synthesize observations

1. identify patterns in observations.
2. state the concerns clearly.
3. bring concerns to the director's attention.
4. ask for help if necessary.

Step 3: Modify the homebase

1. make program modifications called for from informal observations.
2. evaluate your concerns after attempting program modifications; if problem persists, notify the director.

Step 4: Ask the director for an observation of homebase and child. Keep the director well-informed.

Step 5: With referral from the director and with parental consent, contact an outside resource person.

1. create a program plan involving the parent, director, teachers, and outside resource people.
2. maintain ongoing communication between all parties.
3. schedule frequent meetings to evaluate progress or lack of it, with a timetable for improvement.
4. if the plan is unsuccessful, encourage and assist the parents to find alternate child care.

Step 6: The center is unable to met the child's needs and/or the child is unable to function successfully in a group setting.

1. determine the time period for termination of care (e.g., six months, a year, when the child turns three).
2. give the parent at least two weeks' notice that care will no longer be available.

3. help the parent understand that the termination resulted from the program's inability to adapt to the child's needs. It was not the child's failure.

We know that there will be toddlers who struggle with the group setting. A systematic approach of careful observation and a strategy for change has the best chance of helping the child and making life manageable for the staff.

Biting

You can see it in the eyes of staff and parents when an epidemic of biting breaks out. A tension hangs over the room like smog, a demoralizing haze of fear and anger and anticipation: When will it strike again?

Children biting other children is an unavoidable consequence of group child care, especially with toddlers. It happens in the best of programs (but it happens more in mediocre programs). When it happens and continues, it's pretty scary, very frustrating, and very stressful for children, parents, and staff.

Group living is hard—people rub up against each other and children in child care need and want attention from adults. Sadly, negative attention is more desirable than being ignored. A bite is powerful and primal: quick and effective, usually inspiring immediate and dramatic reactions. Size and strength are not required; even an infant can inflict a very painful bite. Once begun, biting is hard to get rid of quickly. The child often bites again, another child imitates, and soon it's an epidemic. Parents become very upset about biting, and the problem escalates.

Why Do They Bite?

Biting is a horrifying stage some children go through and a major problem or crisis for the group. Yet at the same time, for the biting child, it's a natural phenomenon that has virtually no lasting developmental significance. *It derives its significance from the group care setting.* It sounds obvious but if the child was not around children very much, he probably wouldn't bite—because neither the causes nor the opportunity would likely be present. *Biting is not something to blame on children, parents, or caregivers.* A child who bites is not on a direct path toward becoming a discipline problem, a bad person, or a cannibal. Yes, biting is an antisocial act, but it is an act of an individual not yet equipped to be fully social, just beginning life as a citizen.

So why does one child bite and another child does not? There are a number of possible reasons that children under age three bite, none of them the fault of a bad home, bad parents, or bad caregivers. Sometimes we think we have a good idea what's causing the biting, but most of the time it is hard to guess what is going on in the child's head. Some of the likely reasons suggest ways of handling the biting:

◆ *teething.* When teeth are coming through, applying pressure to the gums is comforting, and babies will use anything available to bite. Obviously, if this is a likely cause, then a teething ring or objects to bite will lessen the infant's need to bite other people.

◆ *impulsiveness and lack of self-control.* Babies sometimes bite because there is something there to bite. This biting is not intentional in any way, just a way of exploring the world.

◆ *making an impact.* Young children like to make things happen, and reactions when they bite someone are usually pretty dramatic.

◆ *excitement and overstimulation.* When some very young children become very excited, even happily so, they may behave in an out-of-control fashion. Natasha loves moving to music, and after a session in care with music and scarves and everyone twirling and enjoying themselves, it is very predictable that she will bite someone if an adult does not help her calm down.

◆ *frustration.* Too many challenges, too many demands, too many wants, too little space, too many obstacles may lead a child to bite, especially before he or she has the capability to express frustration through using language.

The "Politics of Biting"—Who Is to Blame?

There is no blame, but *the program should accept responsibility for biting and other hurtful acts like hitting and scratching* because it recognizes biting as a natural developmental phenomenon, like toileting accidents or tantrums.

What does accepting responsibility mean? It means that we have chosen to provide a group setting for children who are at an age when biting is a not uncommon response to life in a group. It is our job to make the program work for all children, removing the stresses that often lead to biting. Some children become "stuck" for a while in a biting syndrome, and it is frustrating for the parents of victims that the caregivers are unable to "fix" the child quickly or to terminate care. Empathizing with their feelings of helplessness and their concern for their children is essential while you let them know about your efforts to extinguish the behavior quickly. Balance your commitment to the family of the biting child with that to other families.

Parents are neither responsible for a biting child nor always a significant factor in the "cure," other than in working with staff on a strategy for change at the center and in reducing, where possible, any stress a child may be feeling in his or her life (but note: this stress may have little to do with the cause of biting).

It is the center's job to provide a safe setting in which no child needs to hurt another to achieve his or her ends and in which the normal range of behavior is managed (and biting is normal in group care). The name of a child who bites should not be released because it serves no useful purpose and can make a difficult situation even more difficult. *Punishment doesn't work to change the child*: neither delayed punishment at home, which a child will not understand, nor punish

Biting: A Crisis for Parents

When a homebase is under a siege of biting, everyone suffers. It is important to keep in mind the perspective of parents.

Memoirs of a Parent of "That Child"

I still have vivid memories of that horrible period that began when she was nineteen months old. It was awful every day, walking into her room and waiting to find out whom Jenny had bitten. Four bites in one day, one in a week, twenty-five in June alone. Life was hell. We slunk in and out like the parents of a criminal. Was it us—some flaw in our home or some mutant gene?

Jenny was such fun as a toddler, this tiny red-haired mop top, with great bouncy enthusiasm. Even at her biting worst, she was happy. We never saw her bite at home; there weren't very young kids around.

We would have these meetings with her caregivers and the director. We were all desperate. Even though we were doing everything we could, we all became defensive, sometimes disbelieving each other. Maybe she was bored (their fault), troubled (our fault), immature (her fault).

I knew that other parents were upset. After all, their children were coming home with Jenny's imprint (thankfully, this was before the time of AIDS). I saw them look at Jenny, at us. Finally one mother began yelling at me, shoving her son's arm in my face with the incriminating two red half circles.

And then at about twenty-two months, Jenny stopped biting. Part of it was all the stuff that the staff were doing and that we were doing at home. But probably she just grew out of it. Now I look at Jenny and see this good high school student with lots of friends, and I can laugh about what we went through. But I remember then wondering how she could ever have a normal life.

The Other Side of the Mirror: "My Child, the Victim"

If I can't keep my baby safe, keep him from being some other kid's snack substitute, what kind of mother am I? One day there is a bite on the cheek, the next day on his arm, and then even a bite on his bottom. The caregivers would sympathize with me and then say, "Biting is normal at this age." Yeah, I know that toddlers bite, but mothers protect and I couldn't protect my kid. It may be normal to bite, but it is not normal to be gnawed on every day.

"We're doing all we can," they said. So? Was I supposed to live with that? I wanted those biters out. How long was I supposed to let my child suffer at fourteen months old? I was told that "Stevie is so curious and friendly that he is the most common victim." I blew up. So it's his fault?

I left the center with hard feelings. Not because it was the center's fault, or even because they wouldn't throw out the biters. They were trying so hard to solve the problem, but they didn't seem to understand what it was like to be in my shoes. We had to leave.

ment at the center, which may make the situation worse. In the dire case where a child becomes so stuck in biting behavior that he or she must leave the program, it is as much the program's failure as the child's or the parents'.

Before the Biting

The emotional fallout that biting occasions can be reduced by communicating to parents before biting occurs:

◆ prepare parents for the possibility that any child, including theirs, can be either a biter or be bitten. Tell them before the fact, as early as the intake into the center. If it is a real possibility, don't hide it.

◆ make sure parents are aware of all the steps that you take to minimize biting and to end a biting crisis. They need to know that your understanding of biting as a natural and common phenomenon does not mean that you throw up your hands in resignation.

◆ know how long you will continue to work with a child stuck in a biting pattern, and communicate that to the child's parents right away. Fear of a sudden loss of child care adds to the tension. Again, it is better if parents know this before a crisis occurs.

When Biting Happens

In all biting situations, regardless of the likely cause, it is important that adults show strong disapproval through words and manner. Caregivers can try to minimize the behavior by

◆ letting the child know in your words and your manner that biting is unacceptable; reserving your sternest manner and words for acts such as biting.

◆ avoiding any immediate response that reinforces the biting, including dramatic negative attention. The biter is immediately removed with no emotion. Use words such as "Biting is not okay—biting hurts" and focus the caring attention on the bitten child. The biter is not allowed to return to play and is talked to on a level that he/she can understand. Communicate that you understand the child's frustration (or needs for exploration or teething relief) and are willing to help him or her achieve self-control.

◆ working with the biting child on resolving conflict or frustration in a more appropriate manner, including using language if the child is able to. "When you feel like biting, use words," "I'll help you not bite" (don't assert, "I'll not let you bite" unless you can deliver on that promise).

◆ examining the context in which the biting occurred and looking for patterns. Was it crowded? Too few toys? Too little to do? Too much waiting? Is the biting child getting the attention and care he/she deserves at all times or only when he or she acts out?

◆ changing the environment, routines, or activities if necessary.

◆ trying to observe a child who is a short-term chronic biter to get an idea about when he or she is likely to bite. Some children, for example, may bite not when they are angry or frustrated, but when they are very excited.

◆ not casually attributing willfulness or maliciousness to the child. Infants explore anything that interests them with their mouths, and that includes other bodies and limbs!

◆ observing the group closely until the problem is found if biting continues.

◆ empathizing with all the children and parents and staff involved. It's a difficult situation for all.

Epidemic Response

When biting changes from a relatively unusual occurrence (a couple times a week) to a frequent and expected occurrence, it should be considered an epidemic or a health emergency—a serious threat to the well being of the children in the room (including the biter[s]). In health emergencies, we apply extraordinary resources to the crisis. Do the following:

1. the staff in the room should meet with the director or other supervisor or support staff on a daily basis throughout the crisis for advice and support and maintain a perspective devoid of blame directed toward children, parents, or staff.

2. chart every occurrence, including attempted bites, and indicate location, time, participants, staff present, and circumstances. (See *Incident Chart* page 159.)

3. evaluate the immediate staff response to each biting situation for appropriate intervention that ensures:

◆ comforting the injured child and treating the injury.

◆ cool, firm, disapproving response to the biter that does not inadvertently provide reinforcement to the biter.

4. analyze the chart and profile the behavior patterns and the environmental context of frequent biters and frequent victims.

5. "shadow" children who indicate a tendency to bite. In addition,

◆ anticipate biting situations.

◆ teach nonbiting responses to situations and reinforce appropriate behavior in potential biting situations.

◆ adapt the program to better fit the individual child's needs.

6. "shadow" children who have a tendency to be bitten.

◆ anticipate biting situations.

◆ teach responses to potential biting situations that minimize the chance of becoming a victim.

Incident Chart

Homebase _____

When?		Where?	Who?		Who?				Surroundings?	Why?
Date	Time	Location	Initiator	Behavior	Target(s)	Behavior	Activities	Circumstances	Comments
7/1	9:50	Block area	Hannah	Bite on rt. cheek	Clarissa	Trying to play with Hannah	Block play, trucks	Waiting for breakfast - noisy	Clarissa suprised Hannah—she was hungry

©1996 *Prime Times: A Handbook for Excellence in Infant and Toddler Care*; Redleaf Press, 450 North Syndicate, St. Paul, MN 55104. 800-423-8309.

7. consider early transition of children stuck in a biting behavior pattern to a changed environment if developmentally appropriate (and allowed by licensing).

8. consider changes to the room environment. Analyze the room environment, schedule, routines, and expectations of children and staff to minimize:

- congestion
- commotion
- confusion and disorder
- competition for toys and materials
- child waiting
- child frustration
- competition for adult attention
- child boredom

9. avoid large groups and break into small groups.

- use other spaces in the center, the playground, and walks.
- within the room spread out the activities and the staff to avoid bunching up (also using the nap area).

10. look for ways to promote the children's sense of security and stability:

- "no surprises": maintain a predictable schedule and ensure that children understand and anticipate the progression of the day.
- ensure PRIME TIMES with each child's primary caregiver.
- ensure warm, cozy, semisecluded "places to be."
- avoid staffing changes.
- develop and maintain individual and group rituals.

11. look for ways to engage children more effectively in the environment:

- analyze choices perceived by children.
- analyze the developmental appropriateness of choices.
- provide duplicates of toys and materials and multiple options for activities.
- consider increasing the motor and sensory choices available.

12. look for ways to calm children after periods of excitement:

- relaxed transitions.
- calming music.

◆ calming physical contact with caregivers.

13. analyze grouping children to avoid combinations that may lead to conflict or biting.

◆ avoid grouping biters and likely "victims" together.
◆ avoid grouping children who will compete for toys.

14. if necessary, bring in outside observers to help you analyze the entire situation (not just the biters).

Maintain Positive Relationships with Parents

1. Let all the parents know that there is a problem and everything you are doing to improve the situation. (See *A Note to Parents on Children Biting*, p. 164.)

2. Remind them of your philosophy of working with children in crisis.

3. Work together as partners with the parents of both biting children and frequent victims to keep them informed and to develop joint strategies for change.

4. Prepare the parents of the child who bites for the worst if suspension or termination from the program is possible and suggest they make contingency plans. Having to leave the program is a terrible consequence; having to leave with little warning is even worse.

"I Dreaded Going to Work"

The lead teacher in a room undergoing a rash of biting described what it was like:

You don't know how lousy it feels when biting gets out of control. Four bites today, three bites yesterday, six bites last Friday. I went through periods of feeling like a terrible teacher. I didn't want to face the parents of the children who weren't biting. I'd get angry at the biting kids and see Ben and Becca as if they were these little monsters and want to kick them out. And I was even more angry with their parents! They had to do more, take more responsibility, be more structured, more loving, more something. All of these feeling swirled around, although only my husband had to hear the wails and moans. I knew the feelings weren't fair, and it took all my professionalism to stuff them down.

Hanging on during an Epidemic

Magic feathers helped Dumbo fly, but there are no magic feathers to solve a biting crisis. Sometimes nothing works, and children grow out of it or leave the program. Doing all of the above should help alleviate or shorten the crisis. Maintaining good relationships with parents during a biting epidemic requires all the trust and goodwill built up by good program practice.

Because it is a natural and inevitable occurrence, like illness, earthquakes, and floods, all we can do is prepare for biting and maintain perspective while it is happening. It is the time when our expertise, professionalism and character are put to the test.

Terminating Children from the Program

When do you decide that you can no longer serve a child? It is always a painful experience for parents, staff, and child. Terminations should happen only when the program has done what it could to adapt the program to fit the child. The stronger the partnership with parents, the more effort to adapt the program, the more likely it is that all children will fit. But equally important, strong relationships mean that if the program cannot serve the child, the decision will be mutual or at least less acrimonious. Use the procedure outlined above when the child's behavior raises questions about whether the program is appropriate.

Temper Tantrums

Going to pieces, getting out of control, or having a momentary breakdown are all ways of describing temper tantrums. Unfortunately, these are common experiences for toddlers (and older children—and some adults!). Tantrums can be quite powerful and therefore frightening, not only to other children and adults but also to the child who is having one. They typically come as the culmination of fatigue, frustration, or confronting a number of obstacles or barriers. They are fueled in toddlers by their inability to use words to express their strong feelings. Imagine a bottle of champagne that has been jostled and shaken to the point that it finally blows its top with a powerful explosion. When that is finished, it is still and flat. With a temper tantrum, a seemingly insignificant event can be the "straw that breaks the camel's back."

Responding to Temper Tantrums

Temper tantrums, like crying, are real expressions of distress, not usually something the child puts on deliberately. Most toddlers in the throes of a temper tantrum need help to get out of it. The sort of help will vary with the child. Some children need to be held to get back in control. But for others, being held will feel like restraint and will only fuel the tantrum. These children, however, may respond positively to an adult staying close by and talking calmly. Adult anger is not an appropriate response to a tantrum, which calls for calm firmness that lets the child know the adult will help him or her regain control. A tantrum can be physically and emotionally exhausting, and afterwards, the child may want to engage in a quiet, soothing activity such as looking at books, sand or water play, or even a rest or sleep (you may want one, too).

Unfortunately, there are always a few toddlers who have learned that temper tantrums are effective ways of securing something they want. Usually these tantrums are more controlled than the ones previously described. In these cases, as long as the child does not hurt anything, the caregiver may decide to ignore the behavior. As is true with biting, temper tantrums should never be a successful way of getting something a child wants.

A Final Word: Life in Group Care Is No Picnic

Is this approach to discipline too soft for babies, delaying their learning the hard facts of life about waiting, sharing, taking turns, stopping themselves? No, because even in the most accepting, gentle, individualized program, group care creates numerous occasions that require of children extraordinary self-control, delay of gratification, and other behaviors that we want to cultivate. We do not need to build in extra opportunities that require children to test their self-control.

It's easy to get in power struggles or battles of will with children, even with the youngest babies. Group living is tough, especially with a collection of little egos struggling for self-control and intent on exploring how the world works. The key is for staff to help each other maintain perspectives that accept much of the troublesome behavior as natural while trying of course to smooth the waters and come up with strategies toward building more peaceful tomorrows.

EXERCISES

1. Observe an infant room and toddler room. In each room, what "illegal" behaviors did you see? Note the following for each incidence:

◆ was the behavior observed by staff?
◆ why do you think the behavior occurred? What was the situation, the child's exploration, the child's mood?
◆ was there a consequence?

2. In those same rooms, look for any unnecessary "No" conditions that work against the creation of a "Yes" environment.

3. Make a list of the limits or rules that operate in an infant or toddler homebase. What is the rationale for each? Do they have to do with adult convenience or the well-being of children? Are they justifiable?

REFERENCES

Gonzalez-Mena, Janet. *Multicultural Issues in Child Care.* Mountain View, CA: Mayfield Publishing, 1993.

Sandoval, M., and De La Roza, M. "A Cultural Perspective for Serving the Hispanic Client." In *Cross Cultural Training for Mental Health Professionals.* Ed. H. Lefley and P. Pederson. Springfield, IL: Charles C. Thomas, 1986.

Snowden, L. "Toward Evaluation of Black Psycho-Social Competence." In *The Pluralistic Society.* Ed. S. Sue and T. Moore. New York: Human Sciences Press, 1984.

Tobin, J., Wu, D., and Davidson, D. *Preschool in Three Cultures.* New Haven, CT: Yale University Press, 1989.

A NOTE TO PARENTS ON CHILDREN BITING

In even the best child care program, periodic outbreaks of biting occur among infants and toddlers, and sometimes even among preschoolers. This is an unavoidable consequence of young children in group care. When it happens, it's pretty scary, very frustrating, and very stressful for children, parents, and teachers. But however unfortunate, it is a natural phenomenon, not something to blame on children, parents, or teachers, and there are no quick and easy solutions to it.

Children bite for a variety of reasons: simple sensory exploration, panic, crowding, seeking to be noticed, or intense desire for a toy. Repeated biting becomes a pattern of learned behavior that is often hard to extinguish because it does achieve results: the desired toy, excitement, attention.

Here is what we do to try to extinguish the biting behavior:

1. When a child is bitten, we avoid any immediate response that reinforces the biting, including negative attention. The biter is immediately removed with no show of emotion and caring attention is focused on the victim. The biter is not allowed to return to play and is talked to on a level that he/she can understand, then redirected.

2. We look intensively at the context of each biting incident for patterns. Was there crowding, overstimulation, too few toys, too much waiting, other frustration? Is the biting child getting enough attention, care, and appropriate positive reinforcement for not biting? Does the biting child need help becoming engaged in play or to make friends?

3. We work with each biting child on resolving conflict or frustration in an appropriate manner.

4. We try to adapt the environment and work with parents to reduce any child stress.

5. We make special efforts to protect potential victims.

DEALING WITH BITING IS A PROGRAM RESPONSIBILITY

The program accepts responsibility for biting and other hurtful acts and for protecting the children. It is our job to provide a safe setting where no child needs to hurt another to achieve his or her ends. The name of a biting child is not released because it serves no useful purpose and can make an already difficult situation more difficult.

Biting is a horrifying stage some children go through. It is, however, *a common phenomenon* that has virtually no lasting developmental significance.

A child who bites is not on a path toward being a discipline problem, a bad person, or a cannibal. There are a number of possible explanations for why some children bite. None of them is due to a "bad" home, "bad" parents, or "bad" teachers. Most of the time, it is hard to guess what is going on in the child's head.

Parents are neither responsible for a child becoming a biter, nor always a significant factor in the "cure," other than working with staff on a strategy for change at the center and for reduction of any stress the child may be feeling.

PUNISHMENT DOESN'T WORK TO CHANGE THE CHILD

Neither delayed punishment at home, which a child will not understand, nor punishment at the center, which may make the situation worse, helps. What does help are immediate, logical consequences: being deprived of what he or she sought and denial of positive outcomes to the biting, such as adult attention.

BALANCING PROGRAM COMMITMENTS TO ALL THE CHILDREN

Some children become "stuck" for a while in a biting syndrome, and it is frustrating for the parents of victims that we are unable to "fix" the child quickly or terminate care. We try to make every effort to extinguish the behavior quickly and to balance our commitment to the family of the biting child to that of other families. Only after we feel we have made every effort to make the program work for the biting child do we consider asking a family to withdraw the child.

Group living is tough. When biting occurs, we are all challenged to maintain a broader perspective and to pull together.

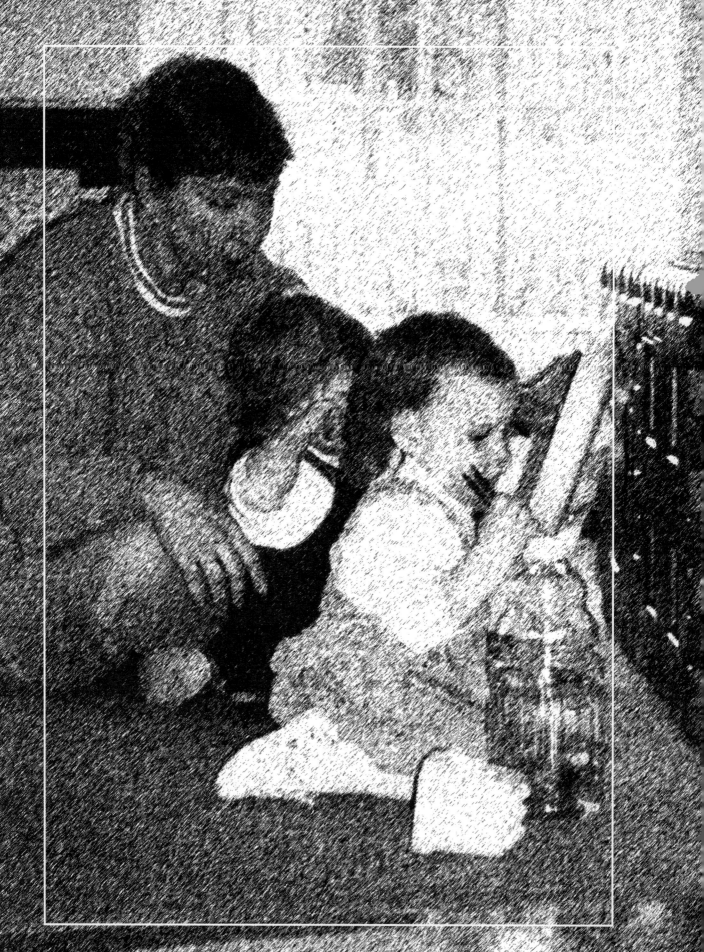

Chapter 10

Safe and Healthy Environments for Infants and Toddlers

excellence

A safe and healthy environment designed for infant and toddler exploration and challenge without threat of serious injury or illness. Parents and staff have confidence in the continuous monitoring of the physical environment, equipment and materials and in the careful caregiving practices and appropriate supervision of children.

Providing Safe Care

Certainly infants and toddlers are the most vulnerable children in group care. They are so new to the world! Neither their bodies nor their minds have accumulated the experience that over time will make the world of unseen germs and potential accidents a much safer place.

Daily living in a group setting presents continual opportunities to exchange germs and to incur various injuries. The more warm and relaxed the setting, the more possibilities for transmission of disease. The more encouragement of active sensory and motor learning, the more apparent risk of injury.

Can child care centers be safe and healthy for their youngest inhabitants? Yes—with an understanding that safe and healthy do not mean a sterile world free of germs and bumps and bruises. A safe and healthy center is one that minimizes a child's exposure to illness and the threat of injury while providing for all of that child's developmental needs.

Health and safety issues often test the strength of the parent-staff partnership because there is often no easy answer, no clear compromise, but plenty of strong feelings. The mutual respect, trust, and empathy that parents and staff build up are often required when issues of illness, exclusion, and child accidents arise.

Health Policies and Practices

Babies are highly susceptible to respiratory and gastrointestinal ill-nesses. Their immune systems are undeveloped and their drive to mouth and touch everything leads to a lot of transmission of poten-tially infectious matter. It is common for many babies in group care settings to have eight or more illnesses during the first year of life: five or six respiratory (ear, nose, and throat infections) and two or three gastrointestinal (stomach) illnesses. In a program with poor health and sanitation practices, children may experience even more illnesses. Children in group settings with good health practices probably experi-ence about the same number of illnesses in their childhood as children cared for primarily at home. However, more of those illnesses occur in the first two years due to earlier exposure.

Healthy settings depend on

◆ thoughtful, strictly followed sanitary routines that are regularly monitored and evaluated. Careful diapering and toileting proce-dures, regular hand washing, and proper food handling are key areas.

◆ careful attention to the stress placed on each child and to adapting the environment and routines to reduce the stress.

◆ policies regarding staff and child illness and contagious conditions that minimize the likelihood of infection.

Model Child Care Health Policies (1993) is an excellent reference to develop comprehensive health and safety policies. It is available in book form or on disk from NAEYC. Included are sample health forms, detailed guidelines for admission and exclusion, and monitoring forms for health and sanitation. *Model Child Care Health Policies* was developed by the Pennsylvania Chapter of the American Academy of Pediatrics in conjunction with another excellent resource, *Caring for Our Children, National Health and Safety Performance Standards: Guidelines for Out-Of-Home Child Care Programs* (1992), published by the American Public Health Association and the American Acade-my of Pediatrics. *Healthy Young Children* (1991) is a third essential resource on creating a safe and healthy environment.

Daily Admission and Exclusion

When is an infant or toddler too ill to be in child care? This is probably the most difficult and sensitive health issue and often becomes a source of tension between parents and staff. It is a concern to every-one: the parent, who may not be able to work the staff, who have to care for the child; the child, of course; and the other parents, who look at each sick child as a potential threat to their child's health. There is a natural tendency to look at the same child and reach different con-clusions. The parent who can't afford to miss another day of work sees a recovering child who "will do fine." The caregiver who has to care for a child who is unhappy or has diarrhea sees an "obviously ill child" who should be at home.

There are always issues over how strict and flexible exclusion policies should be. Guidelines developed by the American Academy of Pediatrics *Model Child Care Health Policies* and *Caring for Our Children* are based on ensuring the health of the individual child and all children in the group. These guidelines point out that exclusion often has little effect on the spread of many respiratory and gastrointestinal diseases because children are infectious before they exhibit the symptoms of the disease. This is a critical point that cannot be emphasized enough. *By the time the ill infant or toddler is actually showing signs of illness, the infectious material is in general circulation.* Excellent sanitation will reduce the spread, but given how infants and toddlers explore the world, some germs will spread no matter what we do.

From *Caring for Our Children* :

> Exclusion of children with many mild infectious diseases is likely to only have only a minor impact on the incidence of infection on other children in the group. Thus when formulating exclusion policies, it is reasonable to focus on the needs and behavior of the ill child and the ability of the staff in the out-of-home child care setting to meet those needs without compromising the care of other children in the group (pp. 80-81).

But exclusion is necessary at times:

> Chicken pox, measles, rubella, mumps, and pertussis are highly communicable diseases for which routine exclusion is warranted. It is also appropriate to exclude children with treatable illnesses until treatment is

"That Child Does Not Belong Here!"

Caregivers usually prefer strict black-and-white policies that exclude children with most signs of illness, particularly infants. Many centers have policies with no flexibility. One instance of diarrhea, one reading of temperature over 100 degrees, and it's "Please come pick up your baby immediately," even if it's 2:00 P.M. and the child is due to be picked up in a couple of hours, even if the child is resting comfortably. A program that looks at the child in the context of families and recognizes the realities of parents' lives will understand the guidelines cited above and behave differently. "Able to participate in the program" is a key factor that calls for judgment. In a program that accommodates differences in pace and schedule and has cozy places to pause, a mildly ill child may not require exclusion.

Local health practitioners often have different standards that come into play when parents relay the advice of their pediatrician. Parents may be advised by a pediatrician to keep their child out five days because of a particular illness, while another will counsel that it is acceptable to send the child to care once the fever breaks or the child is on medication or the child is able to participate in the program. Because pediatricians have a range of views and expertise on out-of-home child care, it is valuable to have *Model Child Care Health Policies* and *Caring for Our Children* as your definitive resources and to swear by them.

received and until treatment has reduced the risk of transmission. The presence of diarrhea, particularly in diapered children, and the presence of vomiting increase the likelihood of exposure of other children to the infectious agents that cause these illnesses.

Undiagnosed rashes and infestations such as head lice usually warrant exclusion until treatment is underway.

Daily Admission Procedures An important part of the greeting process is assessing the suitability for group care of the infant or toddler that day and communicating with parents about current medications. Children arriving with symptoms that suggest possible illness should be referred to the lead teacher or director for possible exclusion. If a child who may be mildly ill is admitted, it is advisable to request that the parents leave numbers where they can be reached and to call during the day to report on their child. Some programs provide beepers to parents who are hard to reach. Ask the parent to indicate on the daily experience sheet (see page 284) any special health considerations as well as other information pertinent to the child's care and to fill out any medicine administration request forms. In turn, use the daily form to let the parents know that day about the child's disposition and behavior throughout the day and about any administration of medication.

When a Child Becomes Ill at the Center It is always important to contact parents as soon as possible when a child shows signs of most illnesses, even if these are minor and the child does not have to be sent home. Let them know the child's condition. Understand that parents are not always able to drop everything and leave work. It is wise to save requests for immediate pickup for conditions that warrant it. Some mildly ill infants and toddlers simply need to rest and snuggle and be kept comfortable until parents arrive; others are unable to be comforted even with one-to-one care. Ask a parent to come immediately if you are unable to keep the child comfortable or when those conditions listed above require exclusion.

Children's Health Records

Every child in care should have a health appraisal form completed by a pediatrician. Most states require this form to be in a child's file before or shortly after enrollment. This form must confirm the child's good health and suitability for group care and verify that required immunizations have been completed. Immunizations must be kept up to date. It is a good idea to require annual health appraisals for each child.

The health appraisal form should also provide complete information on any special health needs. If special care is required, a special care plan should be developed by the parent, pediatrician, and center, detailing any special care required, including diet.

Medications

The administration of medication is an important aspect of child care health practices that requires careful attention to detail. Infants and toddlers can easily be harmed by the failure to develop and follow proper procedures. While some centers do refuse to give medication and require parents to come to the center to do so, that practice seems unfriendly to both children and working parents. Important aspects of a medication policy (but always follow the rules outlined by the state licensing agency) include the following:

◆ medications for children must be accompanied by a parent-signed medicine authorization form with the child's name, doctor's name, dates for administering the medicine, doses, name of medicine, reason for medicine, and name of pharmacy. Some states may require a doctor's signature as well.

◆ medicine must be in the original pharmacy container. Urge parents to request a second container from the pharmacy so the original can remain at the center.

◆ nonprescription medicines should be administered following the above procedure. Because many over-the-counter medications do not have standard doses for children under age two or three and instead recommend consulting with a pediatrician, a standing order from the child's pediatrician for use or a specific note from the child's pediatrician for that medication or preparation should accompany the parent's permission. Some states may require a doctor's signature as well. NOTE: Sunscreens are important to use to prevent children from burns but require parental permission and instructions for use like any other over-the-counter medication.

Each center should work out a medicine administration routine that ensures

◆ appropriate storage of medicine easily accessible to the caregiver but not accessible to children, refrigeration of many medications.

◆ caregivers carefully trained in administering medication. This includes awareness of center policies and immediate recording of administered doses in a log and on parents' daily experience sheets.

◆ whenever possible, schedules should be structured so that medicine can be given around lunch and late afternoon (i.e., three times per day, with parents giving the first dose).

◆ authorization forms should be good for only one medicine. One form must be completed for each medicine. No medicines should be given without an authorization form.

Always make sure that your policies conform to the health and licensing rules that your center is governed by.

Staff Health Records

In order to ensure that staff are both physically fit for their jobs and free from contagious illness, center employees should successfully complete a preemployment physical, including a Mantoux or chest x-ray testifying to the applicant's good health and satisfactory immunization record.

Staff health records should include results of the preemployment physical, physical updates at regular intervals, records of work injuries, instructions for special needs, and emergency instructions with information on the staff member's special health needs (e.g., allergies), physician, and contact instructions. Again, check your licensing rules for additional requirements.

Staff Illness

Staff illness is often nearly as sensitive an issue as child illness, given the frequency of exposure to illness and the difficulty of finding substitutes. Staff should not attend the center if they are known to be in the contagious stage of an illness, if they are physically unable to perform their job because of illness or injury, or if their job is likely to exacerbate an illness or injury.

Management of Infectious Disease

The critical factors in infection control are rigorous sanitation and appropriate response when an infectious condition is discovered.

Every center should have a trained staff member capable of reviewing symptoms for infectious illness. When a contagious condition is suspected, contact the parent and outline the requirements for the child (including when exclusion is necessary and when return to the center is possible). Center policies should detail the steps to take to prevent the spread of the illness (e.g., identifying ill children, disinfecting the environment, and changes in sanitation practices or routines). When appropriate, a sign notifying the other parents of exposure, symptoms, and precautions for this illness should be posted or a letter should be sent to parents.

HIV/AIDS, Hepatitis B, and Blood-Born Pathogens   Blood-born pathogens are bacteria, viruses, and other pathogens carried in the blood and sometimes in other bodily fluids that cause illness. The best known are HIV (Human Immunodeficiency Virus) and Hepatitis B Virus (HBV). Every center should have written policies on the admission, exclusion, and care of children with HIV, HBV, and other viruses transmitted by blood. Because of the seriousness of the illnesses and the fear that they generate, up-to-date knowledge about both transmission and proper precautions is critical. The center should take care that all staff and parents understand the issues.

As of this writing, there have been no known instances of HIV transmission between children in child care. The likelihood of transmission is believed to be close to zero and does not warrant exclusion from child care. There has been one documented case of HBV transmission. The low likelihood of HBV transmission does not justify exclusion of children unless they have serious problems with dermatitis or bleeding.

The most important response to the threat of blood-born pathogens is to adopt the universal precautions recommended by health authorities for handling exposure to blood- and blood-containing body fluids. *Caring for Our Children* details the proper use of nonporous gloves, hand washing, and disinfecting blood-contaminated areas.

Sudden Infant Death Syndrome (SIDS)   Some infants are susceptible to Sudden Infant Death Syndrome, also called crib death. It is an invisible, nondramatic killer that is not prevented simply by better surveillance. Research has shown that putting infants to sleep on their backs or, to a lesser extent, on their sides, may reduce the incidence of SIDS, as will eliminating pillows from cribs, and the use of bean bag chairs. Sharing information about sleeping positions with parents is advisable and requesting a release if they choose to have the infant sleep on his or her stomach is advisable.

Child Abuse and Neglect   Caregivers at all infant and toddler programs need training to identify possible cases of child abuse or neglect. Caregivers are mandated reporters legally required to notify child protection authorities of suspected instances about abuse or neglect. The potential ramifications of reporting on the parent partnership and staff relationships are so serious that knowing what behaviors or patterns of behavior, injuries, and conditions suggest abuse or neglect is critical. Training is usually available from public health departments.

Common Health Conditions of Infant and Toddlers

High Fevers   Infants and toddlers run high fevers more easily than adults. Fevers over 102 degrees are common in response to viral infections of the throat and ear. It is important to pay attention not only to the temperature of the child but also to his behavior as well to determine the seriousness of the situation. A child with a high fever who is acting sleepy and apathetic is much more of a cause for serious concern than the irritable child who is fairly active and eating well. Fevers can be brought down by bathing in tepid water and, with parent consent, the appropriate dose of acetaminophen (No-Aspirin, Tylenol).

Vomiting, Diarrhea, and Dehydration   Dehydration is a life-threatening concern, particularly for infants. The body needs fluids and vomiting and diarrhea can quickly cause dehydration. Outward signs of dehydration are dry mouth, dry and papery skin, crying without tears, and sunken eyes. Caregivers and parents should always take diarrhea and vomiting seriously.

Small amounts of clear liquids, ice, frozen juice chips, or Popsicles to suck on, gelatin pudding, and cold, flat sodas will help hydrate the child and settle an upset stomach.

Middle Ear Infections   Anyone familiar with babies is soon aware that ear (and to a lesser extent, throat) infections are common in infants and toddlers, both as byproducts of colds and on their own. The telltale sign of pulling on ears and fever should lead to a doctor's visit because ear infections can lead to permanent hearing loss. Some toddlers with a large number of infections will ultimately have tubes put in their ear to drain fluid and pus.

Avoid feeding children prone to ear infections while they are lying on their backs. Be alert to any sign of hearing loss or problems with speech. When children have tubes, keep water out of the child's ears to avoid introducing new infections.

Common Colds   Colds are infectious diseases caused by hundreds of different viruses. Germs are everywhere, spread by people before any symptoms become evident. Colds are not caused by cold weather, rain, drafts, or how we dress. You can get one cold after another from different viruses, and they can last for up to two weeks. Runny noses, stuffy noses, coughs, and low fevers are symptoms. Rigorous sanitation and limiting contact with large populations may reduce the number of colds the child is exposed to, but unfortunately no matter what we do, colds tend to run through group living environments.

Diaper Rash   Prolonged wetness, rubbing from wet diapers, and urine and feces combine to create diaper rash. The best treatment for diaper rash is to let the child sleep without a diaper and to give sitz baths, using a small amount of vinegar. Change diapers often and increase the child's intake of liquids, particularly acidic fruit juices like cranberry juice.

Thrush   A severe form of diaper rash that can also occur in the mouth, thrush is caused by a fungus and appears as milky patches on the skin. It requires antifungal medication.

Teething   Teething occurs around six months and may cause irritability, biting, and drooling. Drooling often leads to diarrhea, since the extra saliva causes babies to overdigest their foods. Chilled rubber teething rings or teething biscuits, bagels or cold large carrots are good chewing alternatives. Massaging the baby's gum (wash your hands before and after) will soothe the child.

Sanitation Policies and Practices

Hand Washing

Hand washing is the single most critical aspect of good sanitation in an infant/toddler program. In a good program, staff feel as if they are washing their hands all the time. To protect against the spread of illness, all participants in the center should wash their hands with soap and running water on arrival, before eating and after toileting, after diapering or assisting children with toileting, when cleaning, administering medication, after nose blowing, or following contact with any body fluids or contaminated material. It is also recommended that staff wash their hands before entering an infant or toddler room after being around others. Hang a poster on proper hand washing techniques at each hand washing sink.

Children should wash hands before and after meals, after diapering or using the toilet, after coughing or sneezing, after visiting other rooms, and before/after other contact with body fluids. Caregivers should wash the hands of babies and help older children, teaching them proper techniques (see *Healthy Young Children*).

Save Money: Use Bleach

There are a number of commercial disinfectants available, but chlorine bleach and water is as effective as any of these. Use 1/4-cup of bleach per gallon of water. Mix daily and throw out unused solution.

NOTE: *Disinfectant is only effective when the surface is allowed to air dry.* Disinfectant kills germs by oxidation. Wiping dry after use negates the disinfectant's effects. The solution is not harmful to skin.

Using Latex Gloves

It is necessary to use disposable latex gloves when changing children who have diarrhea or very messy diapers; when changing the diaper of a child with gastrointestinal illness; when contact with blood-containing fluids is likely (especially if a caregiver's hands have open cuts or sores); when cleaning materials or surfaces contaminated with body fluids such as blood, vomit, or feces. But it is not necessary to use gloves for every diaper change. In fact, it may even be harmful because staff may forget that the gloves only protect hands. If they touch other surfaces while wearing gloves, they may contaminate those surfaces.

Staff should bring latex gloves on trips and to playgrounds to be used in the event of injury.

Diaper Changing

Even in the best designed facilities, it is a challenge to diaper a group of children and not contaminate the surroundings. In developing the routine, consider the following:

- ◆ diapering should take place only in designated areas.
- ◆ a poster outlining proper diapering procedures should be displayed at the diaper change table.
- ◆ diaper changing areas should be sanitized (sprayed with bleach solution or other disinfectant) after each use and allowed to air dry. Clean soiled areas with hot, soapy water, wiped dry first, and then sanitize.
- ◆ keep all diapering supplies near the changing table and out of children's reach.

◆ remember that diapering is a PRIME TIME during which eye contact, play, conversation, and contact are important.

Diaper creams and powders are not necessary for most children and are actually discouraged by many health professionals, although parents may wish to use them. If used, be careful not to share them between the children and prevent inhalation of powders and corn starch.

Diapering Routine

All diaper routines should be adjusted to the particular setting, but the essential steps are similar:

1. Wash hands and gather supplies needed for changing, including any change of clothes.
2. Put a clean sheet of "diaper" paper (e.g., nonporous paper like examination or computer paper) on the table.
3. Place child on changing table. Always keep a hand on the child.
4. If gloves are needed, put them on before continuing. NOTE: gloves should be required in instances when contact with blood or gross contamination is likely.

5. Remove and double-bag soiled clothes and put them out of reach of the child. Remove diaper. If using a disposable diaper, fold inward and place in a covered, lined, foot-operated can. If cloth, double-bag the diaper and place in container out of reach of the child and away from clean clothes.
6. Cleanse diapered area of child with wipes or wet paper towel and dispose of wipes in can.
7. Powder or cream diapered area only if requested by parent.
8. Wash your hands.
9. Re-diaper and clothe the child.
10. Wash child's hands.
11. Remove and dispose of diaper paper.
12. Wash changing table and pad with soapy solution, sanitize, and air dry.
13. Wash your own hands.
14. Record diaper changes on daily experience sheet. Note diaper rashes or uncommon contents.

Toileting

Toilets should always be kept visibly clean and be disinfected daily. Potty chairs are strongly *not* recommended by health authorities because of the risk of spread of infectious disease. Unfortunately (and often necessarily), they are widely used. When used, potties should be emptied, cleaned, and disinfected after *each* use by staff wearing latex gloves. Great care should be taken to avoid contamination in the potty cleaning process. Ideally, potties are cleaned in a utility sink not used for other homebase purposes.

After accidents in which clothing is contaminated, dispose of feces in the toilet (if it can be done easily and in a sanitary fashion) but do not rinse contaminated clothing. Instead, double-bag it and send it home with the child.

Nap Time Hygiene

Infants should each have their own cribs and toddlers their own cots or cribs and blankets that are labeled with their names. Change crib sheets daily and sanitize mats and cots weekly. Bumper pads (if used) should be laundered every two weeks. Blankets should be washed weekly or when soiled.

Cribs or cots should be separated by at least 24 inches or by a barrier that prevents transmission of infectious material.

Soiled Clothing

Children's soiled clothing should be bagged in plastic bags until washed (either at home or at the center).

Toy Washing

Ideally, once a toy or cloth item has been used by a child, it is removed from circulation until sanitized or laundered. Toys may be sanitized in a dishwasher or washed in warm soapy water, dried, then sprayed with a disinfectant, and air dried. Each room should have a system of separating contaminated and clean toys. A dishwasher for toy washing accessible to infant and toddler rooms (which is often located near the washer and dryer) is a great help.

Food Handling and Mealtimes

Disease is easily transmitted during food preparation and meals unless strict sanitary procedures and continual monitoring are observed. Most important:

◆ homebase procedures for bottle and food preparation, feeding, storage of food, and cleanup should be detailed in writing, posted, and monitored by a health and sanitation professional.

◆ from a health standpoint, food handling and diapering ideally should be carried out by different caregivers. Because this is rarely possible, it is critical to keep the two functions distinct and separate by distancing changing areas and food areas and by thorough hand washing. For a healthy center, caregivers *must* develop a state of mind that makes taboo any trend toward a casual transition between the two.

◆ food, juice, and milk should be stored appropriately. All partially used food or drink should be discarded. Clean up any spills with hot, soapy water and disinfect the area.

◆ food spills during mealtime should be wiped or vacuumed up immediately.

Trash Handling

Trash should be emptied as needed, but at least once per day. Dirty diapers should be stored in foot-operated covered containers kept away from children. Food waste should be disposed of in lined, covered containers. Clean trash cans with hot, soapy water and sanitize frequently. Seek assistance from public health or other health agencies to ensure the best possible practices in your situation. Also, regularly monitor your actual practice, and of course, keep your sense of humor.

Nutrition and Health

Ensuring adequate nutrition and sensible food policies and practices is important for healthy development. Guidelines for healthy nutrition are widely available; *Healthy Young Children* is a good resource.

"No Sweets at Birthday Parties?"

Baby birthdays are universally prized events. Food policies can often turn into a battleground when adults differ on what standard of nutritional purity apply, what foods should be presented, how much children should have to eat, and what foods are appropriate at holiday and birthday celebrations. "Expert advice" may divide staff and strain the parent-caregiver partnership. Centers with food programs may have to balance a concern for good nutrition (low fat, high fiber, few sweets, lots of fruits and vegetables), ethnic variety, parents' concern about children not getting enough to eat if they don't eat what they eat at home, and of course, cost. What do you do?

A good program will accept the challenge and strive for balance and moderation. All of the occasionally conflicting concerns mentioned above are legitimate. What is important is defusing the righteousness that seeps into attitudes and recognizing that group life involves compromise.

Birthdays and holidays are times that typically are celebrated with treats. Centers might encourage parents to minimize the use of sweets and empty calorie foods and to celebrate in other ways with special decorations and activities. But here too, a "pure" policy is at odds with the culture and will lead to more conflict than warranted by the positive effects of the policy.

Feeding: Breast, Bottle, and Baby Foods

Infant feeding should be based on parent instructions. The best food for infants is breast milk, and caregivers need to be supportive of mothers who wish to breast-feed. There should be a comfortable place that meets the mother's requirements for privacy to breast-feed and to pump breast milk.

Because of the range of parental preferences and individual differences, even centers with food programs usually ask parents to send food from home. To ensure each child's health and safety:

- accept only formula in original containers and reconstitute it according to package directions.
- prepare formula using water heated in bottles to the child's preference in bottle warmers. *Never heat bottles in a microwave oven.* Microwave heating is uneven, and a bottle warm to the touch may contain scalding milk that permanently damages the child's esophagus (about the width of a straw in a young baby).
- label each child's bottles and caps with his/her name.
- discard unused prepared formula at the end of each day.
- refrigerate all prepared bottles.
- do not store defrosted breast milk for longer than twenty-four hours.
- partially used bottles may be kept at room temperature for no longer than one hour and *should not* be put back in the refrigerator for later use. Keep bottles out of the reach of other children.
- place dirty bottles in a basket clearly labeled "Dirty Bottles."
- never serve commercial baby food out of the jar. Use a serving dish and cover. Date and refrigerate open jars of baby food and use the contents within forty-eight hours.

Dental Health

Thumb sucking presents no health or developmental issue unless a child continues beyond five years of age and the onset of permanent teeth. Pacifiers are a matter of parent choice and are only harmful to the extent that they are shared between children.

"Baby bottle tooth decay" is caused by giving an infant or toddler a bottle of milk or juice as a pacifier at bedtimes. Any liquid except plain water can cause baby bottle tooth decay.

At about two years old, children can be taught to brush their teeth with a fluoride toothpaste after meals. When tooth brushing is not possible, drinking water after meals helps to remove food particles from teeth.

A Healthy Environment

Some of the important environmental considerations that help to improve the health of young children:

- good ventilation and lots of fresh air.
- draft-free temperatures of 65–75 degrees.
- adequate humidity (30–70 percent relative humidity).
- a smoke-free environment.
- clean air and water free from toxins and allergens.
- a setting free from infestations of vermin.
- pets (hamsters, gerbils, guinea pigs, birds that are not from the parrot family), free from disease and vermin and kept in clean cages.

Health Education

Young children need to learn about health and safety as a natural consequence of daily care. Infants and toddlers will begin to learn about proper hand washing, sanitary practices in food handling, meal preparation, and toileting procedures from well-planned routines. The curriculum for older toddlers can include developmentally appropriate information about germs and other important health topics. Workshops and written communications for staff and parents are excellent vehicles for health and safety education.

Emergency Preparedness

Emergencies do happen and infants and toddlers are the most vulnerable population at the center. Every center should have a plan for emergencies that includes a plan for each room posted in a central location. Emergencies include procedures for fire, severe weather, environmental emergencies, power outages, and medical emergencies. Plans should include at least the following:

- two diagrammed evacuation routes.
- instructions for each adult in the room.
- a gathering place following evacuation.
- how to call emergency medical help.
- first-aid instruction, including infant CPR.

Both the office and the homebase should have up-to-date index files with staff's and children's emergency information. Each room should have a well-stocked first aid kit that is clearly marked with a red cross to indicate that first aid supplies are there.

Evacuation Drills

Evacuation drills should occur once per month and should be scheduled to occur at times that might present problems, such as toddler nap times. For safe evacuations,

- all adults should have assigned roles, with support staff generally helping in infant and toddler rooms.

◆ infants and other nonambulatory children should be transported in cribs designated as evacuation cribs with reinforced legs and wheels (or in a crib substitutes such as mail carts).

◆ blankets, jackets, shoes, and emergency information should be stored in a manner that permits quick removal during a fire drill.

◆ designated staff should check each room prior to leaving the building.

◆ a designated person should account for each child and adult listed in attendance that day.

Medical Emergencies

Medical emergencies are not uncommon in child care. Emergency procedures should be posted in every room and by every phone. Sufficient staff should have up-to-date training in first aid and infant CPR to ensure that a trained staff person is available at all times. First aid training should include management of dental emergencies. Frequent "refresher" training is required to achieve an actual state of preparedness.

A designated staff member should assess all injuries and identify who should administer first aid, carefully following specified procedures (for example, see p. 100 in *Healthy Young Children*).

A first aid kit should be available in a convenient but secure place well-marked with a red cross in each homebase, in the kitchen, at playground doors, in any vehicles, and in the office.

First aid kits and children's emergency information cards should accompany all outings, both on the playground and off the center property. A designated staff person should ensure that first aid kits are well stocked.

Reporting Injuries

All significant injuries should be described by an observer on an incident (or accident) form, with a copy sent to parents. Parents should be called and informed of injuries. When the injury is more serious than day-to-day scrapes and bruises, call parents and alert them to the injury and to the care the child has received. Minor bumps and bruises may be reported in an Ouch or Bump report, and a copy given to the parent and put in the child's file.

Biting should be treated like any other injury. If it is minor, complete an Ouch Report. If it is more serious, call the child's parents and complete an incident report.

In the event of a very serious injury or emergency, the parent should be notified either simultaneously with the emergency medical service (EMS) or after the EMS has been called.

Tracking Injuries

Preventing injuries depends on having an accurate picture of what is actually happening—where, when, why, and who. It is important to maintain a central file of incident reports and not to disperse them in the children's files. They should be reviewed regularly and analyzed to identify hazards, problem times or locations, and children who seem prone to problems, and to take steps to prevent future injuries.

Transportation

Transportation safety requirements tend to be regulated by law. Infants and toddlers should ride in an approved safety restraint rated for their weight. Vehicles used for group transportation should be equipped with a first aid kit, a telephone, and preferably be accompanied by a back-up vehicle.

Providing a Safe Experience

Safety is of course a top priority for every program. Infants and toddlers don't recognize most of the danger that accompanies daily living. Yet if young children are to actively explore, investigate, and use the skills they are developing so rapidly, they will inevitably experience the normal bumps and bruises of childhood that come with exploration and physical learning. The challenge for staff is to strike a good balance between safety concerns and a rich learning environment. Your job is to minimize the chance of accidents, however small, and to make sure there is virtually no threat of serious injury or harm in the form of cuts, concussions, and broken bones.

Remember—anything that *can happen* probably *will happen* over the span of hours, days, and years that a program operates. A center with twenty-five infants and toddlers will have more than 20,000 instances of diapering. In five years, what are the odds of a child falling off a changing counter if there is no focus on safety? Eliminating accidents depends on

- a staff that is trained to continually "think safety" and to keep informed about possible hazards.
- an environment continually monitored and evaluated for safety concerns.

Major Safety Hazards

Not surprisingly, infants and toddlers are susceptible to a host of dangers from their drive to explore the world with their mouths and bodies:

Ingestion (choking, poisoning, internal burns)
- small objects
- pushpins (particularly colored pins)
- pills and medications
- toxic plants
- toxic liquids
- plastic bags and balloons

◆ large food pieces (e.g., carrots), nuts, popcorn

◆ allergic reactions to foods

◆ too-hot foods and liquids

Falls
◆ changing tables

◆ stairs

◆ climbing on storage units, stacked chairs, tables

◆ platforms, lofts, climbers, couches

Falling objects
◆ unsteady storage units

◆ poorly attached cabinets

◆ equipment with hanging cords

◆ heavy equipment or toys stored on upper shelves

◆ desk- and table-top items

Cuts, eye injuries
◆ sharp corners and edges on doors, cabinets, furniture

◆ sharp objects

◆ protrusions that poke (handles on windows, knobs, etc.)

Pinches
◆ doors, cabinet doors, car doors and windows

◆ rocking chairs or glider chairs

Burns and electrocution
◆ electrical outlets, exposed wires

◆ hot liquids (tap water, coffee and tea, soup, grease)

◆ hot foods (especially uneven heating in microwaves)

Safety Depends on Staff Awareness

It is easy to become desensitized to unsafe conditions. Safe settings depend on staff being vigilant about safety concerns:

◆ checking equipment for rough, broken, or unsafe parts.

◆ keeping in mind that babies will use anything available to pull themselves up to stand, to hold on to while walking, or to climb on, so equipment needs to be secure and heavy enough that babies cannot cause it to fall.

◆ ensuring that there are proper surfaces under climbing equipment that cushion falls.

◆ covering electrical outlets.

◆ making heaters and fans inaccessible.

◆ installing child-proof railings and banisters on stairs and other raised areas.

◆ locating medications, purses, and other potentially unsafe materials out of the reach of children.

◆ ensuring that floor surfaces, both indoors and out, are nonskid, especially in areas that get wet or covered with sand.

◆ having places where young infants can safely watch or play safely.

◆ observing the environment throughout the day for hazards (e.g., toys on the floor).

◆ observing children's behavior and adjusting the setting to make play safe (e.g., eliminating items from the reach of a child).

Every program should develop a site safety checklist and check it monthly for safety purposes. (See the sample checklist on page 187.)

Learning from Experience

Often a safety concern comes to light because of an accident or a close call. Our reaction is often to make a snap judgment about cause and effect to try and solve the problem. This may result in unnecessarily limiting equipment or coming up with a solution with more negatives than the original conditions. Instead of jumping to a quick solution, ask yourself:

◆ what happened? what was going on around the incident? Look at the child's behavior and the behavior of other children. Look for crowding, equipment concerns, transition confusion or stress, fatigue, and supervision concerns.

◆ was it avoidable? can you reduce the chance of it happening again?

◆ was there a chance of serious injury? If there was, how can you modify the situation to eliminate the risk?

Accidents Will Happen!

Infants and toddlers will get bumps and bruises. The world has risks, and fortunately bodies are designed to withstand the normal results as children learn to become mobile, active participants in human society. Each program has to draw its own lines on what level of risk is appropriate. For instance, if a program has a rocking chair, sooner or later a child may get his or her fingers pinched under the rocker. Is that reason to not have a rocking chair, which is a valuable piece of equipment in rooms for infants? Perhaps. But probably not in a safety-conscious program where staff make sure the chair is on a soft, pliant surface like a carpet, out of the traffic paths, and caregivers are aware of the problem and particularly observant of young babies.

Many safety problems come not so much from poor equipment choices as from poor planning, crowding, inappropriate use or location of equipment, and children not having enough to do.

The Politics of Risk

It is one thing for us to write that children need to be allowed to explore the world and risk the normal bumps and bruises of childhood. It is quite another to be a caregiver talking to an upset parent with a bruised child. The program as a whole has the responsibility to help parents buy into a vision of active learning and to trust the program's ability to protect their child from unreasonable risk. Caregivers cannot be left to struggle with the issue alone.

A Final Word: Health and Safety—A Work in Progress

A coherent approach to health and safety in group care for infants and toddlers is always a work in progress. New information and conclusions come forth from health professionals, and changes in public perceptions and events at the center change the attitudes and opinions of parents and staff. The right balance of challenge, safety, strict health policies, and accommodations to the real world will change. The key to creating a safe and healthy center that is a great place to be a child and a place that parents can feel secure is to never stop thinking about it. Always ask yourself how you can improve sanitation and reduce the spread of disease, eliminate accidents, and be better prepared for emergencies.

EXERCISES

1. Observe a number of diaper changes and potty training episodes, watching carefully for possible contamination and lapses in safety

2. List health policies that are incompletely written down.

3. Discuss what constitutes acceptable risk with three or four caregivers in relation to motor activities that may lead to bumps and bruises indoors and out.

4. List those areas of the site where accidents are most likely. What times of day are most likely to produce accidents?

REFERENCES

American Public Health Association and the American Academy of Pediatrics. *Caring for Our Children, National Health and Safety Performance Standards: Guidelines for Out-of-Home Child Care Programs.* Washington, DC: American Academy of Pediatrics, 1992.

Kendrick, Abby, Kaufmann, Roxanne, and Messenger, Katherine. *Healthy Young Children: A Manual for Programs.* Washington, DC: NAEYC, 1988.

Pennsylvania Chapter of the American Academy of Pediatrics. *Model Child Care Health Policies.* Washington, DC: NAEYC, 1993 [available in book form and on disk].

Site Safety Self-Inspection Checklist

❏ Date inspection was made: _____   ❏ Person performing inspection: _____

❏ Center: _____

Comments
(check if satisfactory:
if not, indicate action
taken or planned)

CENTER WIDE

Floor surfaces are smooth, clean, and do not cause trips or falls. _____

Walls, ceiling are clean and in repair. No peeling paint, damaged plaster. _____

Children are always under supervision. _____

No poisonous plants, vermin, or disease-bearing animals (no turtles, parrot family birds, or harmful pets). _____

Trash storage is covered. Sanitation is adequate, especially in food service areas, on cots or mats, dust traps. _____

No smoking in facility. _____

No precariously placed small, sharp, or otherwise hazardous objects. _____

Plastic bags are safely used. _____

No use of plastic balloons. _____

Decor is pleasant and in good shape. _____

No tacks or pushpins in use. _____

Heating and ventilation are working. Pipes and radiators are inaccessible or covered to prevent body contact. _____

Outlets are covered or grounded. There are no dangling or covered extension cords or window blind cords. _____

Safeguards are in place to prevent children from entering unsupervised or hazardous areas (including places children can climb on, through, under, etc.). _____

No pest strips or poisons are in use. _____

HOMEBASES AND MULTIPURPOSE ROOMS

Medicines, cleaning agents, tools, and teacher supplies are inaccessible to children. There are no aerosols in the room. ____

First aid and emergency kits are present in rooms and adequately supplied, no medicine cabinets are unlocked. ____

Temperature and humidity levels are comfortable. ____

Hot water does not exceed 110° F (43° C), soap and towel supplies are adequate, disposal is sanitary. ____

Mealtime sanitation procedures are posted and followed. ____

Exits are clearly marked and unobstructed. Easy access to emergency phone. Emergency contact information is current. ____

Locked doors to closed spaces can be opened by an adult. ____

Cots/cribs are labeled. Linens, mats, cribs, cots, and blankets are clean. ____

Toys and furnishings are in good repair and free of pinch or crush points, exposed bolts, or sharp edges. Toys on floor do not cause hazards to walking adults. ____

Feeding chairs have wide bases and safety straps and are kept clean and sanitized. ____

Infant swings have secure chairs and safety straps. ____

Diaper-changing procedure is posted. ____

Changing area is clean with adequate supply of changing pads and disposable sheets. ____

Toy washing is done daily and soiled toys are removed from action. ____

Soiled diapers are disposed of in a sanitary manner in a foot-operated covered container. ____

No use of microwaves for child foods or bottles. ____

No bottles in cribs. ____

No use of bean bag chairs. ____

No use of walkers. ____

CORRIDORS AND PUBLIC AREAS

Gates and gate equivalents are safe. ____

Monitoring of entrance for strangers is constant. Emergency phone numbers are posted near the phone. _____

Doors are operational with panic hardware on emergency exits. _____

KITCHEN AND STORAGE AREAS

Children are not allowed in the kitchen area. _____

Water for dishes is at least 170° F. Water and sanitizing agent are used for sanitation. Plumbing works properly. _____

Trash storage is covered and kept away from food storage and preparation areas. No storage near furnace or water heaters. _____

Cleaning agents, tools, and utensils, including matches, are stored away from food storage and are used safely. Toxic materials are in original containers separately stored away from food. _____

First aid and emergency kits are available and adequately stocked. _____

Fire extinguisher is charged. Staff know how to use it. _____

Food is dated and rotation methods are used. _____

Refrigerator temperature is 45° F. _____

Frozen foods are stored at 0° F or below. _____

Handled leftovers are discarded. _____

Food is stored on shelves; containers are labeled; insect-resistant metal or plastic containers (not plastic bags) are used. _____

Personnel are healthy and perform appropriate, frequent hand washing and wear clean clothing. _____

Surfaces are clean, free of cracks and crevices. _____

No wooden cutting boards are used. _____

Eating utensils are free from cracks and chips. _____

Pot handles on stoves are turned inward. _____

BATHROOM AND LAUNDRY ROOM

Hot water is less than 120° F; soap and towel supplies are adequate. _____

Trash storage and litter are adequately controlled. _____

Cleaning agents are inaccessible to children.   ____

Windows, doors, ceilings, and walls are clean and well
maintained. Floors are not slippery.   ____

There is no electrical equipment near water.   ____

Exits are clearly marked and neither obstructed nor cluttered.   ____

OUTDOORS AND PLAYGROUND

Daily procedures to ensure areas are free of litter, sharp objects,
and animal waste.   ____

Traffic safety is assured.   ____

Staffing plan to ensure no crowding and adequate supervision.   ____

Play equipment is smooth, well-anchored and free of rust,
splinters, and sharp corners. No exposed, uncapped screws or bolts.   ____

No "S" hooks or other open hooks. Swing seats are lightweight,
flexible, and noncutting. Equipment is placed in safe location.   ____

Sufficient developmentally appropriate play experiences.   ____

No entrapment spaces between 3 inches and 8 inches.   ____

No pinch or crush points on equipment.   ____

Fences/natural barriers prohibit access to hazardous areas and
keep animals out.   ____

No stagnant pools of water.   ____

Sunscreens are used and shade is available.   ____

Poisonous plants and stinging insect nests are removed.   ____

Street traffic controlled. Pick-up and drop-off procedures are safe.   ____

All safety procedures are followed on walks and field trips.   ____

OTHER

Sand, pea gravel, or fiber is 8–12 inches deep, checked daily for even
spreading, and free of litter or waste.   ____

Part 4

Quality Learning

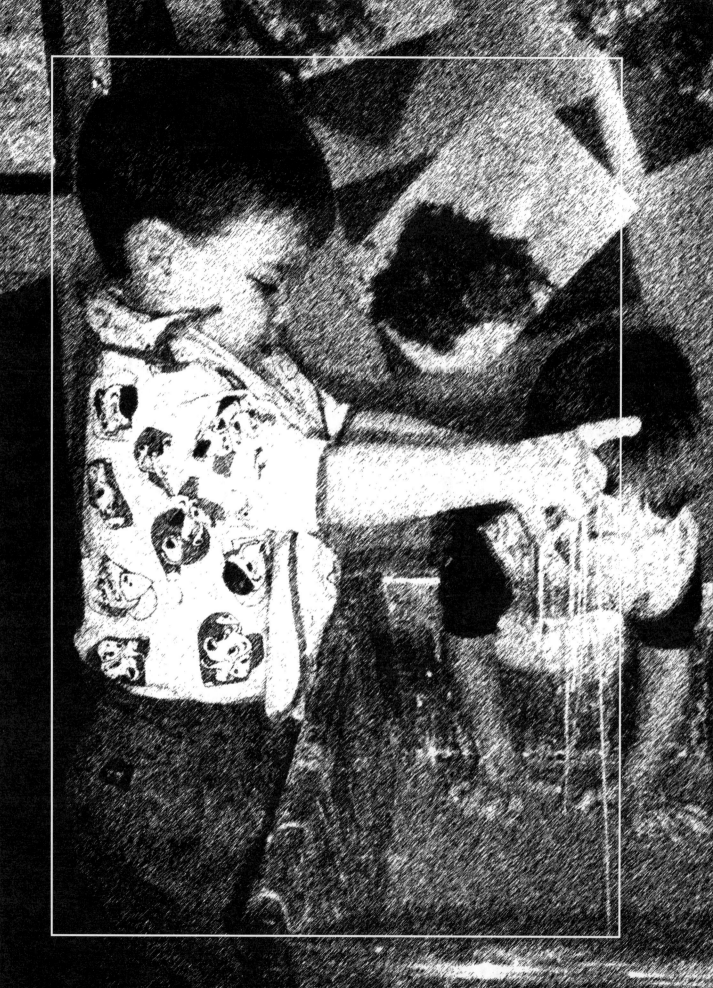

Chapter 11
The Learning Environment

An environment organized for active, hands-on, developmentally appropriate, individualized learning for each child. The "world at their fingertips" maximizes built-in learning and independent access by children, offers a full range of appropriate experiences, and allows staff to concentrate on PRIME TIMES for caring and learning. Staff understand that caring and learning are inseparable. They are sensitive to the learning experiences occurring naturally in day-to-day living.

Curriculum and Learning

The concept of a learning environment recognizes that learning is more than the outcome of curriculum. The child's entire experience with the program is important; there is no clear separation between learning and caring, play and work—certainly the child doesn't fit education into a tidy time or space.

The learning environment is designed to

◆ empower each child to become a confident, lifelong learner and a secure caring person.

◆ promote all aspects of development: large and small motor, cognitive, perceptual, social, emotional, language, creative, and expressive.

◆ nurture a positive self-concept, which includes acceptance of cultural and family background.

◆ be free of racial or sex role bias or stereotype and to encourage children to accept and enjoy diversity.

◆ provide a wonderful place for a childhood.

Curriculum is the term used for the way the learning environment is planned and organized. The fundamental premise of the curriculum is that children are active learners who learn best from activities they plan and carry out themselves. Children are recognized as scientists and builders, as acrobats and artisans who need active experience with the world of people and things and opportunities to plan, set goals, and take responsibility. It is understood that the *spirit* of learning, not the content, is the prime concern.

Staff are expected to provide the environment and the materials that children learn from and to be there to stimulate questions and curiosity. Staff support and encourage children and help them find new answers and new challenges. Caregivers also help children achieve the confidence and self-discipline to develop increasingly more sophisticated skills and knowledge.

An environmental approach to education means that furnishings, equipment, materials, the ways time and space are structured, and all the ways adults and children behave, teach children what the world is like, how it works, what they are capable of, and their important place in the world. Schedules, learning centers, learning built into class-room furnishings (e.g., different patterns, textures, and furniture to interact with—not ABC rugs), and outdoor play areas are planned to allow children to independently explore, discover, and learn through developmentally appropriate play.

The Infant-Toddler Curriculum

The first two years of life are when children need to acquire what psychologist Erik Erikson called basic trust, a pervasive sense of the essential trustworthiness of oneself and others. This is the sense of safety and security that comes from responsive, predictable care from familiar others to whom one is attached. Without this sense, the world is far too scary a place to cope with and learn about.

Each child also needs to develop a sense of autonomy, a sense of being a separate, independent self. This comes from being treated as an individual and being allowed increasing opportunities for independence. The toddler's "No" is an assertion of autonomy that leads to freely saying "Yes" and to developing the power to begin to control body and feelings.

Only when children feel a sense of personal power—"I can affect (influence) things"—and competence—"I can achieve things"—can they step out into the world as active learners and problem solvers prepared to cope with what will come.

To ensure that each child develops a strong sense of basic trust, autonomy, power, and competence, the curriculum needs to be based on two concepts: PRIME TIMES and a world at their fingertips. Together, these two elements ensure individualized care and active, developmentally appropriate experience.

Encouraging PRIME TIMES

A well-designed learning environment allows staff to focus on PRIME TIMES, those moments of one-to-one or small-group care and learning that lie at the heart of healthy development: caring, nurturing, learning moments, or conversations, during which there is total engagement with people and things. A rich built-in learning environment allows caregivers relaxed time to feed, diaper, dress, ease into or out of sleep, or otherwise nurture a child: to touch, to talk, to listen, to play all the call-response games the child sets in motion. Because language is important for even very young babies, these are also PRIME TIMES for learning. As a teacher, you must take advantage of these moments.

A World at Their Fingertips

Young children need a safe world rich with opportunities to actively explore and enjoy: to see, hear, feel, touch, and move; a world where, according to psychologist Jerome Bruner (1973), a child "is encouraged to venture, rewarded for venturing his own acts, and sustained against distraction or premature interferences in carrying them out" (p. 8).

Infants and toddlers are sensory-motor beings. They explore the world with their senses and their developing motor skills. Long before they understand concepts like "under" or "far" with their minds, their bodies are learning to navigate the up and down, over and under of the physical world.

Infant and toddler environments are planned and organized to maximize

- large and small motor experiences: for younger babies: looking, reaching, grasping, holding, crawling in, out, over, under; for toddlers: gripping, throwing, manipulating, walking, climbing, pushing, pulling.
- sensory experiences: explorations of texture, color, sound, size, shape, smell, taste, weight.
- cognitive experiences: object permanence, spatial relationships, classifying, collecting and dumping, cause and effect experiences, problem solving.
- language: adult-child conversations, labeling, books, music, rhyming, and sound explorations.
- social experiences: caregiver-child one to one, child-initiated interactions, guiding and modeling positive peer interactions.
- expression: art, movement, doll and soft toy play, imitation and beginning dramatic play.

With all these, the emphasis is on what the child gains in the process of engaging with people, equipment, and materials rather than on creation of a product or a result.

The Importance of Natural Experience

An exclusively child-oriented world peopled by children and women, filled with bright plastic things and pictures of animals and fairy tale characters, is a very limited and artificial world in which to spend forty to fifty hours a week. Instead, the best child care emphasizes a focus on natural experiences, ones that have meaning in the life of the center such as cleaning, food preparation, caring for other people, animals, and plants, and laundry rather than on artificial, contrived experiences.

There is an effort to bring the real world into the center as well as to get the children out and about into the community around them.

High/Scope's Key Experiences for Infants and Toddlers   Not all experiences are equal, and the learning environment is designed to promote those experiences essential to development. The High/Scope Foundation (1995) developed a list of key experiences for the period from birth through age two and one half to help caregivers plan for and guide the child's experience in the program (pp. 1–4). Key experiences describe how infants and toddlers explore the environment, learn about themselves, and begin to interact with others in their world.

High/Scope's key experiences are organized into categories based on their Piagetian approach to curriculum. Each experience is illustrated with an anecdote. Note that the anecdote may apply to other key experiences. For example, two babies playing peek-a-boo are having a social experience, a presentation experience of object permanence, and a movement experience.

Social Relations
Bonding: building significant relationships with primary caregivers

Daniel goes over to Mindy (his caregiver).

Building relationships with peers and other adults

Henry and John, laughing, play a brief game of peek-a-boo around the basketball pole at outside time.

Expressing emotions toward others

Matt goes over to Rebecca, who has just returned after a week's vacation, and gives her a kiss.

Responding to the needs of others

Matt hugs Christopher, who is crying because his mom has left.

Sense of Self
Distinguishing "me" from other people and things (for example, recognizing one's own image in a mirror)

Mitchell waves at his image in the mirror as he sits on the floor in front of it, touching first his face and then the reflection of his face in the mirror.

Asserting oneself—making and expressing choices, preferences, and decisions

Kayla is playing with blocks spread out in front of her. When another child attempts to take two of her blocks, Kayla says, "Mine" and moves the two blocks closer to herself.

Solving problems encountered in exploration and play

Lizzie eats her dry cereal out of a paper cup at snack time, pouring the cereal into her mouth as if she were drinking it.

Communications
Listening and responding to sounds, voices, words, sensations and facial expressions

Kelly looks at Tracy (an adult) when Tracy speaks to her and smiles at Tracy's voice.

Communicating with movements, gestures, facial expressions, sounds, and words

When Tejas's book falls on the floor from the chair in which he is sitting, he says, "Uh oh."

Participating in the give-and-take of communication—both verbal and nonverbal

Dee (an adult), is rocking Austin, while looking into his face and singing to him. She begins singing the sounds "La, la, la," instead of the regular words to the song. Austin looks up at her and says, "La, la, ma, ma. . . ."

Using language to fulfill needs

Lyle says, "Help me" as he brings his shoes over to an adult after nap time.

Enjoying speaking and being spoken to

> *At a circle time, Julia chimes in as the group sings a rhyming song:*
>
> *Adult: One, two . . .*
>
> *Julia: Buckle my shoe.*
>
> *Adult: Three, four . . .*
>
> *Julia: Shut door.*

Listening to stories, rhymes, and songs, and exploring books and magazines

> *Danielle looks through a familiar storybook, saying some words quietly to herself.*

Movement

Moving the parts of one's body (reaching, grasping, pointing)

> *Lying on his stomach, Matt reaches for and bats at a beach ball.*

Moving one's whole body (rolling, crawling, cruising, walking, running, balancing)

> *At outside time, Jamie and three other children jump up and down in the empty plastic wading pools.*

Moving with objects

> *Gina pushes a car on the floor and crawls after it.*

Moving to music

> *When Blake's caregiver sings "Sally the Camel," Blake bobs up and down as the numbers are sung and moves his hips from side to side to the words, "Boom, boom, boom."*

Exploring Objects (Prerepresentation)
Exploring objects with one's mouth, hands, feet, eyes, and ears

> *Hope takes her pacifier out of her mouth, looks at it, changes her positions, and puts back it back in her mouth.*

Searching for hidden objects and people—discovering object permanence*

---

* Author's note: in other words, recognizing that an object continues to exist even when it is outside one's sight, e.g., if it is partially visible or completely hidden.

Lizzie continues to crawl toward a cup, even after her caregiver has put it behind a chair, out of Lizzie's sight.

Exploring building and art materials (for example scribbling, using blobs of paint, using clay, attempting to make a circle)

Nick colors with chalk on a chalkboard that lies flat on the floor. He makes long, curved scribble lines at one edge and leaves the center of the board blank.

Imitating the actions of others

Cathy (an adult) is folding diapers for the infants when Karlie comes over and starts folding diapers for her baby doll.

Associating action with objects

Julia rides around on a toy train, making the "Choo-Choo" sound over and over.

Using one object to stand for another

Daniel puts a pot from the house area over his head as if it were a hat.

Responding to and identifying pictures

Carlos sees a picture of a duck in his book and excitedly says "Quack, quack, quack."

Exploring Attributes of Objects: Classification
Exploring and noticing the colors, shapes, sizes, textures, and other attributes of things

Marcus squeezes a soft ball at outside time, saying "Look, I got a wiggly ball."

Exploring and noticing how things are the same and how they are different

Jenny tries to take a blanket another child is using. Dee (an adult) offers Jenny another blanket that is almost identical except that it has a hole in it. Jenny refuses this blanket, saying, "No, Dee, it's broken."

Exploring and noticing how things can be grouped together

Sam brings plastic animals——one by one, eight in all——from all different areas of the room and puts them on the tray in front of Michael. When he is done, he turns away from Michael and claps.

Comparing and Counting
Experiencing more and less

> *While playing with playdough at small group time, Kate observes, "Hey, there's some more," upon discovering some play-dough is left in the container.*

Arranging objects in one-to-one correspondence

> *Keith takes three play people out of a basket and puts each one inside its own little car.*

Using number words

> *While touching the pegs on the pegboard one by one, Tiara chants, "One, two, three, four, five, nine, eight, one, two, three, five, nine, eight, . . ."*

Space
Noticing the location of objects in the environment

> *Michael has finished his snack (which the class had outside). When Bonnie (an adult) asks him to throw away his napkin, Michael walks over to the trash can and puts his napkin in it.*

Exploring and noticing the relationships of objects to other objects

> *Alex comments to the adults who have come outside after him, "You're outside, too!"*

Observing objects and people from different perspectives

> *Jason looks at Jan (an adult) through his legs as he bends over with his hands touching the floor. Jan says, "Upside down!" and Jason responds, "Down!"*

Filling and emptying

> *Samantha fills up her purse with small blocks and carries it around the room with her.*

Taking things apart and fitting things together

> *Zachary fits the small pegs into the pegboard, one at a time.*

Time
Anticipating familiar events

> *Sam brings his chair across the room to the lunch table and sits down, an hour before lunch occurs.*

Noticing the beginnings and endings of time intervals

Raoul is taking turns jumping on the mini-trampoline with Lyle. Raoul jumps several more times, says, "One more minute," then immediately gets off the trampoline and says, "Your turn" to Lyle. They alternate turns for several minutes.

Experiencing *fast* and *slow*

John is pushing another child on the swing at outside time. John says to David (an adult), "I pushin' Henry fast!"

Using Key Experiences   Key experiences are useful to keep in mind as you organize the environment, plan activities, and plan for individuals and interact with children because they cut across curriculum content and focus on the child's development. For the same reason, the key experiences also are very valuable for structuring observations, analyzing and interpreting the behavior of children. Watching children is easy—figuring out what to observe amidst all that is happening is hard. Key experiences provide the structure:

Key experiences: noticing objects in space, object permanence

Seven-month-old Sebastian is moving toward Emma's bottle. He stops when it disappears from sight as it is blocked by another child. He resumes when the child moves on.

Key experience: filling and emptying, prerepresentation—using one object to stand for another, communicating.

Two-year-old Lilly carefully pours her milk into her cup, takes a sip, and then gets up and dumps it out in the garbage. She sits down again, pours more, and dumps it out, this time watching the milk splash in the garbage can —"Rain," she shouts, before her caregiver catches on and ends the waste of the milk.

Using key experiences helps caregivers stay focused on why children do things and "what children *can* do rather than what they cannot yet do or are not doing because they are not interested. Observation makes us more aware of the child's needs and interests at the moment; this in turn leads us to support the child more appropriately" (Post, 1995, p. 3).

Planning the Child Care Center Learning Environment

There are lots of ways to plan curriculum, and teachers usually adapt whatever system is given to them. Whatever the approach taken and the forms used, it is important to get out of the mind-set of lesson plans. Infants and toddlers do not need lessons—they need opportunities for experience that as individuals they can make the most of.

There are five parts to planning the learning environment:

1. Knowing and understanding general child development and individual differences.

All planning should begin with a clear sense of purpose based on our knowledge of the children:

◆ the developmentally important key experiences necessary for maximizing full individual development.

◆ the experiences necessary for each child to have relaxed and happy days.

2. Planning the environment on a bimonthly or monthly basis.

Environmental planning assumes a basic framework of learning centers that changes from time to time:

◆ what learning centers are available?

◆ what props or loose parts are regularly available?

◆ what learning is built into the setting or routines?

The length of time a particular learning center is available will vary based on space availability and child interest. A review of every learning center should be conducted monthly.

3. Planning weekly and daily experiences and activities.

Daily planning will be done in advance as well as during the day, when alterations are needed on the spot.

◆ what experiences are offered each day through rotation of materials in the learning centers?

◆ what activities are planned for each day by teachers?

Planning should be based on observations of the children using the key experiences: their interests, their new skills, their reactions to new materials, equipment, and experiences offered, as well as general observations about the use of time and space. (See the Infant/Toddler Weekly Planning Form, page 219).

4. Monthly experience review.

   Every month, caregivers should look back on what actually happened as a basis for planning changes in the experiences offered by the homebase.

   Are experiences developmentally appropriate for the entire range of children?

Do experiences offer the right balance—

◆ across curriculum areas (e.g., motor, art, dramatic play, construction, etc.)?

◆ for individuals and groups?

◆ new challenge and practice/mastery?

Are the experiences actively nonsexist?

Do the experiences reflect the cultural diversity of the community in which the program operates?

The monthly review should be done by all the staff, if possible. Staff should be encouraged to observe and evaluate the program continuously and to jot down notes or comments while they work. These observations are invaluable in planning for the group or for individual children.

5. Planning for individual children

Individual planning ensures that the program works for every child:

◆ is the primary caregiver aware of the child's current interests, needs, and strengths?

◆ does the caregiver have a list of goals and desirable experiences that are based on observations of the child's development, experiences in the setting, and discussions with parents?

Planning for your primary-care children is an ongoing process, supervised by the lead teacher. Goals are established to ensure the individual child's experience is developmentally appropriate and suits the child and parent's needs and interests. Diagnostic goals to speed development are *not* appropriate (for example, knowing all colors, beginning to walk). Use the key experiences to guide observations and planning.

Lead teachers are responsible for ensuring that planning on all levels occurs and that group staff have appropriate, individual child goals and are working toward them. The director and lead teachers have discretion about the most effective planning structure to use to plan for daily and weekly variations of experiences.

Learning Centers   The following are some of the many possible learning centers or activity areas appropriate for infant and toddler rooms (see also chapter 6, Structuring Time and Space for Quality Care). What is possible depends on the actual space and equipment available. As you develop some centers, you should be able to think of others. Remember that an adult label for the area should not restrict the types of activities children themselves want to engage in (e.g., sensory exploration will occur in all areas). Adults should follow children's leads.

NOTE: As discussed in chapter 10, staff should always be aware of the hazards materials present to small scientists who use their mouths to explore: e.g., choking on small pieces and ingesting toxic finishes. Keep a choke testing tube handy when equipping centers.

Infant Reaching/Grasping/Kicking Area
♦ various materials hanging on rope, elastic, or fabric.

Infant Peek-a-Boo/ Object Permanence Area
♦ divider with holes in it, large appliance carton with holes cut in, curtained area. Objects on a string that swing in and out of sight.

Infant Swing Area
♦ swing, cradle, or swinging platform.

Infant Play Pit, Play Pen, or Plastic Wading Pool
♦ a programmed, protected, contained space that the child chooses to play in.

Individual Infant Seat with Tray
♦ An individual play space for activities such as picking up and manipulating small objects that the child chooses—for example, a high chair or car seat.

Climbing Area
♦ couch, planks, low cubes and rectangles, plastic milk crates, mattresses, one or two stairs.

Mirror Area
♦ various mirrors attached to walls, or attached to divider backs.

Infant Blocks
♦ large cardboard/milk carton, plastic foam blocks, sturdy boxes.

Toddler Block and Construction Area
♦ large cardboard, milk carton or cardboard blocks, large plastic or foam blocks.
♦ small unit blocks, Duplo building blocks.
♦ props: wheelbarrows, trucks, wagons, dolls, and vehicles.

Vehicle Center
♦ infants: smooth wooden and plastic vehicles.
♦ toddlers: trucks, cars, trains, props like little plastic people, houses, trees, small rocks and wood, blocks, ramps.

Hauling/Transporting/Push-Pull Area (contents to be used throughout the room) and Collection Points
♦ pull toys, wagons, shopping carts, baskets, bins, buckets, cardboard boxes, toy boxes, mail slots, tubes.

Soft Toy Area
◆ all sorts of stuffed animals.

Dramatic Play
◆ prop boxes, cubbies, small tables and chairs, appliance boxes, flash-lights, old baby equipment such as car seats, changing pads, etc., Ace bandages, paint brushes, bowls and buckets, household items, found or salvaged "junk" that is safe.

Language and Book Area
◆ pictures of objects that have meaning for children, sturdy books (cardboard pages), special picture books that may be used with adult supervision, pillows, couch, chairs, futon, stuffed animals, tape recorder (used with adults).

Home Corner Area
◆ child-sized stove, table and chairs, refrigerator, beds for dolls (important that they be big enough and sturdy enough for children to lie in as well), strollers and buggies.
◆ props: dishes, dolls with pieces of cloth to wrap around them (sim-pler than doll clothes to take off and put on), blankets, saucepans and other cooking implements, handbags.

Costume Area (materials to be used throughout the space)
◆ hats, helmets, carpenters' aprons, goggles, belts, shoes, scarves, mitts, animal noses, wigs, Ace bandages, nets, all sorts of dress-up clothes.

Art and Expressive Materials Area
◆ white board, chalkboard (can be used on the floor), easel, crayons, pencils (chunky for ease of use), newsprint or other large pieces of paper for whole-arm scribbling, Etch-a-Sketch taped to wall or table, thick paints, collage materials, paste, cardboard, wood, tape, tables.

Messy Area
◆ sand table, texture/water table, dish/garden tubs, sinks, smearing surfaces such as a tabletop or linoleum tiles, sponges, brushes, dish towels.

Manipulative Materials
◆ wading pool, pit, table with rim, small rugs for surfaces; unstruc-tured materials such as juice lids, pipe pieces, knobs, wood pieces, stones, poker chips, large washers, shoe laces, straws, manipulative materials from catalogues, large beads to string; any sort of con-tainer such as cans, cups, buckets, baskets, pans, boxes, tennis ball cans.

Action Center
- busy boxes, switches, zippers, Velcro fasteners, locks and latches, doors, pounding benches; ramps, tubes, containers to drop or roll materials into; things to take apart.

Sound Area
- chimes, whistles, instruments, strings to pluck and plunk, shakers, record player or tapes, listening center with headsets.

Animal Area
- rubber or wooden animals, pictures, animal masks or noses, puppets, places for animals to live, props to create fences.

Cozy Areas, Places to Pause
- all sorts of cushions and pillows, couch, bed, throw, beanbag; inner tubes, throw rugs, bolsters, futons, blankets, parachutes, sheets, canopies, boxes, plastic wading pools. NOTE: have more than one cozy area.

Body Image Space
- area that responds to the child's whole body movement: a space filled with beach balls, paper, hanging fabric.

Surprise Area
- place where surprises or new experiences occur. (Of course, this will not be the only place for surprises and new experiences.)

Please Smell Area
- scent boxes, leaves, flowers, plants.

Please Touch Area
- different textures; coldness, hardness: smooth metal, rough bark, ice, sandpaper, velvet, corrugated materials.

Please Look Area
- mirrors, kaleidoscopes, colored plastic, smoked Plexiglas, paintings, videos, wave tubes, fish tanks.

Zoo Area
- birds, hamsters, chameleons, bunnies, fish, frogs.

Outdoor Areas
- hills, paths, boulders, stumps, wading pools, water, tunnels, shrub mazes, footpaths, wagons, push-along carts, ponchos, shade umbrellas (see chapter 12).

Play Materials   There are a huge number of commercial play materials available to choose from. Some of these, while initially attractive to both adults and children, may not prove to be valuable in the long run in an infant or toddler program. When considering the purchase of toys, think about the skills and interests of the children in the program now and in the future and whether everyday materials or "junk" could serve the same purpose. Could the real thing be substituted for the toy version? For example, a real picnic set of plastic dishes is far superior on all counts to a toy tea set. The use of real objects and safe junk provides a good example for parents, demonstrating that the caregivers believe there is considerable merit in play materials that do not cost large amounts of money.

General Guidelines for Toys
Good play materials should

◆ *encourage action* by responding to the child's actions and allowing the child to do something, rather than sit back and be entertained by something the toy or adult has set in motion.

◆ *respond naturally* rather than in a "gimmicky" way (e.g., a bell that rings is more valuable than an electronic busy box buzzer).

◆ *encourage social interaction* as well as be used by a child alone.

◆ *give infants and toddlers choices* as they pursue their own interests with the aim of channeling their efforts toward using emerging skills.

◆ *be versatile* and lend themselves to a variety of uses rather than have a single purpose.

◆ *engage more than one of the senses.*

◆ *complement the overall aesthetic* and quality of the learning environment through color and substance (wood, metal, plastic, cloth).

◆ *appeal to the full range of developmental skills and interests* present in the room.

◆ *fit the fine motor skills* of the age group in mind.

◆ *be durable* (remember: center use is much more wearing than home use).

◆ *be provided in duplicate* (rather than emphasizing subtle variety) to minimize the need for sharing.

Purchasing with a Child's Sense and Sensibility

Often toys are purchased based on an adult world view. The idea that infants and toddlers need variety (more than duplicates) reflects an adult sensibility about the need for novelty. The rapid development of young children has the effect of transforming objects. A few weeks pass in a child's life, and it is almost a new child who returns to an object and explores different dimensions and uses of it.

Adults know "children love primary colors." They do, and all toy makers have that fact emblazoned on their brains. Yet an abundance of primary colors creates a kaleidoscopic chaos that diminishes the attraction of all colors. With our greater cognitive and perceptual skills, we see a brightly colored truck. The child sees another brightly colored plastic object amidst a sea of bright plastic. When you purchase materials, buy both wood and plastic, both pastels and bright colors. Display materials with an eye toward the clear presentation of a manageable number of choices.

Unstructured Materials   These are materials that you won't find in a catalogue: various found, made, or low-cost purchased objects, the uses of which are not predetermined by adults and are only limited by the child's skills and imagination. The objects tend to be simple and perhaps "junk" to the adult eye until a child recognizes the potential of the item.

Some examples include

plastic film canisters	canning jar rings
large washers	juice can lids
fabric pieces	wooden knobs or spools
plastic golf balls	whiffle balls
plastic tubing	clothes pegs
plastic hair curlers	funnels
plastic or metal cylinders	small brushes
wooden dowels	

What do young children do with these? They sort, put together, line up, drop, fill, stack, and on and on. They combine the materials in ways we would not think of. In fact, the best way to approach junk is that if an item is safe, and that means safe to explore with the mouth, then give it to babies and see what they do with it.

Combine these materials with a variety of small containers and store them in containers that require different motor skills to use. Carrying a container without a handle requires different skills than one with a handle, and there are numerous variations of handles: jug handles, wire, fixed, etc.

Possible containers

cups and bowls	margarine tubs
airline food containers	boxes
buckets	baskets
plastic cylinders	utility trays
tennis ball cans	bags

When using unstructured materials, keep in mind the following:

◆ be extra careful about health and safety issues—sanitation, choking, sharp edges, toxic materials or finishes.

◆ rotate materials in different combinations. Facilitate play by putting out different materials every week or so. For example, some jar lids on a plate next to a teddy sitting in a chair suggest crackers for morning snack.

◆ every so often, casually plop down and play with the materials yourself, but don't assume the child will do what you do.

◆ use the materials in a bounded area to reduce the pickup and incorporate them into learning centers.

Building in Learning   The more learning that is built into the environment, the less staff time needs to be spent in set-up and take-down and the less chance that everything will end up in one great pile.

Learning materials can be attached to almost any surface: walls, floors, benches, tables, backs of storage units, railings, doors, fences, rugs, ceilings, windows, the inside of cabinets, and pillars. The advantages of attaching them permanently with screws or bolts or temporarily with duct tape is, of course, that they will stay put.

Some of the many things that can be attached include

◆ busy boxes, cot gyms, music boxes

◆ rattles, squeeze toys, music makers

◆ toy steering wheels, other wheels

◆ beads on wire or string

- peg boards
- puzzles
- lazy Susans (for display, size, rotation)
- pounding benches and mallets
- doors with latches, locks, hinges, and handles
- fabric with zippers, Velcro closers
- cardboard or plastic tubes to look through, make noises with, put, drop, or slide things through
- a metal surface for magnets
- an easel or white board
- real or play telephones
- mirrors; polished, smoked, or colored Perspex; prisms, colored cellophane
- clear, opaque, wire, or woven containers for drop boxes and collection points
- poke-through and peek-a-boo boards
- pulleys and levers
- textured surfaces
- jack-in-the-boxes
- different-sized cans

Should You Plan by Themes?

Curriculum needs to be balanced, based on children's skills and interests, and to reflect all of the experiences children require. While not desirable, a unit or theme structure may be acceptable if staff have been trained in that approach, but there are real precautions to keep in

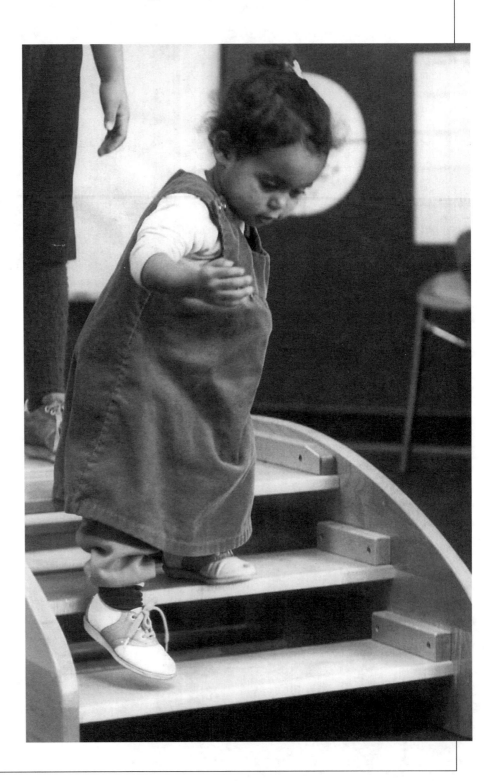

mind. While themes or units do give a central focus that assists staff to plan, they often lead to a reliance on activities and an artificial insertion of activities at the expense of responding to and building on, the children's natural interests. Themes are a convenience for adults—a "hook" on which to base the program for a time, but the meanings of themes are very often lost on infants and toddlers. Before using themes, staff should ask themselves what the purpose is, how the themes are related to the infants' or toddlers' interests, and whether themes are the best way to meet the needs of the children they care for. In any event, themes should never replace or diminish the central focus on planning learning centers for independent use.

Balancing Challenge and Mastery

Play allows children a combination of exploring new objects, practicing new skills, meeting new challenges—all these experiences stretch young children. They enjoy using skills already mastered and savor the comfortable feeling of re-exploring the familiar. It is easy to overlook the value to children of repeating the familiar while consolidating old skills and acquiring new ones. What sometimes appear to adults as boring, repetitious activities may be very important for cementing skills that have recently been acquired. Children also relish the satisfaction that comes from being able to do something that once was difficult or impossible. For example, an eleven month old may spend ten or fifteen minutes putting objects in a plastic bottle and dumping them out again, over and over, delighting in the scatter of the spools as they roll away, the clanking sound as they hit the floor, and the emotional reactions of the adults (whatever those might be!).

Challenging or stretching experiences occur anytime a child is confronted with the opportunity to do something or understand something that demands cognitive, motor, social, or communication skills that have not yet been completely mastered. They are problems to solve. Learning occurs in new situations that are slightly different from those the child is used to. Moderately novel or slightly more challenging toys, equipment, and problems are interesting and motivating to children: "How do I get this new truck to work?" "How can I catch this smaller ball?" Many of these challenges occur naturally, but you should ensure that appropriate challenges are part of the child's daily experience and they build on what a child already knows how to do.

How can we set up an environment so that it has many moderately novel experiences for each child? Primarily by providing a number of choices of appropriate toys, objects and activities, and by letting the child play. Given the chance, children generally move to novel situations and novel uses of materials.

In the end, the best guide to how much sameness and variety is appropriate is the child's reactions. If the child appears bored, disinterested, uninvolved, unchallenged, or fussy, then perhaps new materials and opportunities should be provided.

Infant-Toddler Equipment for Learning

Large Motor
mats/pillows
beach balls
push/pull toys
small wagon
foam rolls
tunnel
carts/strollers
variety of balls
planks
NOTE: no walkers or jump-ups

Additions for Toddlers
stairs/slide
rocking boat
barrels
wheelbarrows
no-pedal trikes
simple climber

Dramatic Play
baby dolls
stuffed animals
rubber animals
rubber people
hats
Plexiglas mirrors
real pots and pans
blankets/tents

Additions for Toddlers
large doll
furniture
dress-up clothes
child furniture
suitcases

Blocks/Construction
fiberboard blocks
foam blocks
buckets/small blocks

Additions for Toddlers
more blocks
large trucks
large trains
snap blocks
waffle blocks

Creative/Art
fingerpaints
block crayons
markers

Additions for Toddlers
chalk
large brushes
chalkboard
playdough

Infant-Toddler Equipment for Learning (continued)

ink stamps
paste

Sensory/Sand/Water/Science
dish/garden tubs
tub toys
sponges
plants
aquariums
bird feeders
animals
wind chimes
electric fans
texture/smell boxes

Additions for Toddlers
buckets/jars
funnels
sifters
measuring cups
pitchers
magnifiers
large magnets
flashlights

Books/Language/Music
cloth books
hardboard books
photos
posters
records/tapes
music boxes
musical mobiles

Additions for Toddlers
picture books
instruments
read-to books
telephones
listening centers

Perceptual/Motor/Games Manipulatives
cradle gyms
busy boxes
rattles
prisms
pop beads
poker chips
sorting boxes
simple puzzles

Additions for Toddlers
stacking/nesting toys
large peg boards
lock boards
pounding bench
jars and lids

The Power of Small Changes

In planning for infant and toddler learning, our mind-sets get in the way. It is easy to forget that real learning is not always the result of huge teacher efforts.

Small variations or adaptations in the learning environment can create, expand, and elaborate learning experiences. Walking along a 12-inch-wide plank flat on the ground, then raised to a slight incline, then level 6 inches off the ground, than raised to a slightly steeper incline offers a whole continuum of challenges to toddlers. A couch pulled away from the wall to create an angular space, then covered with a blanket or made windy by a fan provides different spatial experiences. Providing bigger and bigger balls for rolling, or larger and larger buckets creates different learning opportunities.

But is this really teaching—just moving a plank or a couch, adding larger buckets? Yes, because it creates learning about the world and its properties. Caregivers also learn about the infant's or toddler's own skill level. And your interaction as the child undergoes the experience is certainly teaching if you build off the child's play with responsive language and encouragement.

Alike and Different: Valuing Diversity through Children's Literature

Helping children learn to value the uniqueness and diversity that is all around them is a significant challenge for all who live with and teach children. For very young children, this includes helping them to feel good about themselves, giving them opportunities to learn about others, and helping them experience and value the ways we are alike and different.

The most personal and powerful way to teach diversity and inclusiveness is to model them in our lives, our homes, and our programs and communities. One of the ways we do this is through the stories and pictures we select to share with children. Seeing people like oneself in print is a powerful affirmation: "I must be OK; there are pictures in this book of people who look like me, doing the things I like to do." When we share pictures of children of all races and cultures doing what children all over the world do, we validate the similarities as well as the ways in which each is unique.

Some good examples are listed below in the Resources section of this chapter.

A Final Word: Between Order and Chaos

It is not difficult or expensive to create a learning environment for young children. Their restless urge to discover and master will make a laboratory out of any setting that has sufficient loose parts and motor opportunities. But it takes a lot of skill to design the environment that provides a safe laboratory for experimentation for children *in groups* —one that strikes a balance between a too-stifling order and a too-flexible chaos.

EXERCISES

1. Develop three new prop boxes for a toddler dramatic area.

2. Program twenty different learning experiences in a plastic wading pool.

3. Create three new built-in learning experiences.

REFERENCES

Bruner, Jerome. "Organization of Early Skilled Action." *Child Development* 44 (1973): 1–111.

Post, Jackie. "High Scope's Key Experiences for Infants and Toddlers." *Extensions* 9:4 (January/February 1995): 1–4.

RESOURCES

Bailey, Debbie. Photos by Susan Huszar. *My Mom* and *My Dad*. Spanish versions: *Mi Mama* and *Mi Papa*. Buffalo, NY: Firefly Books, 1994.

By means of superb photographs and simple text, each book explores these family members in diverse family and cultural settings. Photos include nurturing parents involved in everyday family routines acknowledge and affirm diverse family settings. Spanish version shares the photos of the English version.

Kissinger, Katie. Photos by Wernher Krutein. *All the Colors We Are: The Story of How We Get Our Skin Color.* Bilingual, English/Spanish. St. Paul, MN: Redleaf Press, 1994.

"People have many different skin colors." When children understand why we look different, they are free to appreciate the uniqueness of the people in their world. Although the text may be beyond the understanding of the youngest children, infants and toddlers can enjoy the superb photographs that celebrate all the colors of the human race.

Oxenbury, Helen. *Clap Hands, Say Goodnight, All Fall Down.* New York: Simon & Schuster, 1987.

———. *Tickle, Tickle.* New York: Simon & Schuster, 1987.

Cute. Charming. Roly-poly. Oxenbury's cherubs sing, run, and bounce their way through the pages of four big board books for infants and toddlers. The children are so lifelike that you almost expect them to bounce off the page and into your arms. Each book features caregivers and children from a variety of ethnic backgrounds celebrating everyday infant and toddler experiences.

Reiser, Lynn. *Margaret and Margarita/Margarita y Margaret.* New York: Greenwillow Books, 1993.

There is Margarita, who speaks no English. There is Margaret, who speaks no Spanish. When they meet in the park, they bridge the language gap, learn about and appreciate one another, and celebrate with the help of their favorite stuffed animals.

RESOURCES FOR WONDER

◆ *InsectLore* A unique company that sells butterflies, tadpoles, and all sorts of science-nature products. P.O. Box 1535, Shafter, CA 93263. (800) 548-3284.

◆ *Edmund Scientific* All sorts of science and discovery equipment. 101 East Gloucester Pike, Barrington, NJ 08007. (609) 547-8880.

◆ *Bear Blocks* Carpeted, planks and blocks to create ever-changing spaces. 1132 School St., Mansfield, MA 02048. (800) 424-2327.

◆ *Fancy Foote-Works* Custom-built environments, lofts, and play equipment. 549 Moscow Rd., Hamlin, NY 14464. (716) 964-8260.

Infant/Toddler Weekly Planning Form

Week of: _____ Theme (if any): _____

Experience/Skills/Concepts to Emphasize: _____

Changes to the environment	Large Motor	Dramatic Play	Sensory/Messy
	Construction/Blocks	Small Motor/Manipulatives	Language/Books
	Perceptual	_____	_____

	Monday	Tuesday	Wednesday	Thursday	Friday	Comments
Songs, stories, games						
Special activities						
Outdoor						

Quick Evaluation of an
Infant or Toddler Learning Environment

How can you tell if your baby's homebase is a place where infants or toddlers learn what they need to learn?

Here's what infants or toddlers might ask if they could choose their own setting for maximum learning:

Will I be held when I want to be held or need to be?

How many places are there where I can:
pull myself up? _____   reach? _____   kick? _____   jump? _____
climb up? _____   climb in? _____   climb over? _____   climb on? _____
go through? _____   go under? _____   go in and out? _____   see myself? _____

How many different places are there for me "to be" and explore—places that feel different because of light, texture, sound, smell, enclosure, and sight lines?

When you put me in an infant swing or bounce chair, am I only there for a short time? Can I get out when I want to get out?

How often do I get out of the room?

How often do I get outside?

How often do I go for stroller or cart rides?

How often do I get to get out of the stroller/cart and walk/crawl around?

How often do I get to play with messy things such as water, sand, dough, paint?

Are there duplicates of toys?

Are there a variety of toys, "stuff," and real-life objects that I can reach?
Are there duplicates?

What is there to: transport? _____   push/pull? _____

collect/dump? _____   throw? _____

Do I get to feed myself as soon as I can hold a spoon, bottle, or cup?

Do I have to wait to be changed or use the toilet?

When I talk my talk, will someone listen and talk back?

When you talk to me, will you look at me and use words I am learning to understand?

Will someone read to me, a lot?

Will you make me feel special and appreciate me for who I am, the way I am today?

Chapter 12

Infants and Toddlers Outdoors

excellence

The outdoors provides a great place *to be* and *be with* a very young child. Infants and toddlers safely experience on a daily basis all that the outdoors has to offer them for exploration and experience:

✔ a place for motor and sensory exploration
✔ a place for environmental experience
✔ a place for nurturing interaction and adult-child "conversation."

Why do infants and toddlers need a playground? Why do they need to go out at all? After all, what can they do besides fall down, get trampled, eat the flora and fauna, and get bitten, wet or sunburned? Not only that, children's noses run and it takes forever to get snowsuits on or off.

What does the outdoors offer that the indoor setting cannot? Fresh air, new worlds to explore, and a wider field of play:

Climate. The outdoors has weather: wind, sun, rain, fog, clouds, snow, warmth, and chills.

Landscape. Outside, we have hills and knolls, hedges, ruts, holes, streams, surfaces of different textures, descriptions, and levels; vegetation of varying color, smell, texture, and growing characteristics.

Openness. Outside there is vastness, a sense of infinite boundaries even if only in one direction, up. Openness creates a sense of freedom (although imposing fences can heighten the feeling of confinement).

Messiness. Outdoors we can be much freer to be messy (or perhaps more appropriately, more earthy).

Wildlife. The world of uncaged birds, squirrels, bugs, worms, and other life forms is outside our windows.

People. Outdoors there are people in their natural habitats, working, living, playing, traveling.

For caregivers, the outdoors offer a change of scenery and a different stage for being with babies. Child care can be mind numbing in its routine and its confined sense of place. While adults vary quite widely in their appreciation of the outdoors, going outside is necessary to add variety to the adult's as well as the child's day.

In the interests of convenience and ostensible safety, we can be left with a pretty sterile experience. Much of the inherent value of being outside can be lost. Keep in mind the unique value of being outdoors.

Designing Infant and Toddler Outdoor Areas

Imagine a playground for infants and toddlers. *A what?* You may not be able to conjure up a lot of images. Playgrounds are typically rough-and-tumble places where running, jumping, climbing, hurling, the traffic of miniature speeding vehicles, and general wild abandon flourish. Life in the fast lane is no place for a baby.

Okay, what about an infant/toddler *park*? Again, it probably seems strange to think of an outdoor place for children under three years old.

Let's start over. Imagine outdoor places that would be wonderful for you *to be with a baby*, that would enable you to enjoy the world outside the walls of your room while taking pleasure in the growing power and competence of a child. What comes to mind now? Probably images of parks with sun and shade, flowers, gentle breezes, grassy hills, winding pathways and places to relax, talk, and appreciate the sounds of birds, water, and crickets, and babies.

Now return to the idea of a baby playground. Imagine an outdoor arena for baby play: a setting that encourages the visual exploration of a four month old, the reaching and grasping, rolling and leaning of a nine month old, and the stepping and toddling, pulling and pushing, hauling and dumping, and exuberant exploration of older babies. If we begin with the idea of somehow adapting playgrounds for older children we may get nowhere or somewhere that doesn't work. If instead we begin thinking about what we want babies to experience and what we want to do with them, we may end up with something entirely different.

Centers will vary in their potential for providing outdoor play areas. It is important to make the best use of what you have, remembering that even small spaces such as planter boxes, patches of ground, or sidewalks can be sites for quality outdoor experiences.

Design Considerations

Good playgrounds are designed to fit children, staff, and the beliefs and values of parents. They are also designed to accommodate individual sites. Because the amount of space is often less than desirable, good playgrounds are usually versatile and flexible. Experiences change as new props are added such as planks, pillows, boxes, parachutes, balls, blocks, and toys. Changes in the sensory characteristics of the playground alter with the seasons.

The Nature of Infants and Toddlers

Outdoor design has to take into account the nature of babies: little scientists investigating with their eyes, mouth, hands, other senses, and entire bodies. Their curiosity is not tempered by much experience with the world to protect them.

Toddlers are newly mobile, and their bodies rarely are as capable as they imagine them to be. While most older children are pretty good at protecting themselves, toddlers just don't have the experience to judge what they can and can't do. And toddlers are oblivious to the safety of others.

The challenge: creating an outdoor world that doesn't make infants and toddlers ill, frightened, or injured. All too often, playground supervision is viewed as mere surveillance instead of good design with equipment and activities that ensure that children can engage in play. Good design and thoughtful adults can meet the challenge.

The Nature of Caregivers

Caregivers are human. If there is no shade or windbreak, if access to the outdoors is inconvenient, if keeping the children safe and healthy appears to require considerable effort, if there is no comfortable place to sit or lie down with a baby—in short, if it feels like a hassle to get out and an unpleasant experience to be outside, use of the outdoors will be minimal.

Caring for infants and toddlers outside is a difficult job and very different than it is with older children. *Going* out with infants and toddlers may require more forethought when there is no easy direct indoor/outdoor access: How will I change diapers? Bring which bottles? What sunscreen? Whose nap times are coming up? Preparation may be extensive: stuffing children into snow suits, filling the diaper bags, finding the strollers. *Being* out requires a level of grounds-keeping found elsewhere only on putting greens, a watchfulness associated with the Secret Service, and a tolerance for periodic inactivity like that of Ferdinand the Bull. Appreciating a six month old's grooving on the sounds and sight of water dripping from the gutter only lasts so long.

The Nature of Parents

Active outdoors learning for babies is a new concept for most parents. Much like staff, they may need to be sold on the value of outdoor play. The idea of their child mucking about in sand, mud, and water or scaling the heights of a miniature climber may take some time to get used to. However, when you guide parents to observe their child as the persistent little scientist that he or she is, and they understand the safety precautions you have taken, most parents will come to understand the value of outdoor play.

Playground Health and Safety

Most accidents are the result of falls, bumps, blows, cuts, and burns from metal equipment, or of ingestion of toxic or chokable materials. The cause of most accidents is not equipment failure so much as poor playground design, equipment selection, use, and maintenance. Developmentally inappropriate equipment—wood structures that splinter, low-quality equipment that becomes increasingly dangerous as it wears out, and metal equipment that both freezes and becomes dangerously hot—are all too common. Important considerations include these:

◆ *Sufficient Square Footage*: too-small space results in too few play experiences and crowding.

◆ *Drainage*: good drainage is essential on playgrounds for young children.

◆ *Nontoxic Landscape*: all vegetation should be checked by poison control; staff should be alert for the growth of mushrooms.

◆ *Resilient Surfacing*: the ground beneath any surface higher than 18–24 inches that children are able to reach should have a resilient surface that meets Consumer Product Safety Guidelines.

◆ *No Crowding*: when crowding occurs with active toddlers, any equipment becomes dangerous and accidents follow.

◆ *Good Layout and Zoning*: defined play areas, clear pathways, and challenging equipment placed on the perimeter are important. Areas such as swings and bike paths into which children might accidentally wander in and get hurt should be on the perimeter. Young babies must be out of the traffic flow.

◆ *Safe Equipment:* it is essential that equipment meet all Consumer Product Safety Standards in regard to exposed surfaces, spacing (strangulation), materials, design, and location.

◆ *Developmentally Appropriate Equipment:* equipment should be scaled to the size and skills of babies and provide sufficient challenge to toddlers. When children are bored, they seek challenge and stimulation and end up using people and things inappropriately. The result is unsafe motor play, biting, and other aggressive acts.

◆ *Maintenance and Monitoring*: accidents happen when equipment is not constantly monitored for signs of wear (worn chains and loose fasteners, etc.), exposed hazards (concrete pilings, bolts, splinters), and hazardous materials (buried objects in sand, animal feces, etc.).

Special Needs and ADA

Infant and toddler playgrounds need to be accessible to children and adults with special needs. Pathways should be accessible to wheelchair-bound adults, which also allows these areas to be used by buggies and carts. The design should ensure that children with special needs will be able to have the same or equivalent experience as other children.

Who Goes with Whom? Separate Play Areas for Infants and Toddlers?

With limited space and/or a limited budget, how do you partition a playground? What area is fenced off, who gets a swing set, to whose scale are climbers and slides built, and where is the water play? Usually this boils down to where do the two year olds go—with the babies or the preschoolers? And what is there for them to do?

A separate, fenced (or otherwise divided) area for children under two years old makes good developmental sense. But there should be ample large-motor challenge for toddlers. If this area is also the play area for two year olds, the twos should have frequent use of the preschool play area for older children so that they can have challenging experiences. However, teachers should be prepared to supervise and restrict the use of developmentally inappropriate equipment.

If there is a separate area for infant and toddlers, there should be climbing equipment scaled to toddlers.

Designing the Landscape

The basic dilemma: the infant/toddler landscape has to be safe to eat. Shrubs, flowers, and trees can be toxic in all stages of growth and should be checked with the local poison control office. Sand areas that attract cats, wooden objects that grow moss and mushrooms, and gravel all present problems that need to be thought through.

Ideally, outdoor spaces for young children will offer a variety of stimuli. Some are listed below. See also the outdoor activity center on page 230.

◆ *Surfaces:* grass, sand, wood. There will be gentle inclines to roll down and toddle up, grassy knolls to feel secluded in, and flat surfaces to strut and wobble upon. Wooden platforms and decks are desirable because they drain quickly and allow outdoor play when the ground is wet. Resilient quality synthetic surfaces also drain well.

◆ *Textures*: smooth round boulders, coarse bark, smooth sensual wood, soft and not so soft pine needles and other vegetation are good to feel and rub up against.

◆ *Color and Scent as Seasons Change*: trees and shrubs complement each other and transform themselves as seasons change with (non-toxic) falling leaves, cones and blossoms, and peeling bark.

◆ *Places to Be*: round boulders and shrubs create miniature grottoes and secluded baby-size groves to go in/out, over, and around; shady spots and sunny spots; open areas and tight hideaways.

◆ *Pathways*: pathways with destinations and loops not only structure traffic patterns but in themselves can be central sites for learning and exploration. Toddlers love to go, come, go and come, come and

go, endlessly. Pathways provide motor challenges and sensory exploration for babies as they crawl, toddle, push, or haul. Pathways may be as simple and inexpensive as a dirt footpath demarcated by stone borders or simple railings, a gardenlike path using wood rounds, pavers, aggregate concrete rounds or squares, or a multisurfaced system with a mixture of resilient and hard surfaces: planks, logs, rubber surfaces, and brick. (Be mindful, however, that pathways designed as the only route to an area or as emergency escape routes should also accommodate emergency cribs and wheelchairs.) Pathway railings create additional play—remember trailing your hands along picket fences? A railing may be made from rope, two-by-fours, timber, pickets, or other materials.

◆ *Barriers*: barriers, like pathways, direct the traffic flow and enclose activity areas. A creative use of barriers that restricts children to developmentally appropriate areas by requiring certain skills to surmount them allows for self-regulation. Jerry Ferguson (1979) used tunnels, slatted wooden surfaces, shrubs, and other means at Pacific Oaks to naturally regulate the whereabouts of crawlers and freewheeling toddlers. Tiny retaining walls of rock or wood that babies can lean against, scale, explore with fingers and bellies; and gates that open and close combine learning and crowd control.

Structures on the Landscape

◆ *Roofs, Canopies, Umbrella Mounts*: shade is essential. If there are not sufficient trees, then canopies, lawn umbrellas, and awnings become prime alternatives.

◆ *Swings*: opportunities to move in space, alone or with a trusted adult, are provided through use of swings with baby seats, porch swings, hammocks, and cradles. Soft rubber and plastic swings are much safer than ones of wood and hard plastic. Fully enclosed "surround swings" are appropriate for infants, and bucket swings for toddlers. NOTE: Swings can be overused and become restraints.

◆ *Skeletal Structures*: set up permanent installations of ladders, hurdles, and benchlike structures. These are in themselves motor structures for climbing on, over, under, etc. They can also be much more: skeletons that change by adding planks, ladders, fabric, and so on.

◆ *Fabric and Flapping Things*: banners, parachutes, wind chimes, branches, and so on make wind visible and audible.

◆ *Decks or Platforms*: wooden flooring outside offers a flat surface that drains easily, and is thus a good place for water play and outdoor play when the ground is wet. A raised platform offers babies chances to "get high" and explore new vantage points.

◆ *Slides*: slides off platforms or slides set in a hill eliminate most of the risk and leave the thrills and spills.

◆ *Half-buried Tires*: tires provide minitunnels, places to sit or lean on, pathway railings. They can be painted to reduce surface heat.

◆ *Play Houses, Crates*: anything with a roof is a playhouse.

◆ *Tunnels, Overhanging Trees, and Shrubs*: anything to be in, under, and go through.

◆ *Young Infant Area*: an enclosed area that encourages reaching, grasping, kicking, and so on, as well as a variety of visual, auditory, and other sensory experiences, perhaps with fabric, branches, or falling water.

◆ *Sound Structures*: miniature shrines with materials that react to wind or touch with sound and motion.

◆ *Sandboxes*: children love to play with sand, so use sandboxes with covers to reduce unsafe play with sand.

◆ *Sprinklers, Water Tables, Tubs, or Elevated Waterways*: elevated wooden, metal, or stone troughs provide water in motion, as do sprinklers. NOTE: Wading pools are unsanitary and should not be used.

◆ *Diaper Tables*: in warm climates, outdoor diapering will maximize outdoor play.

◆ *Platform Climbers*: multilevel platform climbers allow the experience of being up high and can be designed with ladders, stairs, and ramps.

◆ *Dead Trees and Stumps:* anything to pull up on, straddle, and climb safely on.

◆ *Wobbly Structures*: boards on springs or tires, logs, and planks barely off the ground, fastened to frames with chains; anything with a slight wobble.

◆ *Logs, Benches*: places for adults to sit on or up against while observing or nurturing babies.

◆ *Stored Equipment and Materials*: planks, ladders, parachutes and other fabric; wagons, wheel toys, wheelbarrows, pillows, balls, sand/water toys, and creative "junk."

Outdoor Activity Center

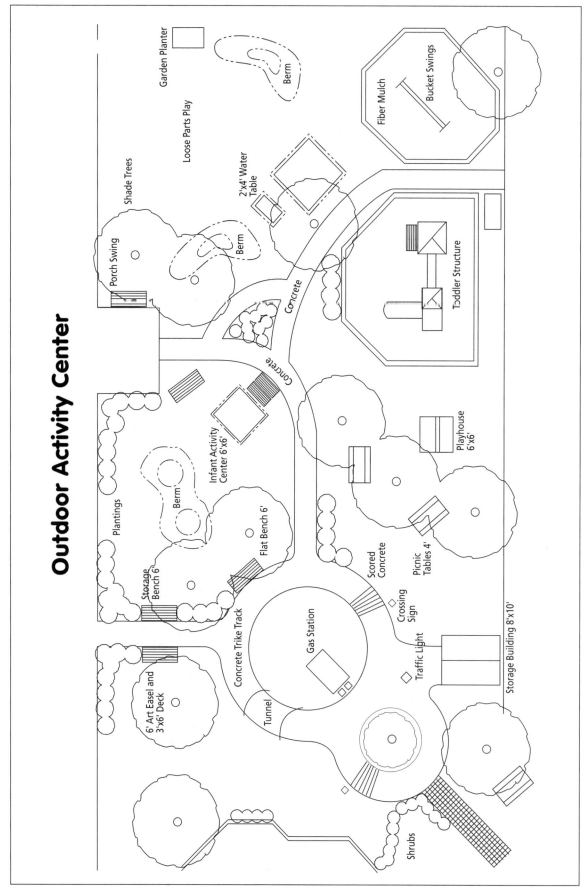

Equipment for Play

The following equipment can transform outdoor space:

◆ *Transporting*: toddlers love to transport—themselves, toys, equipment, anything at all. Sacks, backpacks, utility trays, and buckets, are all valuable loose parts to have on a toddler playground for children to haul around. Riding toys, wagons, wheelbarrows, shopping carts, and carriages are all good vehicles for toddler transport and fulfill their primal need to collect and dump.

◆ *Pushing/Pulling*: play lawn mowers and pull toys (and remember that beginning walkers push more readily than pull because it's hard to both walk and look behind you when walking is a new skill).

◆ *Riding*: pedalless riding toys and small trikes.

◆ *Rolling, Kicking, and Throwing*: different-sized balls and wheeled toys.

◆ *Dramatic Play*: provide dolls, hats, purses, and Educubes.

◆ *Sand Play*: buckets, funnels, tabletop surfaces.

◆ *Construction Play*: blocks of cardboard and plastic.

◆ *Art Play*: brushes, chalk, dirt, and clay.

◆ *Water Play*: use hoses, sprinklers, water tubs. Do not use wading pools or other containers of standing water that children can climb into together because the water can spread germs.

◆ *Projecting*: toddlers project themselves into space with their lunging, lurching bodies; they throw and kick objects ahead of themselves. Provide beach balls and other large balls, anything they can push, and small balls to kick and throw.

◆ *Place making*: use tarps and parachutes to wrap climbers and playhouses à la the artist Christo. This not only adds interest but also teaches toddlers that they have the power to change environments. Toddlers love working out the physics of places with their bodies.

◆ *Loose Parts, and More Loose Parts*: "loose parts" are materials that can be used together, combined collected, sorted, separated, pulled apart, stacked, lined up, dumped, etc. Natural materials: rocks, stones, wood, leaves, sand, water; toys: wagons, wheelbarrows, carts, fabric, backpacks, rope, chain, containers, blocks, dolls, brushes, sponges, ladders, stumps, etc. Loose parts are almost anything safe and not fixed in place; allow children the freedom to use them in inventive ways. They can be stored in stuff sacks, backpacks, utility carts, and duffel bags for easy use.

◆ *Being*: adults will be outside with babies more when the environment is convenient and comfortable. Pillows, hammocks, waterproof pads and blankets, infant carriers, and, if possible, portable changing areas will increase outdoor time.

Wonderful Wheelbarrows and Wagons

Wagons and wheelbarrows are nearly perfect pieces of educational equipment for young children. They require both motor and cognitive learning because maneuverability changes depending on the load and the surface, and they also satisfy the urge to haul and dump. At one center a child struggling with a wheelbarrow looked up at the teacher and said angrily: "Teacher, wheel missing." While the teacher was tempted to put away the wheelbarrow as developmentally inappropriate, she realized that the child's struggle to make it work was the learning.

Balancing Health and Safety with Play

What concerns are important enough to be inflexible about? When is it necessary to accommodate to real life? After all, children will ultimately be exposed to germs and they will get bumps. Every center has to decide what matters to the staff, in concert with health officials and regulatory agencies. Two common concerns come up:

◆ Children need water play yet standing water transmits germs. Water that children can sit in is much less sanitary than using water tubs that they only place their hands in. Individual tubs transmit the fewest germs, and changing the water often reduces exposure. Circulating the water in a wading pool reduces transmission, but serious health concerns are still present.

◆ Many attractive shrubs are mildly toxic. A child would have to eat a lot of unpleasant-tasting leaves or berries to get sick. Should you plant these shrubs? Probably not, for even though the chance of harm is minimal, the attractiveness of the shrub is not worth the "No's" and the need to frequently explain that they are not harmful to anxious parents and staff. There are always other shrubs that present fewer problems.

"Get That Out of Here!"—What Does Not Work With Infants and Toddlers

Some of the equipment that does not work well with infants and toddlers:

◆ trampolines

◆ teeter-totters

◆ belt swings

◆ pedal trikes

◆ single-chain tire swings

Being Outside with Infants and Toddlers: The Caregiver's Role

The success of infant/toddler outdoor time ultimately depends on the adults in the setting: caregivers who recognize and encourage the scientist and explorer in each baby and accept the ups and downs that ensue. At the same time, they must keep a watchful eye on and nurturing presence toward babies for long periods of relatively uneventful time.

What Do Caregivers Do Outside?

Caregivers watch, interact, and worry. Many infant and toddler caregivers have trouble allowing babies to explore. All their instincts tell them to catch the baby before he stumbles, to protect him from even the slightest scratch or risk of discomfort. Without the assurance that babies will be safe, caregivers often severely restrict what their charges are allowed to do. To achieve confidence that babies will be safe, caregivers should observe the following:

1. Remember sunscreen, hats, towels, etc.

2. Look for health and safety hazards.

3. Plan experiences and locations that avoid crowding and toddler swarming.

4. Encourage active engagement with the environment and participate in the exploration.

5. Provide equipment and props that enhance the outdoor experience.

What Should Caregivers Not Do Outside?

"It drives me crazy to go out on the playground and see the staff just talking to each other," lamented the director. "It's not a break." Outside time should not be a chance to visit with other staff. All too often, it offers the chance to see staff from other rooms and adult needs take precedence over children's play. Reasonable break times should replace playground "breaks."

Walks, Rides, Field Trips, and Community Resources

Centers without playgrounds may have to develop other alternatives such as using sidewalks, available yards, and available parks. Centers can create a "playground in a box" by filling a cart with planks, balls, crates, blankets, parachutes, and other equipment.

Strollers, buggies, and carts are wonderful vehicles to use when taking children on walks. But remember, toddlers can walk and babies can crawl. Don't substitute the passive ride for the active outdoor experience. Combine the two.

Toddlers and even infants can enjoy field trips as long as the adults with them also enjoy themselves. Safe transportation in car seats in center vans or parents' cars to a change in scenery can add variety to daily life. Remember, field trips don't have to be to exotic locations like zoos. In fact, exotic locations are more likely to present problems.

Trips to parks, expansive open areas, beaches, fire stations, and so on will provide more satisfying adult-child experiences. For safety's sake,

◆ stay away from crowded areas or places that you have never been before.

◆ always have extra hands available.

A Final Word: Go Outside!

In many regions of the modern industrial world, society is evolving an increasingly more indoor culture. It is important to resist this trend and to help children develop an appreciation for the outdoors.

EXERCISES

1. Explore the outdoor area at your center on your bare feet or knees.

2. Pick an outdoor location and then close your eyes. List all the sensory experiences you have. Go to one or two other outdoor locations and do the same.

3. List the play opportunities available at any one time in your program and evaluate them against the list of potential experiences above.

4. Watch a child under three explore a backyard, a deck, or a stoop. What does he or she do?

REFERENCE

Ferguson, J. "Creating Growth-producing Environments for Infants and Toddlers." In E. Jones, ed. *Supporting the Growth of Infants, Toddlers, and Parents*. Pasadena, CA: Pacific Oaks College, 1979.

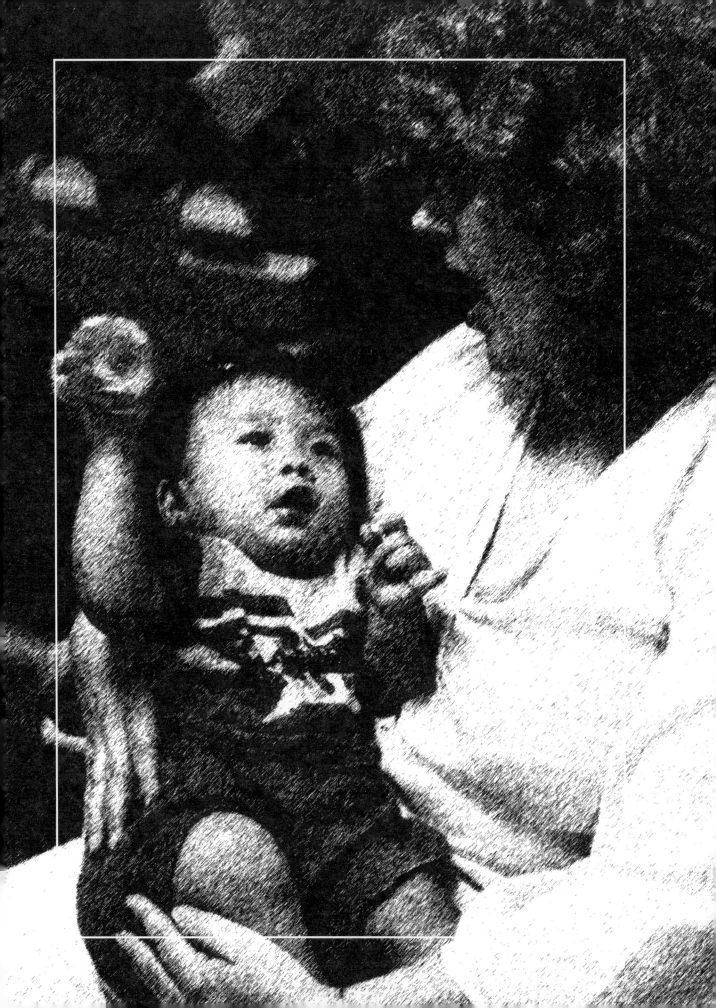

Chapter 13

Interactions with Infants and Toddlers: The Caregiver as Teacher

excellence

Caregivers recognize and understand the PRIME TIMES for learning interactions with children and maximize the one-to-one moments that they can create throughout the day. Interactions are authentic, responsive to the children's invitations, and follow their interests and developmental capabilities. Group activities are scaled in frequency, size, and duration to the children's development.

Introduction

What does it mean to teach infants and toddlers—to be an infant or toddler teacher? The fact that the words don't really seem to fit have led some to abandon the term and title and instead to use the term *caregiver* or *educarer* or *infant/toddler specialist*. While *caregiver* is certainly an appropriate term, in the real world of parents and schools, it reduces the status of those who work with infants and toddlers. Like it or not, the term *teacher* confers educational legitimacy. *Educator, educarer,* and *specialist* are too little used to do the same.

Why the concern over teaching? Because education is an inseparable component of good care and because learning happens all the time, including during routines and transitions. But only rarely does teaching in the sense of instruction play any part in very young children's experience. *Infants and toddlers acquire new skills and understandings about the world and themselves through play, exploration, and living each new day.* Good caregivers value and encourage play as natural and integral parts of their experience in day care. While caregivers need to be aware of children's emerging skills and probable next developmental steps, they do not need to program artificial activities and special exercises to teach these skills.

In chapter 12, we discussed the role of the caregiver as *architect and engineer of the environment for learning:* preparing *a world at children's fingertips* and maintaining environments for free and structured play. In earlier chapters, our emphasis was on the *caregiver as the adult who provides the security and stability that free the young child to explore, be curious, and get involved in play.* Infants or toddlers who are not sure that their needs will be met or who have to adjust continually to new caregivers, places, and routines will not get involved in active play and exploration.

The third critical role of caregivers and the focus of this chapter is that of *supporting children's learning through interactions, interventions, and language.*

Follow the Child

An infant or toddler's play has a serious purpose. It is the child's attempt to gain those skills and understandings needed at this point in his or her development. Play should be driven by the child's interests and timetable, even if they appear to be focused on only one kind of play. This is often an emerging motor skill. For example, occasionally a baby who is learning to crawl may be interested almost exclusively in crawling for a few days and only rarely can anything else hold the child's attention. "Getting into everything" is driven by new mobility and dexterity and by the important realization that the world is rich with objects to explore.

Curriculum, the organization of what we do with infants and toddlers, should be based on general guidelines, information about development in the first three years of life, and sensitive awareness of the styles, interests, and competencies of individual babies. *Curriculum is the framework and rationale for doing what you do, not a list of activities.* Teaching is responsive support for the child's drive to learn expressed through play.

Playing with Children

The most important teaching happens when adults care, play, and work alongside children. These create PRIME TIMES. Good teachers stay with the children: on the couch, on the floor, on the grass—sitting, lying, sprawling at their level, playing alongside them, listening, conversing, touching, observing, and paying attention to the right moment for engaging a child and the moments when it is simply better to watch. At the same time, caregivers are looking after the physical and emotional safety of each child, observing development and identifying strengths, and, of course, keeping an eye out to manage group behavior. Clearly, the idea that "playing" with children is easier than "instructing" children is way off base.

Play with a caregiver is a PRIME TIME and has many benefits. The child learns a number of things:

◆ *I am special.*

◆ *I can trust people.*

◆ *We are in this together.*

◆ *It feels good to spend time with people.*

◆ *I have lots of ways to get attention (a smile gets a smile in return).*

Daily Life Is Filled with Education

Not only are the hills alive with the sound of music, but life is also filled with language, math, science, and the other content areas of education. The *rhythmic whirring* of the washing machine is a musical experience, as is the *steady beat* of the rain on the window. Putting the *two* sheets in the dryer is math. The sheets are *wet* and come out *dry.* There are *two big* sheets and *three little* washcloths. Put them *in* the dryer and take them *out. Smell* the *warm* sheets, *help sort* and *fold* the laundry, and *push* the laundry cart *into* the *room.*

It is important to hear the music and to take advantage of the language, number, and classification opportunities around you. On the other hand, don't be so concerned about education that you miss the pure enjoyment and texture of everyday life. If you are constantly articulating, enhancing, elaborating, reflecting, classifying, and counting, genuine pleasure and authenticity will fade, and children—and you—will overdose from teachable moments.

Guidelines for Quality Interactions

Playing with children as an adult differs from playing with them as a child. While you participate in the activity, you are also responsible for keeping up the flow of interest, recognizing efforts, finding the novel experience, asking questions, and thinking ahead to the next transition. Good planning makes all these possible.

The caregiver's role changes with the age of the child. In general, the older the child, the easier it is to know how to play with her, as she becomes more of a participant and less of an observer. At the same time, as babies get older, they become more capable of entertaining themselves. Caregivers need to be aware of this because the natural tendency is to spend more time than is appropriate with the older babies and less with the younger ones, particularly if there is any external pressure to teach.

Interactions Should Be Responsive and Reciprocal

Both adult and child initiate, respond, and influence each other. Even very young infants initiate social interactions through crying, looking, visual following, and later through vocalizations and gestures. From birth, babies also respond to social approaches from adults. Distressed infants will often quiet when they are picked up. They become still as they listen to a caregiver talk or sing, and they smile and coo contentedly when touched and talked to.

Responsiveness to the child's social initiations is critical. All social overtures by the child should be responded to. It is never appropriate to ignore an overture from a baby—for example, by refusing a block being offered, ignoring a smile or a wave, or not answering a babble or some other verbal communication.

Caregivers have to be careful not to overwhelm babies with their own activity. Rather, opportunities should be created by adults for babies to respond to. Responses should be encouraged by showing pleasure or by responding in turn. For example, a caregiver helping a baby stand up from a sitting position does not repeatedly pull the baby up to standing by the arms and then sit the child down again. The caregiver might do this a few times, then wait to feel the baby pushing up or trying to pull himself up by holding onto the adult. Playing is not something done *to* babies: it is done *with* them.

Adapt the Play to the Child's Cues

Signs of interest become more obvious as babies get older. Babies' moods and behavior will suggest the most appropriate kind of play; when they are becoming tired or are at loose ends near departure time, they might enjoy close, quiet times with their caregiver and their favorite books.

Babies will also give clues about their interests. For example, an infant who is mouthing everything should not be given materials that are unsuited for chewing on. A toddler who has discovered the thrill of hurling objects through space needs lots of materials that are suitable and safe for throwing. Stackers need objects to stack, climbers need things to climb, and toddlers driven to fill and dump or transport objects need appropriate materials for their activities.

Good caregivers are flexible enough to drop their preconceived plans and follow babies' leads. For example, Than has nine-month-old Jerry in her lap and is helping him learn to play pat-a-cake. Jerry claps his hands together for the first two lines of the verse but instead of "rolling it and patting it," he begins to pat his cheeks, then his knees. Than understands this as an initiation, a creative variation by the baby—and drops pat-a-cake at least temporarily to imitate Jerry, expanding on his variation by naming cheeks and head and hands as he touches them.

In an example with older toddlers, Jack has set up a painting activity for his two-year-old group. Large appliance cartons have been placed outside, and thick, bright paints and large chunky brushes are nearby. A basin of soapy water, some sponges, and cloths for cleaning up are also available. The toddlers are mildly interested in painting the cartons but very interested in the soapy water and sponges. With great enthusiasm, they begin "cleaning" some nearby large play equipment. Jack, though disappointed, is flexible enough to allow this to become the activity and to provide some additional cleaning supplies. Caregivers must guard against getting so invested in the activity they have planned that they forget the child!

Interactions Should Involve Many Different Ways of Communicating

Communications with infants and toddlers include looking, talking, moving, holding, rocking, touching, singing, smiling, laughing. One of the marvelous virtues of body carriers (Snuglis, slings) is the responsive communication that occurs when caregivers move about and work with young babies secure on their chests. As the baby moves or gurgles, the caregiver can respond with a reassuring sound, touch, and adjustment of her body to the baby's movement. Overuse of body carriers is a concern only if a child goes from the carrier to the crib, high chair, or other restraining equipment.

Recognize the Individual Style of the Baby at Play and Adapt Your Style to It

Some children need more help than others to get involved. Children who tend to stand (or sit) back may need the support, encouragement, and possibly the help of an adult to become involved. They do not need pressure, however, and individual differences must be accepted. Eighteen-month-old Camila typically watches from afar before trying something new and often dabbles on and off before becoming fully engaged. In contrast, Emma throws herself into whatever is available and needs help not to flit from one novel experience to another.

Be Authentic

Infants and toddlers become quite adept at recognizing artificial enthusiasm and interest. When there is a discrepancy between your words and body language, it may confuse, cause anxiety, or ultimately lead a toddler to discount what you say.

Help Infants and Toddlers Learn New Ways to Master and Meet New Challenges

With careful observation, caregivers can give babies just the amount of help they need to meet challenges, whether those consist of crawling out from under a table or zipping up a coat. They can also demonstrate new or better ways of doing things, for example, testing puzzle pieces or removing a cap from a jar. Demonstrations are a last resort and should be used only when children are about to give up on solving a problem. The aim is to encourage babies to be curious, to explore and discover the world.

Show Pleasure in the Children's Play, but Use Praise Discerningly

Showing pleasure and enjoyment in babies' play encourages them to persist. Indiscriminate praise for everything they do has much less impact and begins to sound empty after a while.

Let Children Explore the Uses of Materials

In presenting a new play material or arrangement of equipment and materials, caregivers should let children figure out what to do with it rather than direct the activities. Caregivers join in or suggest new possibilities only after children have had a chance to try it out. Children should not be deprived of the fun of discovering what can happen when they act on their world—that a mobile dances to its own music when you touch it, that pulling a string attached to a car will bring it closer, that water will not "stack" higher than the sides of the container, that balls bounce but that a round piece of playdough does not.

Sensitive caregivers rarely say "No" in play with babies, reserving it for occasions when they might harm themselves, someone else, or something in the environment. One of the major goals of play in the child's first three years is to nourish curious, assertive approaches to the world. To accomplish this, caregivers must allow children freedom to explore in a secure setting.

Encourage Infants and Toddlers to Persist, to Work Hard, and to Achieve Reasonable Goals

Good caregivers provide challenges that are difficult but achievable for *each* child and encourage the child to work at them. They should intervene with help before babies get upset and quit but not before children have "wrestled" with the problem.

Sooner or later, children with interesting, challenging environments are bound to find problems they want to solve but can't. Children are stuck when they cannot figure out their next move. Adults can then step in and provide the smallest possible bit of encouragement, the tiny link or boost that allows children to move forward again. Year-old Sarah is struggling to climb out of the wagon and is "rescued" just as she is about to dump herself out head first. David gives up the same task without as much effort as Sarah, and Mia will never stop until she is successful. Giving the right kind of help in the right amount at the right time is a characteristic of caregiver excellence.

Sometimes the caregiver can encourage other children to help or motivate the child: "Jesse and Gina, let's help Byron find that car."

Infants and toddlers have valid reasons for stopping an activity; they may be tired of it or the activity may be too difficult for them. There is no reason to persist in trying to maintain children's interest if there are signs that they are no longer interested in the activity.

Help Infants and Toddlers Enjoy Other Children

Infants' and toddlers' interest in relating to each other exceeds their ability to do so. Caregivers need to remain physically close to ensure that most interactions are pleasant ones. At the same time, they are modeling and talking about appropriate ways of interacting. The environment can assist caregivers in helping children get along. Infants and toddlers often play better *near*, not *with*, each other, sharing experience but not materials. Caregivers facilitate learning when they pro-

vide duplicates of toys, tubs for each child, back-to-back toddler easels rather than side-by-side ones, and one- and two-child tables rather than group tables.

Keep Children Safe and at the Same Time Allow Them to Take Risks

Children exploring their emerging physical powers need to be able to stumble and take tumbles. Occasional minor bumps and bruises are inevitable, but more serious injuries are not acceptable.

The Importance of Language

Language does more than simply represent our thoughts and feelings; it shapes and directs our thinking and emotions. A language-rich environment is important in encouraging cognitive development during the early years.

Babies are tuned in to language from birth. The first feeding begins the lifelong give-and-take of communication that ends in dinner parties years later. Infant gurgles; adult smiles or murmurs. Adult soothes; infant sighs. From sighing, cooing, and babbling to first words, a baby learns that language is a powerful tool in human society. Children learn language by being with people who encourage their efforts to communicate and who look for opportunities to communicate with them.

Talking to Infants and Toddlers

Children learn language not only by being in a noisy, language-filled environment but also by direct, personal communication and *eaves-dropping*—listening carefully to the dialogues of others. Caregivers should seize opportunities to talk one-to-one to children and to eliminate unnecessary noise.

There is little value to baby talk. From birth, infants should be talked to in a natural manner. We sometimes oversimplify the ways we say things ("See, big dog"), almost as though we have toned down our speech to speak as the child does. Of course, avoiding baby talk does not mean ignoring the cooing and babbling of young babies; this is valuable conversation for the youngest speakers.

In helping young children learn to use language, it is too easy to lapse into teacher talk or artificial uses of language. Sometimes we ask artificial questions, the answers to which are too obvious: "What color is that?" "Where's the ball?" Or, in our enthusiasm, we may talk too much, bombarding the child with our chatter so that there is no space for him to respond. The child may just turn off and tune us out.

It may not feel natural at first to converse with a young baby who does not understand words or who cannot respond with words. However, this feeling is soon replaced by pleasure at the baby's positive response to our words. With practice, natural, authentic conversation with infants becomes second nature.

Developing Language

Children's language development moves from the perceptual to the conceptual, from sensation to thought. Children's thoughtfulness and curiosity arise from conversation or dialogue, from talking *with* adults and being listened to. Children need much more than being asked concrete questions with right answers: "What's that?" "How many?" and "What color?" They need questions that encourage divergent thinking: "Why?" "What if" and "How?"—and a willing listener as they search for answers to problems that they are interested in. Genuine questions, *prompted by children's interests*, and conversations about a world with a past and a future, not just the here and now, are characteristics of a good program. Conversation helps endow events with meaning:

> "Kira's crying," said twenty-two-month-old Joey. "Why is she crying?" asked their caregiver, Ellen, rather than explaining Kira's distress. "Sad!" said Joey. "She's sad that her daddy left, I think," Ellen explained. "What do you think, Joey?"

"The Frequency of Communication in Infancy Matters—Forever!"

Current research on cognitive development points increasingly to the likelihood that permanent cognitive capacity is increased through language interactions. *Limited language interactions may well permanently limit the child's cognitive development.* (Hart, B., and Risley, T., 1995)

Guidelines for Good Language Interactions

"It is hard for teachers of older children to understand how much I talk during the day," says Linda, who has an infant/toddler class. "With young babies, especially, I'm always putting words to their actions and sounds so I am talking for two: 'You really like that milk,' 'Look at you reach for that ball!' I'm always singing, chanting, telling them what I am doing, and reflecting their feelings—of course, I listen a lot, too."

Children learn language in environments where it is valued as an integral tool for expression and organizing the world.

A good caregiver—

◆ *listens and responds:* take conversational turns that encourage give-and-take: talk *with* the child, not *at* the child; watch for times

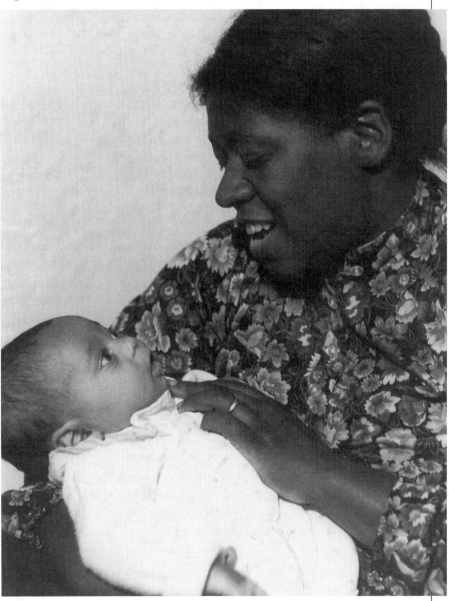

that the child initiates conversation, and then respond. Let the child control the interaction sometimes.

◆ *models:* babies need modeling, not correction. Use words instead of gestures, nouns instead of short-cut pronouns and adjectives like *her, it.* Say, "Take the ball" instead of "Take this"; "Find the red duck" instead of "Go get him"; "Come sit on the chair" instead of "Sit here."

◆ *reads:* reading books with infants and toddlers connects sounds and words with pictures. Even young infants enjoy the interaction with the caregiver, the sounds and the pictures, as well as the story line. You cannot start too early using books with babies.

◆ *labels:* give names to things and experiences. When a baby makes sounds or points, connect the experience to words. When the baby laughs at the sight of the biscuit, say "You like the biscuit, don't you?" When the older baby points and says, "Ba," say something like, "Oh, yes, look at the ball." When a baby is hungry, upset, or delighted, use language to label the emotions: "Oh, that makes you so happy when you find the ball." This is using language in a natural way to teach.

◆ *extends:* as babies combine sounds, caregivers can extend their sounds into words without correcting them. When the nineteen month old says "Kitty there," you can respond, "Yes, the kitty is right over there by the apple tree."

◆ *plays with sounds and words:* language is a marvelously expressive tool. Whispers, squeaks, chants, rhymes, songs, and other playing with sounds encourage children to explore the range and the pure fun of language.

◆ *comforts with language:* use words to help children identify their strong feelings and to make them feel better. Language is a powerful tool that can affect our feelings quite dramatically.

◆ *provides objects and experiences to talk about:* animals, people, familiar objects, and make-believe always spur language.

◆ *uses directives carefully:* "Come here," "Let's go out," "Time to eat," "Please clean up," and other phrases that direct children's activities often fill the environment with language. A high proportion of responsive comments and questions are characteristic of good caregiving.

◆ *encourages toddlers to ask questions, clarify, and seek more information:* even before the child has a large vocabulary, encouraging questions by responding to quizzical expressions, gestures, or simple words is important.

◆ *helps children listen to each other and to ask each other questions:* help children attend to other children who are attempting to communicate with them and encourage them to ask each other questions.

◆ *knows when to be silent:* give children the "silent space" to experiment with language. "The more caregivers talk, the better" is only true up to a point.

Promoting Learning

Life in a group doesn't have to lead to lots of planned group activities in which all the children are doing approximately the same thing together. These are largely for adult convenience. *Most group activities for infants and toddlers should happen spontaneously when the children come together, not when the adults decide to have a group.* Remember, for infants and toddlers, two or three children is a group, and three or four children is a large group. As toddlers develop, short group activities can be enjoyable, and there is probably value in relatively brief "touch bases" groups that develop children's sense of the whole group. These can be walks, short stories, songs, "good morning" circles, and mealtimes. But there is no intrinsic developmental value to teacher-directed circle times until children are ready to make the transition to preschool rooms and require social skills. If short circle times seem to work—that is, if children enjoy them, if they don't require coercive direction, and if children don't tune out—then there is no harm in doing them.

Planning Activities

When planning activities, first consider if a teacher-directed activity is the best way to provide the experience, as opposed to making a prop box or learning center available to children. Also remember there are five parts to any activity for children:

1. *Transition in:* how are children going to move into the activity without confusion and waiting?

2. *Entry:* how are children going to understand what to do?

3. *Activity:* will children be able to do what is expected of them?

4. *Wind-up/cleanup:* how do children finish the activity and participate in cleanup?

5. *Transition out:* how do children move on to the next activity?

The more elaborate the activity, the more important it is to break it down and make sure all the pieces are developmentally appropriate, given the time slot and space. Messy activities like fingerpainting obviously require more planning than a flannelboard story or a quick game of duck, duck, goose. But forethought is always important for any activity because antisocial acts (pushing, biting) and overly directive or negative adult attention can occur during poor in-and-out transitions, and the activity may not work well for individual children.

Cognitive Learning

Each time a caregiver encourages motor or perceptual exploration, asks a child a question, or listens seriously to a child's questions, she is promoting thinking skills. The better tailored a caregiver's questions are to the child's interests and current understandings, the more learning the child is likely to do. Asking toddlers to clarify and expand on their responses is important. Some one-to-one games to consider:

- *object-permanence games*: peek-a-boo, where is the ____?, where did the ____ go?
- *anticipation games:* objects in space Where will my hand/ the ball/ the truck go?, events in time What happens next?, actions What am I going to do next?
- *cause-and-effect games:* What happens if we ____?
- *recognition games:* What is that? What does that do? What am I doing?
- *problem-solving games:* Open the ____, find the ____, take apart the ____.

Language Learning

Caregivers can give infants and toddlers words for their increasingly sophisticated actions, feelings, and understanding—what Alice Honig (1985) calls *parallel talk*: "You are trying so hard to hold that rattle." Also important is *self-talk*, talking about what you are doing with and for the baby: "I'm rubbing your tummy now."

The key to successful communications is talking with the child and finding one-to-one opportunities. Talking *with*, not *at*, is important. It's the difference between real conversation with children and noisy, often annoying prattle. Look for their cues and respond to their communications. Respect the child's need for quiet and for solitary observation.

There are lots of simple language games and one-to-one activities to use spontaneously with infant and toddlers (again, be sensitive to their cues):

- *sentence completion games:* "Let's go to the ____." "I just waved to ____."
- *word sound games* (rhyming, chanting): "The cat in the hat with a bat." "The **tr**uck and the **tr**ain and the **tr**ack and the **tr**ee." "The diap**er** and the wip**er** and the dry**er**."
- *counting games*: "One, two, three spoons—one, two, three cups."
- *location games*: "Where is the truck? Under the chair."
- *time and sequence games*: "First we come in the door, then we put away our coats, then we give Molly a big hug."
- *who games*: "Who is that in the rocking chair?"

Large Motor Skills and Development

With foam forms, pillows, planks, large blocks, crates, and cubes, caregivers can offer infants and toddlers an endless variety of locomotor and nonlocomotor challenges. The term *locomotor* refers to moving through space. Nonlocomotor skills like stretching, bending, balanc-

ing, falling, and rising develop in tandem with locomotor skills. The key to helping children learn is to recognize that slight variations are significant—"the power of small changes" that we mentioned earlier. When you create a slightly steeper incline to crawl or walk up, a bumpier surface to roll on, or a larger beach ball to carry, it may have the same effect on infants and toddlers as if you were asked to balance on a plank rather than on a path or to climb into a hammock instead of a cot. Walking up is easier than walking down. Pushing is easier than pulling. Moving *and* holding are a challenge. Stepping, jumping, and running are all challenges that follow becoming confidently upright.

Teaching motor skills means providing support for practice or mastery efforts and for those challenging opportunities that lie beyond them. It does not mean instructing or pushing. Good caregivers are attuned to the individual infant's efforts at reaching, grasping, holding, letting go, and kicking, and the toddler's mastery of pulling, carrying, walking, walking down inclines, throwing, and all of the other new skills that being upright and mobile entail.

Facilitating Perception   Caregivers can best facilitate children's perceptual development by recognizing their explorations, providing ways to extend and enhance newfound discoveries, and providing words for what they are experiencing. Children learn from an increasingly sophisticated continuum of experiences. For example, light to dark, sour to sweet, soft to hard and quiet to loud become differentiated as children develop. Spontaneous and planned comparison games and stories like "Goldilocks and the Three Bears" are increasingly interesting to children as their sensory capabilities develop.

Play that Promotes Social Learning and Emotional Development
Caregivers help children learn social skills while they go about their

lives in a group. As articulate role models, caregivers present children with pictures of social behavior. By noticing and encouraging children's attempts at social play, by acts of joining, cooperating, and caring, and by explaining to children the "whys" and implications of behavior, caregivers promote social behavior. Caregivers can provide words to help toddlers solve problems and to encourage them to help each other: "Will you hold Moira's mittens while she puts on her coat?" (Do not, however, go beyond Moira's ability to even momentarily give up possession.)

Caregivers can help children learn to cope with and control their developing emotions. The struggle for self-control begins in infancy as babies learn self-calming mechanisms: thumb sucking, rocking, cooing. Adult support helps children learn that they can manage the rockier aspects of life. Individual children require different facilitation. *Remember, children are born with fundamental, individual differences in personality.* Jeremy is so enthusiastic that he sometimes overwhelms others and needs help with more relaxed overtures. Sally and Albert both hold back and need encouragement. Leah has trouble when children are too close and does better when helped to carve out a more separate territory. Our job is help them develop, not to change their personalities.

Music and Movement Play   Understanding that music can happen anytime isn't the same thing as playing radios or tapes arbitrarily or idly bursting into song. Too much auditory stimulation is usually more of a problem than too little. Music is a wonderful tool for setting a mood: It can calm children down or inject a sense of whimsy or new energy. Take your cues from the children in using background music and spontaneous singing.

There are activity books filled with songs and finger plays for infants and toddlers, but much of children's music and movement can be spontaneous. Living each day as opera and singing while you work are characteristics of a good infant or toddler room.

Young infants are aware of sounds and soon respond to the emotional content of music. As infants gain control over their bodies, they move in response to rhythms. Toddlers love songs that require physical responses ("Hokey-Pokey," "Ring around the Rosy"), songs about families, and songs that reflect moods (happy, sad, angry, busy, etc.). Waving scarves, banging spoons, playing instruments and other props don't have to wait until a music time.

Dramatic Play   Dramatic play does not have to be confined to a dramatic play area or to the use of realistic props. It is simply the representation of objects, events, or people that the children are familiar with. Imitating adults, flapping arms like a bird, acting out the eating of a meal, popping up like a toaster, holding your arms like Mommy are all examples of dramatic play.

Infants and toddlers enjoy watching and "participating" in the dramatic play activities of older children, often from a lap at the edge of the activity. Older toddlers also enjoy directing and "narrating" the dramatic play of a caregiver who is acting out a familiar scene, such as rocking a baby, going out the door, or cooking. Always have on hand an array of props: hats, scarves, purses, tools, and household items.

Construction/Block Play   Having a variety of blocks available provides caregivers endless opportunities for facilitating learning: large and small, soft and hard, multicolored. Big foam and cardboard blocks can be crawled around, sat on, knocked down, pushed aside to locate an object, stacked in the form of a tower of two or more, made into a house, placed in "falling domino" rows, and used with a plank to form a bench or ramp. Blocks can be covered with blankets or other surfaces to form a bumpy terrain. Small blocks are great unstructured manipulatives, useful for building and for representing many objects.

Adding play people, animals, cars, and trucks as you play alongside children enhances their play, but don't overwhelm children with props. Remember that for toddlers, taking out and putting away blocks is in itself a play and learning opportunity.

Play with Manipulatives   Caregivers encourage small motor and perceptual motor learning by knowing individual children and trying to provide the *right range* of material choices and the *right number* of choices for each child. Having rattles, stackers, noisy squeakers, spoons, blocks, bean bags, and all the other infant toys available to display selectively is important. Observe and show interest in the child's efforts and occasionally changing the experience to find the right moderately novel experience that challenges her: putting the rattle just out of reach, playing catch, or substituting a more complicated puzzle or pull toy.

Art Play   An appreciation for art can begin in infancy. Infant visual exploration of form and color turns into the expression of art as soon as the child begins to smear, poke holes, and pound. Caregivers can help children notice with open-ended questions ("What do you see in that picture?"), give words to the child's visual or tactile exploration ("It's really big, isn't it?"), and provide media to experiment with. Art is not just "pictures" and painting; it is also sculpture and light and motion.

Art for toddlers is not just watered-down preschool activities. Developmentally appropriate art for toddlers is process oriented and for the most part a more sensory exploration of materials and media than product producing. An orientation toward "product" is inappropriate because toddlers don't set out to "make anything" that is worth preserving. Caregivers should not pressure them to think that way.

It is not particularly meaningful for the children to display the results of their art and craft projects. But what about their parents and caregivers? Parents do want to display these efforts on the refrigerator, and many teachers want to create bulletin board displays. The absence of products may be taken by parents as indications that their children aren't doing much.

The way to resolve this dilemma is to recognize and articulate the distinction between "artifact," which is simply visual evidence of the effort, and "art." First, help parents understand what is developmentally appropriate. But also satisfy the parent's need for artifacts by using photographs of children's activities and pieces of what has resulted from the child's process-oriented efforts, e.g., snippets from the fingerpainting or gluing or scribbling.

Toddlers enjoy paint and clay, gluing and pasting. The sound of crinkly and tearing paper and the residual movement of balled-up newspapers are also part of the art experience, as are pounding and kneading clay. Remember that tearing works for making collages as well as scissors.

Infants can explore art materials on a lap, in a high chair, or on the floor. Toddlers (and preschoolers) often prefer to kneel or stand than to sit.

Sand, Water, and Other "Messy" Sensory Exploration   Children respond differently to messy materials: some seem to need to explore one finger at a time; others jump right in. Help each child explore in the manner that fits his or her style.

Sensory exploration occurs naturally during bathing, hand washing, mealtimes, and exploring puddles—anytime there are sensory materials. Offer an abundance of alternatives to off-limits explorations in toilets, sinks, and at the lunch table.

Older infants and toddlers enjoy exploring sensory materials in water tables and tubs. An arrangement where they can play individually near, but not with other children is often best, for example, tubs back-to-back or separated by a few feet. Giving children the power to alter sensory materials (e.g., soap or food coloring to change the water; water to add to sand), props, and tools adds to their play. They can help prepare the activity by putting down a tarp or by assisting in cleanup

with towel and sponge, as long as you don't expect them to accomplish very much.

Outdoors, of course, is a natural site for sensory exploration.

Appreciating Books and Stories Caregivers teach reading both by reading *to* and *with* children, and teach respect for books though handling, displaying, and making efforts to read. Even young infants enjoy being held and having caregivers read to them if their caregivers communicate enjoyment of the experience. Enthusiastic words directed to children, changing pages, exchanges of looks between infants and caregivers establish a pattern that increases in substance later, as words and pictures take on meaning.

Pick books that are developmentally appropriate in terms of pictures, content, and length. Books about families, babies, and frustrations that toddlers can understand (for example, hunger, lost items, separation), and things they see and use in daily life appeal to young children, as do books that create a mood.

Reading almost always works better individually and in small groups; both should occur frequently. When reading to a larger group, it is important to always stay in tune with the children's experience: from where they sit, what do they are see and hear? When children are restless, use questions, act out a role, and anticipate a word ("And the duck began to ____? *Quack!*") to sustain interest, but don't force completion of a story.

Books that children can read by themselves should be durable and clearly displayed. Caregivers should encourage their respectful use. Occasionally reading a book yourself while they are reading their own is good role modeling.

Storytelling gives infants and toddlers pleasure, particularly when the storyteller enjoys the language as much as the content of the story. Use your voice dramatically, play with the sound of words, and occasionally use props, puppets, or flannelboards with toddlers. Infants enjoy listening and watching toddler small groups. Of course, stories that call for physical responses or that can be acted out appeal to children.

Play with Science Infants and toddlers literally em*body* the scientific method. First they observe, followed by endless trial and error and experimentation with everything in their world; they use their mouths and entire bodies, and they see rather than look. Soon their scientific exploration becomes more sophisticated, and we see toddlers conducting fabulous experiments with whatever happens to be at hand in the kitchen, bathroom, indoors, and out.

The best thing that a caregiver can do is to enjoy the world and how it works and share that pleasure with the child: *noticing*, looking at the infinite variety in the worlds of nature and machines, humans and animals, naming, cataloging, and marveling. The smoothness of a stone, bumpiness of bark, the golden leaf with red veins, the boiling, whistling kettle, and the mist on the window are daily encounters with science, as are dropping a spoon, sliding down an inclined surface, filling up a bucket, and pushing a table.

Beyond engineering the rich *world at their fingertips*, caregivers facilitate learning in childhood by encouraging exploration and having at hand materials and tools that enhance the experience. Containers, magnifiers, string, and tape create physics experiments in gravity and resistance; other materials transform lighting. Growing plants, caring for animals and birds, and cooking with children offer other explorations of the physical world.

Cooking   Food is certainly important to infants and toddlers, and cooking is a wonderful activity that involves all the senses and small motor skills. Young infants like to watch cooking, and toddlers can begin to participate in it. For example, they can snap beans, tear lettuce, pour milk, cut a carrot, stir a pot, knead bread dough, and dish out pudding. Small, quick tasks like popping toast in a toaster, pouring pancake batter, using cookie cutters, or pouring salad dressing are easy to do, empower children, and become exercises in cause and effect. Children enjoy imitating the sounds as well as acting out the actions.

A Final Word: Joyous Child Care

Children can learn from everything. Observe them, respond to their interests and explorations, play with them, support them, and enjoy them. When caregivers have fun and take delight in reciprocal play, children experience the joy of being human.

Exercises

1. Pair up with another caregiver and observe each other's interactions with children. Assess your interactions in terms of sensitivity and response to children's cues.

2. Tape-record yourself for 45 minutes while interacting with children (in an infant room and in a toddler room). Assess your language in terms of the guidelines on page 245–246.

3. Select two areas of play that *you* are usually least likely to engage in (e.g., blocks and music) and develop a list of activities you could do spontaneously with a nine month old, fifteen month old, and twenty-four month old.

References

Hart, Betty and Risley, Todd. *Meaningful Differences in the Everyday Experience of Young American Children.* Baltimore: Paul H. Brooke, 1995.

Honig, Alice. "The Art of Talking to a Baby." *Working Mother* 8:3 1985: 72–78.

Part 5

Good Places for Adults

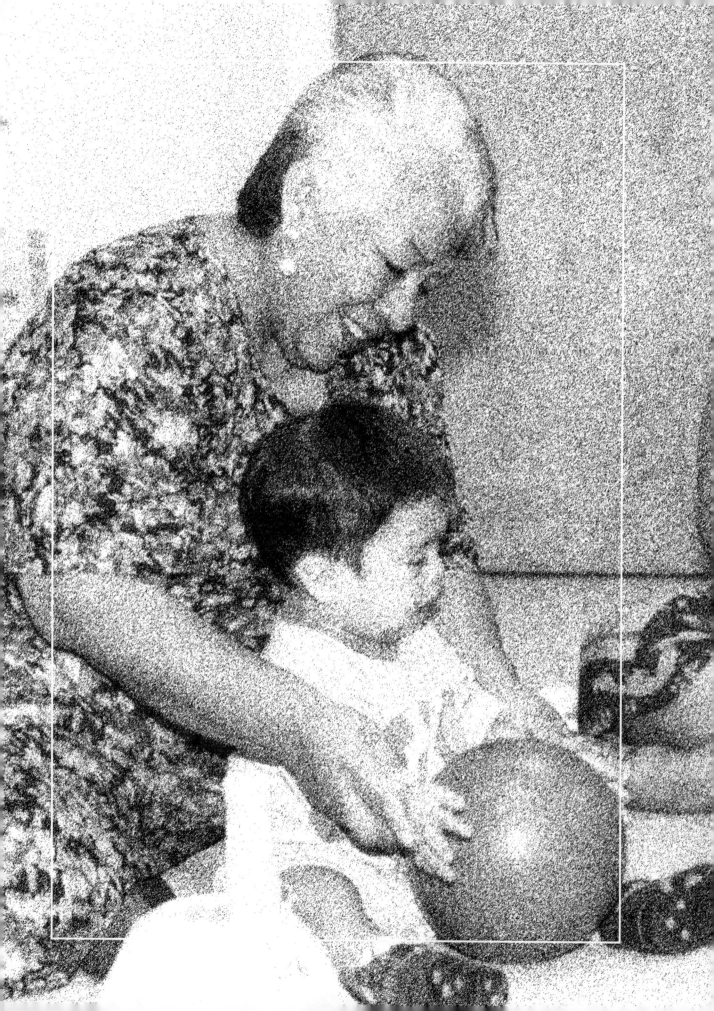

Chapter 14
Partnerships with Parents

Parents are comfortable and secure in the knowledge that their child is receiving excellent care that is consistent with their family needs, beliefs, and values. The program offers services that fit parents' child care needs, and each family feels welcome and a part of the center.

The Program Serves Families

Child care is a family affair, a service for children and parents. Parents are their children's primary caregivers, and our job is to work with parents to meet the needs of their children and their family life. Quality child care is individualized for the child and the family; it provides education that empowers the child. The best centers work hard to empower parents and to help them feel in control of their child's care. The best program is a true collaboration between parents and staff; it recognizes the prerogatives and constraints of both parents and caregivers.

So that parents can feel comfortable, secure, and respected, the staff strive to nurture in both child and parents a sense of belonging to the family and to reinforce primary attachments to parents and other family members. How can we do this? By welcoming parents to the center, involving them in decision making about their child's care, and learning and by nurturing each parent's pleasure in and understanding of their child.

Parents Are People as Well as Parents

A parent introduced to another parent by a teacher as "Marika's mum," responded somewhat tersely, "I have a name, too—it's Jane."

It is easy to fall into the habit of defining child care parents through their children. Worse than the above example is the common practice of referring to the "mom," as in "Mom said that Marika was tired" or "The mom said that Marika needs a nap." Granting parents a separate identity is important in creating a culture of respect.

Child Care Is Not School

Just as it is important not to think of child care as school, it is desirable to stress that relationships between child care and parents is not the same relationship that parents will have with most schools, even nursery schools. Schools generally assume the responsibility of educating the child in the manner they see as most fit and of sharing information about the child's progress. The parents' job is mostly to keep informed and to support the professionals. Parents' presence is usually on the perimeter of the classroom.

Child care is different. If the parent's responsibility is to raise and be the expert on their own child, to make sure the child is cared for in accordance with their values and standards, then in child care, *it is the parent's job to pay attention to and influence the day-to-day particulars of their child's care.* This is an important point, and one that makes many professionals uneasy; sharing information is one thing—sharing power is quite another.

To help make the conceptual shift, suppose that you are a parent with lots of money looking for child care. You may hire a nanny or seek out the specific care you want from the best programs in the area. You would expect *influence* over your child's care, not just information about the care received. Your purchasing power backs up your parental prerogatives. You may want advice and education from the child care professional(s), but you certainly expect that it will be given respectfully, in full awareness that what you do with your child is your choice.

You want control over the care, but as a typical sensible parent, you use your financial ability to find caregivers you trust and whom you rely on for their judgment on most decisions.

About Parents

Parents are people like us: struggling to do the right thing in a busy, sometimes confusing world. Many are thoughtful and sensitive; a few are not. Some are open and easy to talk to, some are more reserved—just like caregivers.

Parents as Customers

One way to understand what a good program tries to accomplish is to consider parents as customers. As with any business or service, the program must meet customer needs and create satisfied customers. Does this mean the program can't have standards and values that sometimes value the program's views of the child's needs over those of the parents? Of course not. Just as conscientious trade workers, plumbers, and doctors won't pander to customers against their own expert judgments, neither should child care staff. It does mean, however, that the foundation of our service is serving customer needs and it is in our interest to define, even sell, our "product," that is, what quality child care is all about, in a way that parents can understand.

Satisfied parents who feel good about their child's care are fundamental ingredients in child care quality.

When parents do their job as consumers, there are inherent tensions. What is our image of a good customer? In purchasing a car, it is the customer who knows what he or she is looking for, peers under the hood, kicks the tires, slams the doors, asks a lot of questions, and doesn't hesitate to return the car if anything is wrong. Extending that analogy to child care, the program and caregivers are the equivalent of the car—to be inspected closely and critically (but not to be kicked or slammed!). When parents behave like conscientious customers, they should be admired and their criticism should not be taken personally.

Good Programs Support Not Supplant

Parents who use care do not want to be replaced in their children's lives. Caregivers are not parent substitutes except in the practical sense of providing substitute care during the hours that parents are unavailable. Having a baby in child care should not be seen by either parents or staff as "handing them over" but rather as engaging in a shared process of providing the best possible experience for the baby, both at home and in care. But good relationships won't happen automatically as by products of caring well for children or of being nice people. They stem from trust built on a foundation of hard work, attention to detail, and good systems for promoting communication and real partnership.

First Steps: Milestones for Whom?

Bobby finally does it—he lurches across the room like a miniature sumo wrestler, and he does so at the center of the room. So what do you do? If you tell the parents, they may well feel left out and cheated of a major milestone: "I wish he had walked for me." What if you don't tell them? Bobby will eventually walk at home. In come Bobby and his parents the next day, united in family pride. However, some parents, knowing that the center generally follows this practice, will want to be told; otherwise, they feel the center may always be holding back information .

Parent Involvement

Parent involvement is an all-purpose term that encompasses parent boards and committees, volunteers, parent education, fund raising, and special events. Each center needs to find the right mix of opportunities for parents to promote comfortable and full partnerships between parents and the center and to enhance the quality of care.

Parents who use day care are almost always very busy and will have limited time to participate in the life of the day care center. The key to parent involvement is to make a variety of ways to be involved in the life of the center available to parents without making them feel these are obligations.

While the parent-staff partnership may include parents participating in a variety of ways in the center, the partnership does not rest on parent involvement. The foundations of the partnership are communication, decision-making systems, and daily interactions that promote shared decisions and mutual trust.

Parent Insecurity Is Normal

Parents of infants are likely to be the most insecure of all child care parents. Most are new to parenting, some are new to marriage, and almost all experience some stress and fatigue due to recovery from childbirth, returns to work, and late night caregiving. Simply leaving the house with an infant and all the necessary paraphernalia for the day may require a major effort.

Some will be ambivalent or regretful about returning to work or school and leaving their child in care. Initially, they may experience the pain and insecurity of separation. After all, they are trusting their most prized possession, their tiny, vulnerable child who is unable to communicate what she is experiencing, to others whom they don't know well.

The pain of separation felt by parents not only does not disappear quickly, it reoccurs throughout the child care experience (and beyond: school, camp, college, and leaving home). In the first two years of life children change so fast, seemingly becoming new people every week. The loss of time with them continues to hurt.

First-time parents usually approach child care uncertain about what to expect, particularly about their own role: how much of a role should their knowledge and wishes play in the scheme of things?

Parents of babies, especially first-time parents, may be anxious about their baby's development and behavior, wonder if he or she is normal, and worry about unusual or undesirable behavior. "Why isn't my Tommy holding a spoon (or walking, talking, playing chess)?" Caregivers' objectivity and experience with lots of babies can be very useful in these situations. We can reassure parents that little Angela's passion for sinking her teeth into the flesh of her playmates will not lead to her becoming a vampire. We know that almost anything a child does is within the diverse range of normal behavior.

Having a child in a group situation with other children approximately the same age is both an advantage and a disadvantage for parents. Parents can't help comparing. Our job is to help them appreciate their own baby's accomplishments, pointing out the child's expanding abilities—in short, helping them to appreciate their child's uniqueness and discouraging them from excessive comparisons of their baby to others. Of course, that means we have to refrain from making comparisons too.

All Parents Are Different

All parents want the best for their children. And most want the same things: success in school, work, and society; self-esteem. But parents have different beliefs and values, and their feelings about the means to these ends are often different. Staff must respect differences and try to accommodate them within the program. When parents' beliefs are incompatible with the program's philosophy and policies, our job is to seek common ground and try to work out solutions.

Parents Are Human (Like Us)

None of us is or will be a perfect parent. We have different failings and make different compromises in balancing the real world of children, work, and family life.

Parents have many roles—employee, student, spouse, partner—with many conflicting demands, some of which at times will inevitably preclude their putting their children's needs first. It is easy for caregivers, whose task is always to put children first, to overlook this and become intolerant or overly critical of parents.

It is not always possible (or desirable) for parents to make all the decisions about allocating precious resources (time and money) on the basis of what is good for their children right now. In the course of our parenting lives, all of us will sacrifice and indulge, behave sensibly and dumbly, be sensitive and thoughtless. This is called being human.

The daily choices parents make are often difficult. In interactions with them and in conversations with other staff members, it is essential to reflect an empathetic and supportive attitude toward parents. It is not our job to evaluate parents and the choices they make.

Although the partnership between staff and parents is focused on the well-being of their children, showing interest in other aspects of the parents' lives and sharing information about yourself builds the relationship. Always, of course, one should respect parents' boundaries and not be too "nosy."

The Kindness of Strangers?

Suppose you are talking with a parent friend and ask her who is watching her child, and she replies, "Some nice blonde woman named Kim and a friend of hers who helps out." Would you feel secure? Parents need to know who cares for their children, no matter how much they trust the center. This includes new staff and substitutes. It should not be acceptable for a parent to arrive and be greeted by an unfamiliar adult.

Use name tags: this may not be necessary in small programs, but it is essential in large ones. The slight formality of name tags can be alleviated by its style.

A staff display, including pictures and short biographies, is important. This does not have to be fancy; in fact, if it is too fancy, it will be difficult to update. It is best to place the display where all parents can see it, not only in a homebase.

Notify parents of staff changes: comings or goings, new substitutes, and volunteers, always *in advance*, even if it's only in the form of a note on the door before they enter.

"They"

Parents easily become "them" or "the parents" not a collection of individuals. In every population, there are a range of individuals from near saints to clear sinners. We usually use the annoying and problematic behavior of the least agreeable to create our "them," against whom we rail with knowing condescension. The parent who willingly places her child in care for sixty hours a week but who only works part-time to pay for facials defines one "they" ("self-indulgent"), along with the chronically late parent ("rude and uncaring"), the one who forgets the diapers ("irresponsible"), the whiner ("obnoxious"), and the one who wants her infant toilet trained ("ignorant"). When some staff get together to talk about parents, one wonders whether they are talking about a mutant species. Usually, however, the staff's bark is worse than its bite. Many staff who rail against parents actually behave in sensitive and accommodating ways when interacting with them. This tendency to create "theys" is certainly not limited to child care workers. It is a natural phenomenon that has to be fought—an occupational hazard of service-related professions. To resist the crea-tion of "theys," all staff should help each other make it taboo to slide into generalizations.

Parents Are Experts on Their Own Child

The parent-child relationship is longer, more intimate, and more intense than the caregiver-child relationship. Parents observe their children across a range of very different settings. Even when parents lack confidence, they inevitably possess insights and information about the child that staff do not. Are they always right about their child? No, their perspective is often distorted by love, hope, fear, and incomplete understanding of development. But our perspective, often wise because of greater objectivity, knowledge of development, and experience with a number of children, is not infallible; we are often wrong as well.

Parents Focus on How the Program Works for Their Child

It would be a much easier job for staff if parents had the same perspective that we do—that is, an equal concern for all children and families in the program and an understanding that there will be inevitable compromises in order to make things work for all children and families in the program. However, this is unreasonable to expect. We don't behave that way in our expectations of services we purchase and parents won't either. For example, have you ever said, "No, don't worry, Mr. Auto Mechanic, I don't mind that my car is not fixed because you did a swell job on all those others"? It is the parents' job to look out for and advocate for their child.

"They Don't Tell Us What Is Happening at Home"

As a consultant, I (JG) sat in the teachers' meeting at the small center and listened to staff talk about the children and families.

"What about (two-year-old) James? He seems to be having a hard time and acting out a lot," asked the director.

"I found out through a mutual friend that his parents are struggling and may split up," his teacher Jane responded. "It explains a lot. I wish his mom had told us. How can we help their kids if they don't tell us what's happening at home?"

I asked the staff what they would have done if they had known what was going on with James's mom and dad. They replied that they would have tried to give James "more" and that they would have understood more. I asked Jane, "Suppose you were going through a messy divorce and you were under a lot of stress. And suppose you weren't getting along with Alice (the associate teacher) because she was on edge because she's drinking too much. Should we put out a bulletin to the parents:

TO ALL PARENTS: The children in Jane's class may behave differently at home because of problems at child care—Jane's divorce and Alice's drinking have resulted in some tension and breaks in the normal routines, but don't worry because care is still good and their on-the-job performance is acceptable. Please try to give your child some special attention because s/he may be feeling a little insecure. We thought this information might help explain your child's behavior.

It is tempting to justify knowing the details of a family's private life because it may help us "understand" or "teach" a child. But we have no *right* to know the ins and outs of family life anymore than parents have a right to know about our private lives in order to monitor program quality or to better understand the center. For the most part, what we need to know is that a child like James is under some unusual stress and needs us at our supportive best. Much of the time, it makes little difference in our response if the stress is due to family "problems," fitful sleep, mild illness, or any of the other possible sources of children's stress. What we try to do is offer flexibility, warmth, and nurturing. If a child is older, perhaps talking about the situation may help him. But in that case, let the child or parent decide that.

Respect for parents demands that unless the situation is one of abuse or neglect, the parents control what information they wish to share. If we come to know something about the family, as professionals we should ask the parent if they mind our sharing the information with colleagues or supervisors. In the case of James, discussing his family situation as a staff, based on gossip and without parental permission, is no less unprofessional than a group discussion about a teacher's private struggles. When we have a relationship based on mutual respect and confidence, many parents will trust us with information about their private struggles.

Parents' Boundaries Differ

Different parents may want very different relationships with the center and the staff. Some want a lot of contact, a great deal of information about the details of child care, and opportunities to share much of what is going on in their own lives with staff. Others maintain a distance, seek and share far less information, and have much less contact. This may be because they want to know only enough to believe that they have made a reasonable arrangement for care. Parents have a right to set their own boundaries, as long as all necessary information for the good care of the child flows back and forth.

However, remember that some parents may simply be shy or uncertain about their role, and staff should always look for ways to put them at ease so that they feel really welcomed and comfortable with the relationship.

Some Parents Will Alienate Staff

Take any ten or fifteen people. A few will be "difficult" and one will be "impossible," and all will be difficult occasionally. It is true of staff and true of parents. The most difficult parents to form a partnership with are those who are critical of the center and staff, irresponsible, always demanding or uncooperative, or who neglect their child. Often, these are the parents who need the most help and support, and they are behaving in ways that are least likely to elicit them. It is the essence of professionalism to serve these parents well.

Some Parents Harm Their Children

Sooner or later, most centers will struggle with the issues of child abuse, neglect, and family dysfunction. Parenting is never stress free, and each of us has the capacity to harm a child, either through acting out in frustration or anger, being overwhelmed by circumstance, or neglecting care. But most of us don't do these things; instead, we somehow manage to control ourselves and care for our children adequately.

Dealing with families under stress is undoubtedly the most difficult aspect of a caregiver's job. Child providers are required by law to report any instances of suspected abuse or neglect. Reporting abuse or neglect—in fact, even deciding whether there is enough to report—is a traumatic experience with potentially huge consequences for the family and the caregiver-parent relationship. Sadness, confusion, anger, fear, and every other emotion may cloud the decision, including doubt about whether reporting is best for the child. The center and individual staff must follow the state guidelines.

This is the ultimate test of the bond between parent and program. If there is a strong partnership and mutual trust, there is at least hope of weathering the storm and continuing to support the child and family.

"They Don't Care"

In child care, we often take *our* institutional limitations as givens, certainly not as signs that we care less about the children. Ratios, center size, foods served, limits of services, staff turnover—"Sorry, welcome to the real world of today's child care." We usually can honestly say that we are doing our best, but we are not always so willing to accept parents' givens. Yet parents' real lives—long work days, finding time for themselves, money problems, difficulties sorting out what is the right thing to do in a diverse, guilt-inducing, materialistic culture—easily bring out the judges in us (particularly if we haven't had to face the world as parents ourselves).

"They don't care" or "They don't care enough" is perhaps the most common hidden thought to lurk in the back of many child care workers' minds every time we look for extra clothes, cope with a sick child, or regret the poor turnout at an open house. This is often followed by, "I wish they would get some parent education," as we piece together an image of the child's family life based on the child's behavior, our disapproving glimpses of parent-child interactions, and reports from the home front. As a director, I (JG) made sure our parent handbook had a section asking that parents label their children's clothing because "Don't they realize how many clothes we have to go through and how alike all the clothing is?" As a parent, I inconsistently labeled my kid's clothing because "Don't they realize how many clothes kids go through and what it takes to label each pair of socks?" As a parent, I regretfully missed open houses and committed all the parent sins, but I still cared deeply about my kid.

All of the Above Is True for Parents of Children with Special Needs, Only More So

"You don't really know what it's like to suspect or discover that your new child is not 'like all the other kids' until it happens to you," Marco explains. He is the parent of a child with a severe hearing disability. *"You are in denial, in shock, and then angry and frightened. It's hard on the marriage, it's hard on her ten-year-old brother, who doesn't understand what's wrong and why. It throws off your social relationships with friends and family—some avoid us, we get sick of sympathy and pity, and some don't understand what it all involves. We have had wonderful child care, but it is always tricky; sometimes they think I'm too pushy, sometimes they feel we don't tell them enough, and sometimes they seem to expect too much. Well-meaning teachers have said things that upset me because they underestimate Sarah, and I've said things that upset them because they think I expect too much from them.*

"I wouldn't trade Sarah for any other kid on the planet, but I also feel for any family in our situation."

Marco is a "difficult" parent, at times abrupt and demanding, at other times aloof. Serving children with special needs means serving parents who also have special needs. Like their children, they require extra patience and sensitivity.

Parents and Caregivers

The parent-caregiver relationship is probably the most challenging aspect of a caregiver's job. It takes sensitivity and skill to maneuver through a delicate relationship with parents, one free from competition over the child's affection and primary claims about knowing what is "best" for the child.

Many parents approach the parent-caregiver relationship with some child care guilt and a confusion of messages about what to look for in quality child care. Many caregivers—some of whom work with children because they feel more confident with children than adults—bring the insecurity that accompanies low pay and status and the same uncertainty about "what is the right thing to do" to the parent-caregiver relationship. Most staff and parents come from an individualistic culture that is not great about sharing love and intimacy. Staff often develop feelings and perceptions that work against a partnership. Those feelings are a natural outgrowth of the complex relationship and are present in nearly all programs.

Competition for the Love of the Child and "Child Saving"

It is hard not to compete with parents for the child's affections. Caregivers become attached to children and take pleasure in their attachment to us. Most parents appreciate the importance of their child being attached to the caregiver. But as Rita Warren (1984) cautioned, "child saving" is the number one occupational hazard for those who work with children: the feelings that we would be better parents and that we somehow have to make up for the parent's real or imagined failings. Parents need to know that the staff who care for their children understand that the parent-child attachment is crucial; that parents are the most important people in their child's life; and that the relationship between the caregiver and the child will not be at the expense of the bonds between parent and child. How will parents know this? In their writing and conversations, caregivers should express respect for and appreciation of parent efforts and the parent-child bond, and not overemphasize the child's bond with the caregiver. It is a fine line for staff because parents also want to hear about how much their child is liked and thought of as special.

Staff Competence and Parent Self-Esteem

The more competent staff are, the more parents may feel insecure about their own parenting unless priority is given to forming partnerships. Caregivers have two somewhat conflicting agendas: first, they want parents to feel secure leaving their baby with them and therefore they want to demonstrate competence and understanding of the child; second, they want parents to feel important and needed. It is easy for caregivers with good intentions to undermine parents by offering unsolicited advice, describing better behavior by the child at the center than the parent experiences at home, or simply by appearing competent and confident when the parent does not feel that way.

Benefits of Partnership

For the child:

The experience of the special people in his or her life working together cooperatively, getting along with each other. A feeling of security.

Consistent, sensitive, individualized care because of information shared.

Greater continuity between life at home and in care.

Parents who feel empowered in caring for their child, which enhances feelings of attachment to the child.

Parents who feel confident about their child rearing.

A passionate advocate.

For the parents:

Greater confidence in their decision to use care and in their parenting skills.

Belonging to a community of people who care about their child.

The opportunity to contribute significantly to their child's experience even when they are absent.

Increased feelings of attachment to the child (in contrast to decreased attachment, which may occur when there is no partnership).

Additional information about and a different perspective on their child.

Continual reassurance they are the most special person in their child's life.

For the staff:

Information about the child from an expert on that child.

A variety of help and contributions.

Affirmation of their importance and support for their work.

The satisfaction of knowing that they may be making a lasting, positive difference in the child and his family's life.

Parents Belong in the Homebase

Parents should be encouraged to visit, linger, take the time to breast-feed or eat with their child. Feeling at home is assisted by knowing the "rules." They need to know where to hang coats and purses and what to do and not to do; for example, diaper procedures and where not to sit. It will also help parents if they have clear information about their responsibilities for their child when they are present and what their role is in relationship to children other than their own.

If parents are made to feel truly at home in the center, some caregivers worry that the environment will become crowded, adult centered, and too busy. This can indeed happen, but it can be corrected if caregivers are alert to the problem and change the environment when it is adult heavy. Staff can take some babies outside or on a trip through the center. If there are traffic jams because of too many parents, the problem should be discussed with parents as a group. They should be asked for good alternatives. Staff should not discourage parents' feelings of belonging.

Staff Behavior Teaches Parents What Is Really Expected of Them

Sometimes center staff make the mistake of assuming that informing parents that they are welcomed and that staff want to talk to them and backing up these claims with written information is enough. Unless this initial information is reinforced on a daily basis by staff, partnerships will not happen. Staff have to take the lead in continuously demonstrating to parents that they desire partnerships.

Staff, especially new or inexperienced staff, may feel intimidated by parents and may find relating to them the most daunting aspect of their work. However, they need to remember that parents also feel daunted by the prospect of using care and wonder how they and their child will "measure up." If staff and parents do not understand how each other feels, they may misinterpret what is actually a lack of confidence, reading it instead as aloofness or unfriendliness, to the detriment of the relationship.

Parents Won't (and Shouldn't) Feel Secure and Comfortable until They Know the Center and Staff

Staff who work in a center will be proud of their reputation for good work on behalf of children and may feel affronted when parents do not immediately appear to trust them. But not only is this to be expected, it is a clear sign of the parent' investment in their child and the seriousness with which they accept their parenting role.

Partnerships Take Time and Work

This is meant in two ways. First, partnerships are not created by decree or by statements in a policy handbook. Like all meaningful

"They Won't Leave Us Alone"

The flip side to "They don't care" is "They care too much" about some things. Cody's mother, Gloria, is a walking negative stereotype of the mother on welfare: high school dropout, overweight, and poorly dressed. A mother of three children at only twenty-two, she keeps appointments erratically and rarely provides an extra set of clothes for her children. Moreover, she has been reported to the state for suspected child abuse for what looked like a burn on her child's bottom. It turned out to be impetigo. When she becomes upset with the center about Cody's care or has questions about his education, staff always respond with an underlying, unspoken, "How dare you challenge us on our care decisions!" The more questions, the more staff outrage.

Some of Gloria's questions and concerns:

◆ when will Cody be taught to read?
◆ why does he get so dirty?
◆ how did he get that bruise?
◆ how could he lose two shirts and a shoe?
◆ why do you let Cody get away with so much?

Gloria is loud and seems ill at ease and "pushy" to the staff. Because of this, many staff do not recognize that her questions and concerns are nearly always appropriate, never frivolous.

Lupe's mother, Marta, is nearly the opposite of Gloria: a forty-two-year-old, fashionably dressed psychologist. Lupe is her only child. Marta is usually late picking up Lupe and is often slow in responding to staff requests. When she asks questions or has concerns, which is frequently, she asks many that are similar to Gloria's. Staff response is less one of "How dare she?" than one of "What a typical, neurotic older yuppie parent." Like Gloria, Marta has questions and concerns that, while numerous and often minor, are never off the wall.

A fundamental parent role is that of child protector. Parents look out for their children, monitor their care, and advocate for quality care and education. In addition, our model for a conscientious consumer of an expensive and important service is someone who looks very carefully and demands satisfaction. Both Gloria and Marta play these roles as well as or better than many "nicer" or more relaxed parents. When a parent is persistent or assertive, she (or he) may well seem obnoxious (at least to us), and we first use stereotypes to discredit her, and then extend our feelings about her to "parents" and create a "them." Staff need to understand that parents' concerns or questions are always valid although some may be ill founded. Making requests or complaints is a legitimate aspect of the parent role.

relationships, they happen over a period of time through ordinary give-and-take interactions. Second, one of the biggest obstacles to forming good relationships between parents and staff is the fact that both are busy. Parents are often rushing at both ends of the day, and these are often the most hectic times for caregivers as well. Each may perceive the other's hurried and busy demeanor as an indication of lack of interest in communicating.

If partnerships are to happen, staff schedules should support parent-staff communication. They need to be in synch with primary care-

Favorites

Nothing gets in the way of parent-staff partnerships more than the perception by parents, whether real or imagined, that caregivers have favorite children or parents, but it's not them! Nothing is also more likely in a setting where personal contact is so extensive. It is inevitable that staff will "take" to some children and parents more than others and vice versa. Staff and parents may have personal relationships outside the center or staff may baby-sit for families. A treasured caregiver may be invited to a child's birthday party.

Some centers discourage any "fraternization" or baby-sitting, but that seems neither realistic nor particularly healthy. Are there clear guidelines to avoid problems?

Not really. These situations require sensitivity and professionalism on the part of caregivers if the professional and personal relationships are to be separate. All parents and children need to feel that they get friendly, respectful treatment and the best from their caregivers.

The best approach is to acknowledge potential problems, accept the difficulty that child, parent, and staff person will have in completely disassociating the special relationships, and be aware of any problematic situations. Caregivers should be open about personal relationships outside the center and staff should as a team keep each other "honest" to ensure that all families receive equal treatment and that no child or parent has cause for complaint.

giving relationships; there needs to be sufficient staffing to allow conversation. Further, communication may have to extend beyond frenetic greetings and departures to phone calls and notes.

Parental Responsibility

All parents have a right to be involved in decision making about their child. Some parents may be willing to leave the decision making up to staff. This may be a sign of confidence in staff, but the wise caregiver should resist allowing parents to hand over responsibility. Many parents are stressed and have multiple roles to fill, and professional staff may take on increased responsibility for the child's care and well-being with good intentions in order to support the parents and lighten their burden. It is important that the center's special efforts to support parents, such as serving breakfast to the children, bathing them, arranging for immunizations and medical or dental checkups, or regularly speaking directly to the child's physician are accompanied by continual efforts to maintain the parents' view of themselves as the decision makers in their child's life.

Parent Requests: A "Why Not?" Approach

All parent requests should be met with "Why not?" thinking and a nondefensive attitude, an approach that grants legitimacy to both the parents' request and the caregiver's limitations. When a parent asks

Partnership Is—

Partnerships are forged when parents' and staff's daily interactions with each other are characterized by
◆ equal distribution of power based on the recognition of the unique contribution and strengths of both parents and caregivers.
◆ mutual respect.
◆ trust.
◆ continuous, open, two-way communication.
◆ shared mutual appreciation, and understanding and liking for the child.
◆ common goals.
◆ shared decision making.
◆ sensitivity to each other's perspectives.
◆ teamwork and the absence of rivalry or competition for the child's affections.

Partnership Is *not*—
◆ parent involvement/participation.
◆ parent education.
◆ becoming friends.
◆ the same relationship with every parent.

for a change in their child's routine, a special activity, or a different way of doing things, we should genuinely ask ourselves "Why not?" Unless a practice is definitely harmful to a baby or absolutely cannot be accommodated in day care, parents' wishes should be honored, even in fairly unimportant matters—for example, when a parent asks that her infant's food always be warmed before feeding.

A mother may request that caregivers not pick up her baby if he cries when he is put down for a nap, especially if the baby has shown many signs of being tired, since she allows the child to cry for up to fifteen or twenty minutes at home. Caregivers should agree to see how this works. Doing so empowers parents and establishes a relationship in which the mother and caregiver can talk openly and honestly about issues related to the care of the baby.

This is different from a "the customer is always right" approach. *"Why not?" does not mean "Yes."* There are many legitimate "Why not?"s that lead to a "No": a practice may be harmful to the child (for example, nap time bottles of juice), the center's budget, the complexity of group. Perhaps caregivers don't know how to accommodate the request; perhaps staffing does not permit it, to name a few. The program has no reason to be defensive about unalterable givens that lead to program limitations.

When you cannot say yes to a request, it is very important to explain the reasons in a respectful manner, never condescending to the parent or implying that the request itself was improper. *Make it clear that it is always acceptable for parents to ask.*

Often, excessive demands by parents come from a feeling of having too little influence over their child's care and a need to exercise some control. In some cases, discussion leading to a compromise will be necessary.

The outcome of a "Why not?" approach is not unmanageable complexity but thoughtful care, a foundation of mutual respect, and, in most cases, increased trust that staff are professionals committed to good care. Equally important, a "Why not?" approach leads to innovation and better care. Parents bring to light important questions and concerns, as well as share their expertise. Parents acting as informed consumers fulfill their responsibility to ensure that their children have the care they deserve.

Giving Advice to Parents

It is important to be cautious in giving advice to parents, making certain that the distinction between opinion and fact is clear to the parents and avoiding the impression that you are evaluating their practices. It may be difficult to refrain from giving unsolicited advice on child rearing, but unless keeping silent harms the baby, it is best to wait until parents open the way for discussion.

Caregivers also need to recognize the limits of their expertise. Absolute opinions on what is the "right" thing to do for a child's development are rarely called for.

The Value of Consistency

How important is consistency? After all, people are different, and the child care setting is different from the home setting. Consistency between care at home and in day care helps a baby feel secure and assists in learning. Just as important, striving for consistency affirms parents and ensures that each child is treated as an individual; for example, asking Jenny's parents how they soothe Jenny.

While achieving consistency is hard because children change so quickly, the drive for consistency fuels the continual flow of information between home and child care. If Jacob is learning to drink from a cup either at home or in child care, sharing this information and coordinating practices will make Jacob's learning process easier and affirm the caregiver's and parents' sense of a joint enterprise.

When families come from cultural backgrounds different from that of the caregiver, there may be home customs that are unfamiliar to caregivers. Understanding and respecting the variety of good practices is essential. We all have prejudices, some of them ones we are aware of, some of them more hidden. Staff may need help to look at their own prejudices about people in order to relate effectively to all families in the center. This is a first step toward working against bias and prejudice, or at least toward ensuring that it does not influence interactions with families.

In general, some diversity in care practices is not harmful to children, and in fact is inevitable. However, it is desirable that nap time, eating routines, use of a pacifier, and discipline be handled somewhat similarly in both settings.

When is consistency critical? First, it is critical when what a child learns makes him dysfunctional in one setting or the other. For instance, if Betsy is encouraged to defend herself in one setting and to seek adult assistance in the other, she will be reprimanded both places for behavior she has been encouraged to develop. Second, consistency is important in situations in which the parents feel that certain practices are crucially important to their child's well-being. These may focus on PRIME TIME, for example, mealtime, or on behavior that demonstrates respect for adults.

Is Good Care Universal?

Every culture believes that what it does is "right." Within a culture, there is such a thing as good care and good child development. But cultures don't agree, which is understandable, because they are products of centuries of history, geography, language, and visions of the future. Child development experts are raised and educated within a single culture. Even within the same culture, experts don't always agree on what is "right."

Throughout this handbook, we have used excerpts from Janet Gonzalez-Mena's book, *Multicultural Issues in Child Care*, to illustrate the many different ways that cultures define good development and good care. Expectations about children, nurturing routines, discipline, and giving praise and affection vary from culture to culture. The way members of a society care for children determines the characteristics of its adults, and the beliefs, values, and practices that hold communities together.

Caregivers always need to remember that often there is a cultural logic to parental beliefs and practices. This logic may be based on cultural practices perceived as just as right as our own closely held truths. Because this is so, we have a responsibility to listen and respect, to adapt practices when possible, and to articulate clearly the logic of program practices when adaptation is impossible.

Establishing Relationships with New Parents

Parents want to like and trust their child care providers. They also want to be conscientious consumers, but many have an incomplete sense of what they should want. The first six weeks are the time to grow the relationship, set expectations for quality, and make sure that any issues come to the surface.

Touring Prospective Parents

All prospective parents should be encouraged to visit the center and observe its program before making a decision to enroll their child. This visit can be very informal, with questions answered and information given. But, as with any relationship, first impressions count. Parents' experience on a visit before deciding to enroll will provide impressions that color their future experiences. The tour introduces your program, staff, and vision of quality to the prospective parent.

Successful Tours

1. Have a script (at least in your head): know what features of your program you plan to cover and how to show your program in the best light.
2. Prepare by experiencing the program through the senses of the parents. "Why is it so cluttered looking?" "What is that smell?" "Why is it so loud?" You are used to the real world of your program and the experience of active learning in a group setting; they are not.
3. Listen to the prospective parents. What are they interested in? What are their concerns? Solicit their questions and concerns.
4. Know your program, its strengths and weaknesses. Know how to present your limitations in a reasonable fashion.
5. Be honest. In a good program, we don't need to hide the limitations of group care or the struggles to produce quality with limited resources, or pretend to be something we are not. If we lead parents to expect something we can't deliver, we will have serious problems after they enroll.
6. Involve the staff. Introduce them and sing their praises. Make sure staff greet both parents and child and show interest in having a new family.

The Intake

Once parents have decided to enroll a child, an intake that includes the lead teacher or primary caregiver should occur prior to entry in the program. The interview should be relaxed, and the parents should be made to feel comfortable about bringing the child or children to the interview.

More than a time to complete paperwork, the intake is a time for parents to share information about the child (see the *Infant/Toddler Needs and Services Plan* on page 118), their desires and concerns, and for staff to discuss the ins and outs of the program. It is a time to find out what expectations parents have of the center, and to make clear to them what responsibilities the center has to them.

It is important for staff to go beyond simply responding to parents' questions, as parents who are new to child care may not know what questions to ask. Staff should be prepared to highlight important information in the parent handbook. (See the sample handbook statement on page 276.) These topics may include

◆ daily routines
◆ discipline policies
◆ learning environment/curriculum
◆ expectations of parents
◆ policies related to illnesses

◆ staffing practices

◆ possible sensitive issues such as biting, diagnosis of special needs.

Misunderstandings in such areas as to when to keep a sick child at home and the need to adhere to agreed-upon pickup times can create tension and ill will that are hard to overcome.

Parents need to know the areas in which staff will be guided by parents' wishes, those areas in which staff and parents negotiate together toward an outcome comfortable for both, and those areas in which there can be no compromise. In fact, it is a useful exercise for staff to look at their program and make lists under those three headings. If the longest list is the no-compromise list, then a look at the program's attitudes toward parents is warranted.

The Parent Handbook

The Parent Handbook is a "bible," a reference book for parents to check when they have a question or concern. (See the sample parent handbook table of contents on page 277-278.) It outlines the center's philosophy, policies, and operations (for example, fees, hours, dates of closing, staffing structure). The handbook says who you are. Reading it, parent should gain a clear sense of what to expect, including the limits of your flexibility. The handbook should be a living document, updated regularly and reflecting current practices. Parents should receive the handbook before or at the intake.

Remember—much of the information in the handbook will become meaningful to parents only as time passes. They may initially be overwhelmed by the amount of information given them and need tolerance from staff while they learn the ropes. Frequently pulling important sections out of the handbook and including them in your newsletter helps to bring policies to life.

Sample Parent Handbook Statement on Parents' Roles, Rights, and Obligations

The Role of Parents

◆ Experts on and advocates for their own children.
◆ Advisors concerning policies, procedures, staff, and curriculum.
◆ Evaluators through polls and surveys.
◆ Promoters of the center.

Parents' Rights and Responsibilities

Rights:
◆ assurance that your beliefs, concerns, and values are sought out and respected and reflected in your child's care.
◆ information about all aspects of the program.
◆ information about all your child's experience in the program.
◆ freedom to visit or observe.
◆ freedom to ask questions of staff (at times when staff are able to respond without interrupting the program).
◆ confidence in the complete confidentiality of all matters involving the welfare of your child and family.

Responsibilities:
◆ knowledge of this handbook and acceptance of its policies and procedures.
◆ volunteering current important information (addresses, medical exams, etc.) and responding to staff's requests for information.
◆ daily review of your child's experience sheet and notes.
◆ exchange of essential information about the care of your child with staff.
◆ respect for staff as professionals who work with you to provide quality child care.

©1996 *Prime Times: A Handbook for Excellence in Infant and Toddler Care;* Redleaf Press, 450 North Syndicate, St. Paul, MN 55104. 800-423-8309.

Sample Parent Handbook Table of Contents

Sample Parent Handbook Table of Contents (continued)

Welcoming New Families

Once enrolled, each new family needs a relaxed and reassuring warm welcome. The first few weeks are critical in establishing a partnership between parents and staff, and staff must take the lead. While staff may sometimes feel intimidated by parents, and new staff may not feel totally confident about their own skills, it is important to remember that parents may be equally intimidated by staff and the newness of the situation.

The teacher or primary caregiver assumes responsibility for introducing the parents to all homebase staff, and homebase staff need to make an effort to put parents at ease. The primary caregiver should be assigned and all necessary preparations carried out before the child's arrival:

- ◆ Assign and label cubby, crib, or mat.
- ◆ Put a picture on the cubby.
- ◆ Make a welcome sign with child's and parents' first names.
- ◆ Post all information necessary to individualize the child's care.

The First Six Weeks Following the first day, each parent should receive a congratulations note from the primary caregiver (see the sample on page 280). In the first few weeks, the primary caregiver should make an extra effort to ask parents how things are going for them and their child. During the third or fourth week, the director should write a handwritten note asking the parents how things are going and extending an invitation to talk (see the sample note on page 280). At the end of six weeks, the primary caregiver should give the parents the six-week questionnaire, read the response, and pass on the form to the director (see the sample on page 281).

NOTE: For parents new to the homebase but not to the center, staff should follow the above procedure, omitting the congratulations note and the director's note.

....

First Day Note

Congratulations!

Your child made it through his/her first day and so did you! The first day is always the hardest. Separation and adjustment should get easier as time goes on.

I want to do what is necessary for your peace of mind. We are in this together, and a sense of partnership should develop between you and me. Don't hesitate to let me know about anything that may be bothering you about your child's care.

_____

Primary Caregiver

....

Director's Note

Dear_____

Just a note to let you know that if you have any concerns, questions, or suggestions, drop in or call me. We are delighted to have Bobby (and you) in the program.

_____

Director

....

Six-Week Questionnaire

Dear_____

Now that you have been in the program for over six weeks, please help us by letting us know how you are feeling about your experience in the program.

1) Do you feel that there is a partnership between you and your child's primary caregiver?

       not at all   very much
       1   2   3   4   5
       Comments:

2) How satisfied do you feel about the quality of your child's care at the present time?

       not at all   very much
       1   2   3   4   5
       Comments:

3) Do you have any questions or concerns?

4) How well do we provide YOU with information?

       not at all   very much
       1   2   3   4   5
       Comments:

5) How well do we listen and respond to your concerns:

       not at all   very much
       1   2   3   4   5
       Comments:

THANK YOU! We welcome any additional suggestions you may have with regard to any aspects of the program. Please return this to the office.

_____

Parent Signature

Maintaining Parent-Caregiver Partnerships through Good Communication

Partnerships are founded on communication. Effective communication is a result of using natural opportunities to communicate and understanding that everyone today is bombarded with information, much of which we ignore or quickly forget. Good centers communicate but don't overcommunicate; they try to understand the best ways to reach overloaded parents.

Daily and Weekly Homebase Communication

Daily Contacts   The core of the parent-caregiver relationship lies in the daily moments of arrival and departure. The partnership hinges on those few moments of interaction. Some hints for successful daily contacts, in addition to those in the discussion of arrivals and departures:

1. Greet *both* the parent and the child as they arrive.

2. If you are busy when a parent and child arrive, greet them and let them know that you will be with them as soon as you can.

3. Be sensitive to cues from the parent about whether or not they are in a hurry. If they look as if they are and there is nothing urgent to talk about, don't keep them.

4. Try to have the room set up in an inviting way so that there is something attractive to engage the child upon arrival. This helps the child make the transition from home to child care.

5. If the parent has a concern and you are very busy, explain this and agree upon a time to talk about it. Remember—you may use the telephone during slow times. If the arrival time for a parent who invariably wants to talk is always hectic, suggest that a slight change in arrival may allow you more time to talk.

6. Communicate a tone of openness. Displaying the menu and the daily program, letting parents know when students or other visitors will be present, informing them of staff changes—all of these communicate the message, "What happens here is your business, too."

7. Invite parents in and be ready for them. Encourage them to breast-feed, play with their child, or simply observe. Help them to feel comfortable.

Daily Experience Sheets   It is important that everyone who cares for a child has a sense of the child's experience, both at home and in the center. Staggered scheduling of staff makes daily experience sheets with written information on the child's experience at the center and at home a critical communications link. But note that these should only supplement lots of informal daily communication between caregivers and parents.

Besides transmitting information, the daily sheet (see page 284) assures parents that their child was well cared for and affirms the program's belief that parents should know about their child's day. A well-written note demonstrates that their child is noticed, well cared for, and appreciated for herself.

In writing daily slips, try to give an accurate sense of the child's day without either sugar coating it or making the parent feel terrible. Always look for something positive—information that will make parents feel happy about their child's experience or proud of their child. Parents will begin to question, however, if it appears that their child *always* has a good day.

If the child has had a bad day, phrase it in an understanding way that focuses on the child's struggle, not on the effects on staff or the other children. For example, "David had a hard time with limits today" is easier on the parent than "David constantly got into trouble." The more parents are informed and helped to know their child's experience, the more respect and support they will give to staff.

Writing daily notes is almost an art. If you need help on a sensitive issue, ask other staff to suggest wording.

Other Written Communication

◆ *Notice Boards and Signs:* Notice boards in the foyer, hallways, and homebase entrance are useful for communicating news, daily events, staff changes, holiday closing dates, visitors, and so on. Notice boards in each room placed strategically near children's cubbies can be used to post menus, daily or weekly programs, general reminders, news of special events such as children's or caregivers' birthdays, an announcement of someone taking her first step, or field trips.

◆ *Parent Mailboxes:* A number of devices are possible for use as parent mailboxes: clips or clipboards on a cubby, mail slots, or fabric pockets are all common. Whatever is used should be easily accessible for parents and staff. NOTE: Solicit parent feelings about which

Parents' Information

Child's Name: _____   Today's Date: _____

Where can we reach you today?   Usual? _____   Other? _____

How did child sleep?   ❑ Well   ❑ Longer than usual

                            ❑ Less than usual   ❑ Woke up in the night

Time child woke up?   Other information

Child's mood has been: _____

What time will child be picked up?   _____By whom? _____

Medication today? ❑ Yes   ❑ No. New bumps, injuries, or symptoms of illness? _____

_____

For parents of infants: Time and amount of last feeding?_____

Any special instructions or information? _____

_____

_____

Staff Information

Medication

❑ Yes   ❑ No

Time

_____

_____

Naps

_____

_____

Child's Mood

_____

_____

Outside

_____

_____

Guess what my day was like?

_____

_____

_____

Bottles	AM Snack	Solid Food-Lunch	PM Snack	Diapering
_____	_____	_____	_____	_____
_____	_____	_____	_____	_____
_____	_____	_____	_____	_____

©1996 *Prime Times: A Handbook for Excellence in Infant and Toddler Care*; Redleaf Press, 450 North Syndicate, St. Paul, MN 55104. 800-423-8309.

communications should be private, such as bill reminders or notes on their child.

◆ *Homebase Letters and Newsletters:* Periodic letters and informal newsletters supplement daily information. Mixing information about activities, tales of development, and parent news with the inevitable reminders of policies and homebase needs makes for a more readable result. A homebase newsletter can be a simple, one-page narrative of current events.

No Surprises: Delivering "Bad" News Nobody likes to communicate unpleasant information. This fact may lead us to avoidance or to inappropriate notes. Caregivers have to think through how best to communicate potentially distressing or complicated information. While a note has the advantage of giving the reader a chance to react in private, verbal communication is often gentler because words on paper have a way of seeming harsher. What approach to use depends on the complexity of the message, the time available, the skill of the caregiver, and knowledge of the parent. Often, a discussion backed up by a simple written note avoids miscommunication.

It is important to anticipate those instances where we would expect a parent to be upset. For instance, when a child has been bitten or injured, call the parents if possible so that they won't be surprised by the child's injury.

When parents find out about changes such as staffing or routines after the fact, particularly by observation, they may well be annoyed or anxious. Letting them know about changes as soon as possible acknowledges the partnership, and, in trying situations, does not add fuel to the fire.

Welcoming Parents into the Homebase through Photographs

Another way of welcoming parents and making their child's homebase their homebase, too, is using photographs of parents, siblings, and grandparents in the room on a regular basis. Pictures of all the members of the child's family in the locker area make it a family space as well as to introduce parents to other parents.

Sample Homebase Newsletter

From the Muffin Room

What a great month we had. We saw the weather change from windy and cool to pretty hot. The first hot spell in many of our lives. We love being out on the grass, picking dandelions. Strolling along in our strollers and toddling along while watching butterflies are two of our favorite things. Swinging outside and putting our feet in the water puddles keep us giggling. We also like bringing out pillows, lawn blankets, sun umbrellas, and wagons.

As we move outside, we are entering the wet and messy season and appreciate the extra clothes you bring. Let us know about any concerns you have about sun and sunscreen.

We welcomed Jonathan and Celina, and said sad good-byes to Alex, Tara, and Barbara. Alex and Tara moved up to the Dandelions, and Barbara moved to a new house with her mom and dad because Ruth got a great new job. Congratulations, Ruth!

Some of the amazing things we love to do these days:

◆ Jackie: Picks up everything he can with his thumb and finger and smiles, waiting for us to stop him before it reaches his mouth.
◆ Jonathan: Loves to be on Betsy's lap and read books.
◆ Kim Lee: Claps and hums and opens up every box she can find.
◆ Celina: Tries really hard to keep that food on her spoon as it heads for her mouth.
◆ Alex: Climbs up the ladder, climbs up the couch, climbs up nearly everything.
◆ Sara: Loves looking around, blowing bubbles, testing her voice for Sally.
◆ Kemal: Collects all the blocks and gives them away, then does it again.

Many thanks to Steven (Celina's dad) for fixing the wagon, and Shirley (Sara's mom) for sewing the pillows. Thank you all for taking the time to chat in the morning and evenings.

"Random Kindness and Senseless Generosity"   Nothing communicates caring and goodwill so much as unexpected acts of kindness and generosity, such as a card on the parent's birthday, an unexpected, appreciative note, an offer of tea, coffee, or a breakfast roll, perhaps a photograph of their child, or marking the anniversary of the family's time in the center. Offer a needed ride to the repair shop or home on a rainy day. If the program seeks out ways to make families happy, the resulting parent-staff relationships should weather nearly any storm.

Parents Communicating Sensitive Concerns   Parents may not always feel comfortable expressing a concern to their primary caregiver or teachers in the room. Instead, they may choose to use the lead teacher or the center director. Channels of communication should be as flexible and open as possible, as long as staff share information with appropriate other staff and respect parents' confidentiality. Such sharing can be very threatening to both parents and staff members.

Staff Expressing Sensitive Concerns to Parents   Lead teachers and in most cases, the director should be involved prior to discussing any concerns that caregivers may have about either child or parent behavior with parents. It is important that staff concerns and expectations are expressed clearly and consistently with the center's philosophy and policies. Concerns about child abuse and neglect should be consistent with reporting policies established by the state. Some states forbid notifying parents of a report prior to its being investigated.

Parent Conferences

Parents should be encouraged to request a conference with the caregiver at any time. In addition, staff should invite parents to a conference at least twice during the year and during the period the child is making the transition to a new group.

It is important that the conference be truly a discussion—a mutual exchange of information, ideas, and concerns, not just a reporting by staff to parents. The tone of the conference should be friendly, relaxed, and informal, with staff communicating fondness for the child and respect for the parents.

The Content of the Conference   Parent-staff conferences are a time to discuss the child's experience in the program. It is time to share information, deepen the relationship between parents and staff, discuss concerns that parents or staff may have, and most of all, a time to appreciate the child. It is also an occasion to recognize the efforts of both parents and staff on behalf of the child. It is important that a conference not become a progress report or primarily a developmental assessment for a number of reasons:

◆ Development *is not* a race. Children do not benefit from achieving developmental milestones at the earliest opportunity.

◆ Development *is not* simply a matter of amassing experiences. Children do not benefit from being pushed to experience more and more.

◆ Caregivers are rarely trained to assess children developmentally and see children in only one setting. The educational goals of a high-quality child development center are not to speed up development but to accomplish other goals:

  ◆ to provide a relaxed, fun, and secure caring and learning environment for each child.

  ◆ to broaden and deepen a child's experience by providing opportunities for new experiences to challenge the child and familiar experience, to master challenges in all areas of development:

     motor

     cognitive

     perceptual

     social

     emotional

     language

     expressive capabilities.

  ◆ to promote a sense of positive self-esteem and self-confidence as a competent and capable active learner and as a member of a family and community.

  ◆ to promote those understandings, dispositions, and skills that lead to success in future schooling.

The conference report form on pages 290–291 is designed to incorporate your thoughts as well as those of the parents and to summarize what you have discussed. You do not have to write down everything you discussed. After the conference, make a copy and give one to the parents.

Goals of the Conference   The goals for the conference should be:

1. For the parent to feel positive about the child and the child's experience in the program.

2. For the parent to feel informed about the child's experience.

3. For the parent to understand why we do things the way we do, and the cooperation we need from them.

4. For us to understand and appreciate the parents' ideas, feelings, and way of doing things.

5. To identify any questions or concerns that parents or program staff may have about possible or necessary changes in routines or practices.

6. To strengthen the relationship and generate good feelings between parents and staff.

Approaching the Conference   Parent/staff conferences can produce anxiety in both parents and staff. The tension is usually there because we all care about the child and worry that we will be in some way judged or found wanting for our piece of the child's experience. Also, parents (and staff) may not know what to expect. In almost every case, if we can relax, conferences can be times of mutual affirmation, respect, and sharing about the child. It will help you to relax if you are prepared for what you will say. It will help the parents if they are sent the conference report form ahead of time as an outline of discussion points.

Preparing What You Will Say   Remember that this is not a report on the child's *behavior* but a discussion of the child's *experience* in a group setting. A child who is having a difficult time may be behaving in a way that is a problem for the staff and the child in the center setting, but the child may be fine developmentally. Adjusting to group, routines, separation, and environment often has nothing to do with the child's normal development. Helping the child may depend on the caregiver's capacity to provide a setting that works for the particular child:

◆ Make it clear that this is a discussion, not a report.
◆ Be positive: look for the strengths and endearing qualities in the child.
◆ Be clear.
◆ Summarize.
◆ Be prepared with specific examples: behavior, situations, feelings.
◆ Be honest about concerns or questions, but recognize sensitivities.
◆ If you have any questions about how to approach a parent about a sensitive issue, discuss it with a supervisor.
◆ Don't be judgmental: report on problems or concerns without judging the child, parents, or program.
◆ *Listen*: you want to know what parents think and feel.

Getting Off to a Good Start   Put the parent at ease by offering coffee or juice. Say something right away that shows that you enjoy the child and respect the parents. Explain the purpose of the conference and stress that you want them to have the chance to discuss what is on their minds.

Parent/Staff Conference Report Form

CHILD_____ PARENT(S)_____

TEACHER _____ DATE_____

Use this form to summarize what was discussed at the parent staff conference. Unless parents or staff feel that complete and precise wording is necessary, feel free to make lists and to use phrases to provide a brief record. Make a copy for the parent, the child's file, and your supervisor.

I. Introduction

A parent/staff conference is a time to discuss the child's experience in the program. It is time to share information, develop a relationship between parents and staff, discuss concerns that parents or staff may have, and most of all, a time to appreciate the child. This form is not a progress report because

◆ Development *is not* a race. Children do not benefit from achieving developmental milestones at the earliest opportunity.

◆ Development *is not* simply amassing experiences. Children do not benefit from being pushed to experience more and more.

We believe that a high-quality child development center has several goals:

◆ to provide a relaxed, fun, and secure caring and learning environment for each child.

◆ to broaden and deepen a child's experience by providing opportunities for new experiences that challenge the child and familiar experiences that the child can master in all areas of development: motor, cognitive, perceptual, social, emotional, language, and expressive capabilities.

◆ to promote a sense of positive self-esteem and self-confidence as a competent, capable, active learner and member of a family and community.

◆ to promote those understandings, dispositions, and skills that lead to success in future schooling.

II. The Child's Daily Experience

1. Daily Life: Sense of Security and Happy Days
   Topics: separation, schedule/pacing.

2. The Child's Social Experience
   Topics: sense of independence, relationship with adults and children.

©1996 *Prime Times: A Handbook for Excellence in Infant and Toddler Care*; Redleaf Press, 450 North Syndicate, St. Paul, MN 55104. 800-423-8309.

3. Program Participation and Learning
   Topics: favorite activities and interests, exploration and learning style, participation in activities and use of materials, problem solving skills.

4. Socialization and Self-Control
   Topics: emerging self-control, frustrating situations for the child, response to frustration and coping styles, program/parent efforts to help child.

5. Special Strengths
   Topics: individual skills, personality factors.

6. Parent(s)/Staff Questions or Concerns

7. Follow-up Goals or Concerns from Previous Conferences

III.   Parents' Experience in the Program

1. General Experience Between Parent(s) and Staff Pleasant and Respectful

2. Good Information Flow Back and Forth Between Staff and Parent(s)

3. Parent(s) and Staff are Responsive to the Requests and Concerns of Each Other?

IV. Parent/Caregiver Goals To Improve The Child And Parent Experience In The Program

1. Child-Related Goals

2. Parent-Related Goals

©1996 *Prime Times: A Handbook for Excellence in Infant and Toddler Care*; Redleaf Press, 450 North Syndicate, St. Paul, MN 55104. 800-423-8309.

Transitioning Children (and Parents) to the Next Age Group

Sooner or later, children move on to the next age group. For some children and parents (and some attached primary caregivers), this is a time of anxiety. For others, it is a time that has been eagerly anticipated, and there are few tearful looks back.

Successful transitions depend on good planning and on recognizing and understanding the perspective of children and parents. Some things to keep in mind:

◆ children cannot move up until there is a space in the next group. Sometimes children get "stuck" in a group waiting for an opening, and sometimes children get moved up a little earlier than expected to take advantage of an opening. Because of this, it is important to make sure the group works for children at both ends of the age spectrum.

◆ care must be taken to avoid giving the impression that there is something competitive about moving up, that it is like graduation or some indication that the child has superior skills and abilities.

◆ most children need more than a few days of visiting to feel comfortable. Preparing for transitions is an ongoing process that begins a long time before the actual move.

Ongoing Relationships Between Rooms   Ideally, even in large centers there is sense of community and relationship between different age groups and different rooms. A child in an infant room will come to know the toddler staff and the toddler rooms through visiting, shared activities, and common space. The same is true of toddlers and preschoolers. Through the newsletter and other communication, parents will come to know about the people and aspects of life that their children will soon enough become a part of.

The Ready List   Once a child is ready to move, whether or not space is available, perhaps a few months before a move is anticipated, staff in the two rooms or modules should make a concerted effort to begin the transition. This involves visiting, along with the primary caregiver, sharing activities, and other efforts to gradually familiarize the child with the new room. At the same time, parents should be made aware of the approaching transition and be given information on the child's soon to be new homebase. Care must be taken to avoid giving the impression that there is something competitive about moving up, that is, that it is like graduation or some indication that the child has superior skills and abilities. (This can't be stressed enough!)

The Last Few Weeks   When a moving date is known, the current primary caregiver and the newly assigned primary caregiver should get together and map out a plan for daily visits to the new group and make sure that parents have all the information necessary to feel secure about the move. Each child's and parent's needs will be different.

The New Group The first week in the new room should follow the routine for the first week of any new child and family: picture on the cubby, welcome sign, first day note to parents, and a reassuring phone call if necessary. It is also important for many children to keep in contact with the old room. "Cold turkey" transitions are not a good idea.

Parent Involvement

Parent involvement is a catchall term that covers everything from real governance to attending a homebase brunch. Ideally, there are a range of opportunities to allow parents to match their involvement to their time and interests.

Parent Advisory Committees No matter what the formal governance structure—public or private owner, corporation, university or social service—some parent advisory structure is important. Why? Because parents are the experts on their own children and involving the consumers of child care will help ensure better care. It also brings parents into the center, and their ownership can lead to support on a number of levels.

Participation in the management of the center may be one option for parents wanting to be involved. While it suits some center managers, boards of directors, and some parents, it should not be viewed as the best or most effective vehicle for parent involvement. If parents are involved in managing the center, it is important that they see themselves as representing other parents as well. There should be mechanisms for canvassing other parents' views and for sharing information between parents and management. Keep in mind that parent participation in management of a center, even management by parents alone, should not necessarily be equated with the idea of partnership discussed earlier.

The Structure of Parent Advisory Committees There is no right way. Unless there is a formal function of governing, elections are usually not necessary and an open system of seeking volunteers and achieving a balance by room and/or age group of children is probably most desirable. Little is gained by limiting the number. A very effective structure is a "parent rep" system. This is a system that assumes parent reps will contact their "constituents" (parents in the same room, etc.) prior to the meeting and solicit concerns, ideas, and appreciations is an effective structure. All parents should be invited to participate in meetings and on committees and task forces. Parent rep meeting minutes serve as vehicles for airing issues, explaining policies, and circulating parents' appreciation of center staff.

Parent Rep Meetings Six to ten times a year, parents representing each homebase get together with representatives of the administration, board of directors (or sponsor), and any interested parents to discuss how things are going and to plan any desired special events or activities. The topics discussed stem from the information collected by parent reps, the director, or others.

Soliciting Information   Parent reps volunteer for about a year. They join with one or more other parents from their child's room to call other parents from the room both to see how things are going and to respond to any specific topics that have been identified by the Director or anyone else. Topics include everything except those that require confidentiality regarding a particular child, parent, or staff person. For example:

◆ *Questions*: "How do you determine when children move up?" "How are parent fees established?" "Why do children have to go out in cold weather?" "Why does it take so long to fill a teaching vacancy?"

◆ *Suggestions or Ideas*: "We'd like the toddlers to go on field trips." "What about extending the hours to 7:00 P.M.?" "Why don't we utilize the multipurpose space differently?" "What about more ethnic meals?" "I'd like to see more language activities in the preschool."

◆ *Concerns or Complaints*: "The bathrooms don't seem very clean." "I worry about the supervision on field trips." "Will my child be ready for first grade?" "Why can't I get my new baby in?" "Is there enough training of teachers?" "Are the staff/child ratios sufficient?" "My child has a handicap. How do I know she will receive the experiences that she needs?" "Why is there so much biting among toddlers?"

◆ *Compliments and Appreciation*: "The toddler staff are really doing a wonderful job." "The new substitutes seem much better trained." "There has been a lot of improvement in the variety of meals." "I think Carrie did a great job helping Addie get through her first few days in the infant room."

Ensuring Positive and Productive Meetings   When there is a commitment to honest discussion and problem solving, parent meetings are positive. There has to be an acceptance that there will always be real issues and concerns and honest questioning of policies and decisions. At the parent meeting, individual concerns become the starting point for discussions of policies and practices. Commitments should be to working through "Why we do things the way we do" and to meeting the needs and interests of parents—a "Why not?" attitude. There should be open recognition that the right thing to do is not always clear or immediately possible and that "We are all in this together," each representing a legitimate perspective.

It is also important to make sure that meetings don't focus on those issues much better handled by individual communications between parents and caregivers or lead teachers and that they don't become discussions of individual performance.

Excerpts from Parent Rep Meeting Minutes

Toddlers: Concerns, Ideas, Suggestions

A parent was concerned about how hectic it was at pickup time and felt she never had time to talk to her child's primary caregiver. A second parent always felt that it was a hassle ending the day on a relaxed note.

Response: It has been hectic lately, and we are brainstorming alternatives. Sometimes by adjusting your arrival and departure times by a few minutes you can avoid a traffic crunch. We are working on tinkering with the environment and late afternoon activities to make the transition more relaxed and to free up staff. Remember—if you want more communication, feel free to call or ask for a phone call mini-conference (or a longer conference).

Two parents felt that transitions from infant to toddler rooms was not as smooth as it could be.

Response: We agree. Unfortunately, "the best laid plans," etc. We had it all worked out and then had to shuffle because of staff illnesses and the change in plans of two families. We will try and learn from this and work out some contingency plans.

A parent didn't understand why we let "sick" children stay. Her child would then get sick.

Response: As we explain in the Parent Handbook, our exclusion policies are based on the American Academy of Pediatrics *Model Health Policies*. It is important to understand that the spread of infection from the illnesses that we are experiencing now (colds mostly) occurs *before* a child shows and symptoms. Excluding any child with a cold who can participate in the program does nothing to reduce the spread of infection. There is a copy of the *Model Health Policies* in each room.

Appreciations

Jenny does a terrific job helping me with Byron's clingy behavior. I was sorry to see Georgia move to the preschool but think Talia is a great addition.

Thanks for the great daily experience sheets.

Parent Evaluations and Parent Polling

Parent evaluations can take the form of annual comprehensive evaluations or smaller, more specific polls. For instance, you may poll parents on the food program, field trips, enrichment activities, and the outdoor policies. Polling and evaluation do three things:

◆ provide useful input.

◆ invest parents in particular issues.

◆ educate parents about issues and policies.

One useful polling structure is a weekly minipoll: one questions that takes under a minute to answer. Some examples:

◆ Are you satisfied with the new breakfast menu?
◆ What's the best thing you have observed this week at the center?

Center Newsletters

A newsletter can be an effective medium for presenting more extensive information on the center's operation, elaboration of philosophy and policies, aspects of the program, and the broader context of child care. A simple newsletter can involve contributions from parents. Perhaps parents can even take responsibility for it.

Parent Events, Large and Small

Centers vary in their ability and desire to create a sense of community and belonging. When planning parent events, remember:

◆ Consider the parents' perspective. Parents are busy and may have little spare time for events. Evening programs are difficult for parents because they conflict with their desire to be good parents and to get their children into bed. For that reason, some centers structure events during mealtimes, so the parents and children can stay at the center rather than have to leave and come back.

◆ Plan a mix of events and don't expect all parents to attend. A homebase tea, a centerwide barbecue, a wine and cheese party, and a holiday program are all good things to do. So arc parent work days, fund-raising events, and parent-child activities. Parents who choose not to attend should not be perceived as problematic or less valued.

Parent Education

Parents often are interested in sessions that give them a chance to learn more about child development and child rearing. The most effective sessions are informal discussions that allow parents to discuss their concerns with "experts" and other parents.

A resource library with books, magazines, pamphlets, and videos is useful.

Parent Donations and Contributions of Time or Skills

Encouraging parent donations and contributions allows parents to feel they are a part of the center and creates a community feeling, as well as producing valuable resources. However, if the practice results in a forced sense of obligation toward or judgment of parents, it may not be worthwhile.

A Final Word: Common Sense and Respect

Good relationships with parents grow out of common sense and thinking through the realities of child care. When we respect parents, focus on their perspective, and sensitively share our own, and think creatively about how to overcome the real challenge of busy people trying to work together, parents become allies and their children benefit.

EXERCISES

1. Come up with a description of an ideal child care situation from staff's perspective. Then do one from the parents' perspective. Compare the two lists.

2. Make a list of those decisions that are granted to

> caregivers
> joint negotiations
> parents

What are major obstacles to partnership in your center? What can do you do?

3. Ask parents when and where they feel most comfortable and most awkward in the center.

REFERENCE

Warren, R. *Caring: Supporting Children's Growth.* Washington, DC: NAEYC, 1977.

Chapter 15
Good Places for Staff

excellence

Staff genuinely enjoy and appreciate the children they work with and feel secure, valued, and respected as professionals. Roles and responsibilities are clear and understood. Teamwork and collegiality are valued and supported. Staff are supported through good supervision, a supportive work environment, and opportunities for professional development.

Introduction

Quality rarely happens unless the center is a good place to work. In the words of an experienced teacher:

> "I have worked in three programs in the last ten years. All had pretty good people but only one was a great place to work. The center, not just the director, just seemed to care about staff—personnel policies, the way staff people treated each other, respect from parents, the staff room (even if it was almost a closet), all made a difference. They expected a lot from us but they were always up front and listened. I think the kids got better care because of it."

She went on to say,

> "Of course, part of being a good place to work was the pay and benefits. It was the real world of child care, so none of the centers paid all that well. But the center I liked clearly was doing all it could to improve salaries and benefits: educating parents about the need for better salaries, looking for more funding, and involving us in some of the decisions that had a budget impact, like whether to switch toddler ratios from one to four to one to five."

Good People for Infants and Toddlers: Staffing the Program

Good programs know how to recruit, support, and keep good people and how to help them become an effective team. As discussed in chapter 3, the organization and culture of the center shape the quality of staff efforts.

Who Are "Good" People? General Qualities of Staff

All sorts of people work effectively in child care, so there is always a risk in defining necessary qualities. Nobody is perfect. However, as a guide to selecting staff, consider these characteristics:

- *Good physical and mental health*: group child care is demanding and children arrive with lots of needs and germs.
- *Sense of humor*: sometimes laughing is the only way to cope.
- *Openness to new ideas and willingness to learn*: There is never a settled "right way" to do things that applies to all children, parents, and coworkers. Quality is a product of thinking and rethinking.
- *Enough self-confidence to be flexible and accept and offer suggestions and criticism*: defensiveness blocks professional and program growth.
- *A maturity that accepts the fact that many days are much the same and the ability to get excited about little things and appreciate small accomplishments*: daily life at child care centers can easily become a rut unless caregivers possess a mature perspective. Like children, they have to find joy in all the small victories and wonders of ordinary life.
- *The ability to function under pressure, to be calm amidst periodic tumult:* faced with crying children, upset parents, substitutes, dirty diapers, and "Jackie ate all the paste," the caregiver has to be an island of calm.
- *The ability and willingness to work with other staff and parents*: adult relations are as important as child relations, so empathy, respect for differences, tolerance, and tact are important.

Qualities Necessary for Working Effectively with Infants and Toddlers

Working with children under three years old is demanding on staff physically and emotionally. In addition, caregivers are faced with outdated attitudes that put them at the bottom of the educational ladder: "What does an infant/toddler teacher *teach*, really? Isn't it just caring for them?" In other words, 80 percent lap, 20 percent brain. In truth, finding good caregivers for infants and toddlers is often more difficult than for older age groups. A good infant/toddler caregiver

- *Likes and respects infants and toddlers and enjoys their company*: appreciates all that they can do now, (e.g., make all sorts of sounds), not just what they will be able to do in the future (first words). Sensitive caregivers appreciate the significance of a shaky baby's reach for a toy, a fifteen month old patting a distressed child gently on the hand, a baby stacking two blocks together or drinking successfully from a cup.
- *Knows about babies and early development*: understands where babies are and where they are heading.

♦ *Can adapt to infant/toddler time:* accepts the fact that the world of infants and toddlers can be very slow, coupled with moments requiring a lot of effort in a short time.

♦ *Is interested in getting to know* each *baby:* every baby must be prized.

♦ *Has the empathy and ability to see the world through the baby's eyes:* retains compassion for separation, teething times, dubious assertions of "No" and "I can do it myself," and all the other times young children are struggling with life.

♦ *Is warm and affectionate:* expresses affection in a manner appropriate for each baby.

♦ *Is creative in play with infants and toddlers:* has the ability to help children explore what the world has to offer and understands *the power of small changes* to keep children interested.

Roles and Responsibilities

Confusion over roles and responsibilities is often a source of tension. "I'm an assistant teacher, Michael is a teacher, and Carol is a lead teacher. We really work like a team here. We share all the work; I help with planning. I have nearly the same qualifications. It bothers me that we have different titles and salaries."

Differences in Roles and Responsibilities

A child care homebase is a complex work and social setting. For it to operate smoothly, all staff must have a deep appreciation of the need for teamwork and be willing to help each other out. There are overlapping responsibilities, even between an experienced, highly qualified staff person and an inexperienced worker with no formal qualifications. Everyone usually changes diapers, interacts with the children, helps set up and clean up, and talks to parents. Often there are only slight variations between staff qualifications. But in two important ways, staff are not equal:

♦ *Authority and Supervision:* the responsibility for the room and the performance of the staff team is invested in the lead or head teacher role and entrusted to the individual with the experience and expertise in leadership and supervision.

♦ *Curriculum Planning:* although everyone contributes, the person who plans the environment and curriculum and determines the child's educational experience should be both the most expert and the most responsible—the lead teacher.

Titles and salaries reflect levels of responsibility. Leadership assumes responsibility for the work of others and for the experience of children and parents, even when the leader is not present. The director is held accountable for the center at all times. If everything collapses when she is on vacation, the director is usually accountable and has to answer questions of poor planning or delegation. This applies also to the lead teacher and the room or rooms she supervises, or to the teacher in charge in the absence of the lead teacher.

Lead Teacher   *Responsible for providing a warm, nurturing, and educational environment that meets the needs of each child. Supervises staff and assigns primary caregivers, performs all necessary administrative tasks as delegated, oversees the development and implementation of daily curriculum, and teams with the director to develop program goals. Works closely with parents to ensure that each child's needs are met and parents are satisfied with the program.*

The lead teacher is in charge of one or more rooms (a useful distinction is to use the term *head teacher* if there is only one room to supervise). Much like the center director role's vis à vis the center as a whole, the lead teacher is a team leader and responsible for making sure all the necessary work gets done through her own efforts and by motivating, supervising, and delegating to his or her staff.

Qualifications   The lead teacher has to be an effective leader and curriculum planner, not necessarily the most accomplished teacher in the unit. What prior experience, training, and credentials can be expected varies depends on the available talent pool. But regardless of experience and training, lead teachers require the following:

◆ *Sharing the Program Vision:*
   a wonderful place to be a child
   individualized, personalized care
   individualized learning environments
   parent empowerment

◆ *Professionalism*: the ability to accept responsibility and to commit to a standard of performance that sets an example and earns the respect of others.

◆ *Leadership*: the ability to inspire others through knowledge, expertise, and efforts in order to maximize the talents, skills, and efforts of the staff.

◆ *Supervision*: the willingness and ability to supervise staff. Good supervision involves communicating clear expectations, providing encouragement and support, delegating responsibilities appropriately, and addressing issues of unsatisfactory performance. Good supervisors are able to deal directly and fairly with sensitive issues.

◆ *Works Well with Adults*: lead teachers create quality experiences for children and parents through their work with the teachers they supervise, not just through what they do directly with children and parents.

◆ *Initiative*: the ability and desire to make things happen, solve problems, uncover and raise problematic issues, and come up with new ideas.

◆ *Home Base Planning Skills*: the knowledge and expertise to plan a high-quality learning/caring environment that offers individualized, personalized learning and caring.

◆ *Respect for Children, Parents, and Other Staff*: the ability to put oneself in the place of others of others, understand their values, ideas, and perspectives, and behave respectfully at all times.

Teachers and Associate Teachers *Teams with the lead teacher to provide a warm, nurturing, and educational environment that meets the needs of each child. Assists in planning and implementing the daily curriculum and assumes responsibility for the group in the lead teacher's absence. Works closely with parents to ensure that each child's needs are met and parents are satisfied with the program.*

Good teachers also share the program vision, perform professionally, enjoy working with adults, show initiative, plan caring and learning environments, and respect and understand the perspective of others. They may also be required to supervise substitutes and assistant teachers.

Teamwork

The highest-quality care is produced by teamwork in which the strengths and talents of all staff are developed and fully utilized. Tasks are assigned based on interest and talent, not locked into roles. For example, organizing and ordering supplies may be assigned to Russ, who is organized to the point of obsession. Selina, a new teacher, may take responsibility for redoing the housekeeping corner, while Nadjia volunteers to look after children's files.

Participatory Decision Making Participatory decision making generally produces better decisions and empowers staff. With power come ownership and responsibility. The key to participatory decision making is that it takes place in a context whose underlying program philosophy, principles, and objectives are clear and shared. Adequate time is made available for discussion.

A staff rep system similar to the parent rep system is a useful structure for involving all staff in decisions and keeping them aware of policies and issues. It offers chances to ask "Why?" and to voice concerns, make suggestions and observations, and express appreciations. With the ability to influence decisions come responsibility and the need to take into account the wider perspective of parents, the center as a whole, and budget realities that otherwise only directors have to worry about.

Recruiting and Selecting Good Staff

Finding and keeping good staff is not easy in an industry that is relatively low paying and has a limited career ladder. Well-trained and experienced infant and toddler staff, particularly those in leadership roles, are perhaps the rarest commodity. Because young women have increasing choices in the workplace and there are still relatively few men entering the field, competition for good people will probably increase. To compete, centers will have to become good places to work and hire well.

Understanding Your Talent Pool

A talent pool is the population you draw your staff from—all the people who might want to work for you. It is defined by a number of factors:

- salary and benefits
- location
- your official qualifications for employees: experience, credentials
- unofficial (sometimes unconscious, sometimes unfortunate) criteria: age, gender, race, personality factors
- your definition of the job

Some centers consciously limit the talent pool to the college educated, but in the selection process they actually become more selective; for example, they always end up with white women between the ages of twenty and fifty. This is usually not deliberate so much as it is a limited vision of who is "best" at the job. Such decisions mirror the staff's own characteristics—their language, style, values, and general way of being. Candidates may self-select themselves out because the center doesn't feel like a compatible place to work. Out of a concern for both diversity and the need to increase the number of potential applicants, those in a position to influence decisions should ask themselves:

- What training or credentials are actually required for the performance of the job?
- Is this a good place to work for an elderly person, a man, a minority group member—is it accepting of differences in interest, physical abilities, personal style?
- Is our definition of "good" caregiving too narrow (too white, female, based around matters of style, preference, and familiarity)?

Who Are "Good People"?

Ida was eighty-nine years old and still working at the day care. To everyone, she was Grandma Ida. She worked her fifteen hours a week for $5 an hour and was by and large beloved. The average age of the rest of the staff was twenty-four. Ida was a good worker, but not surprisingly, she was occasionally old fashioned, not always politically correct ("You sure are all boy, and ornery today, too"), and occasionally crotchety. But she never was offensive or harmful or more than an occasional pain in the neck. When a coworker (age twenty-two) complained to the director (age twenty-five) that Grandma Ida was more trouble than she was worth, the director asked the teacher to think about the worth of a grandmother figure to children largely cared for by young women.

Staff Recruitment

Do all prospective employees know about your center? In most cases, the answer is no. Why do they want to work for you? How do those who do find out learn about openings? Usually the answer to both questions is word of mouth, advertising, and working with local training institutions and colleges. Word of mouth is often neglected when a center is having problems finding staff. Actively solicit current and past staff and parents to spread the word.

Broadening your talent pool often means rethinking how you recruit staff. To attract people from different ethnic backgrounds than you currently employ, you may have to advertise in different locations, seek out employment counselors and training programs, and find the community networking agencies that can advise you on recruiting.

Wages and Benefits

Compensation for child care staff is typically very low. Caring for children has never been valued economically, and historically child care providers have been at the bottom of the ladder, competing with the "free" care provided in families. The educator function of the child care teacher has been perceived as only slightly more valuable than other aspects of the job.

Because almost all centers are supported primarily by fees paid by parents or parent-subsidy dollars, improving the picture is complex. Even with the minimal compensation for staff, child care is a major expense for most families, typically $4,000–$10,000 a year. Changing the status quo will requires major financial support from society, either public dollars or support from employers.

What a center can do on its own is to carefully develop its budget to maximize revenue and to provide the best and fairest compensation plan possible. Providing benefits and annual salary increases to all full-time staff should be a basic fact of life. Centers have to acquire the business skills necessary to plan for possible eventualities rather than merely to react to events.

Selecting Staff

There is no one right way to hire, but there are lots of wrong ways. A good process for caregivers usually includes an initial assessment of the "paper" person presented through a résumé, application, and references; interviews with the director and others, including parents; and some observation of the applicant with children and parents. Involving a number of people is good not only in order to obtain a number of viewpoints but also as a way to invest those participants in the success of the new employee.

How much influence should parents and staff in the room have on the selection? This is a complicated question and depends on the circumstances. Two factors lead to seeking a broader staff and parent input and to not investing the people in a particular room with too much power. Generally, it is useful to assume that you are hiring an employee for the center, not for a particular room because he or she may end up elsewhere eventually. Second, the room may need someone the team wouldn't ordinarily choose—to bring in new ideas, skills, or a different perspective or background.

Selecting the best person available requires a clear sense of what the best might be at that time and involves understanding the what and why of what you are looking for. Educational planning ability, knowledge of a particular culture (e.g., Vietnamese), maturity, energy, parent relationship skills, and so on may be particular needs. Efforts to diversify the staff often fall down because of a limited vision of who can do the job. Our visions are usually filtered through our own biases and our often limited experience with other cultures or experience with disabilities or other individual differences. Visualizing who good people might be in the broadest sense helps to encourage inclusiveness.

Interviewing

Interviews are the time to discover what a person thinks and if her or his values, and philosophy are compatible with the program's. Also, it is important to find out what kind of person he or she is— does he have a sense of humor, does she listen, is he thoughtful? The more relaxed the interview, the more likely you will find out about the real person in front of you. Generally, interviews with more than one interviewer and fewer than five or six are best, with questions scripted in advance. Some useful questions:

Why do you want to work with babies? What do you find exciting about an eight month old (eighteen month old, etc.)?

What is your vision of quality care?

Apply that vision to the question of feeding, toilet training, and coping with biting.

If you were a parent thinking about child care, what would you worry about?

Describe what you see as your relationship to parents in the program.

Describe a difficult situation with parents and how you did (or would) handle it.

Respect for diversity is a talked-about issue. What does that mean to you as a caregiver to children and families and as a coworker?

Tell us about when you had to change your thinking or behavior based on new learning.

What are you excited about learning in the next few years?

Describe yourself as a coworker and what is important to you as a team member.

Choosing the Right Person

When filling a specific position, recognize that you are hiring for the program, not the room, and look to the future. Will this person be able to work with other teams, other age groups, and possibly grow into a leadership role? A new staff member should complement the qualities and strengths of others.

Sometimes an applicant stands out and there is no doubt what an asset to the program she (or he) will be. We only hope that she will take the job. More usually, there are questions about the individual, and the center has to look closely at the candidate's shortcomings. When this happens, keep in mind:

- some personal qualities are subject to change, such as knowledge of child development, appropriate activities, and caregiving practices or language skills. If the center has the time and access to resources and the individual is willing and able to learn, taking a chance in these area offers pretty good odds.
- some important character traits or strongly ingrained beliefs or values are unlikely to change. One's flexibility in thinking and behavior, ability as a team member, and strong beliefs about or attitudes toward parents or children are unlikely to be subject to change.
- the capacity for leadership and supervision is essential in a lead teacher or director. It can be "grown" and often has to be; many applicants will have never had the opportunity to test that side of themselves. But the seed has to be there: the confidence to lead others, the strength to make unpopular decisions, and the ability to adopt a broader perspective.

Supporting Quality Staff

The adult work environment plays a major role in influencing the quality of care for children. It affects the morale, motivation and growth of staff, as well as their level of professionalism. Caregivers cannot focus on meeting the needs of children when their own needs are not being met. Bloom (1988) lists and defines the principal organizational dimensions that contribute to a positive work environment:

- *Collegiality:* extent to which staff are friendly, supportive, and trusting of one another. Measures the peer cohesion of employees and the esprit de corps of the group as a whole.
- *Professional Growth:* degree of emphasis placed on personal and professional growth.
- *Supervisory Support:* strength of facilitative leadership that provides encouragement, support, and clear expectations.
- *Clarity*: extent to which policies, procedures, and responsibilities are clearly defined and communicated.
- *Reward System:* degree of fairness and equity in the distribution of pay, fringe benefits, and opportunities for advancement.
- *Decision Making*: amount of autonomy given to staff and the extent to which they are involved in centerwide decisions.

♦ *Goal consensus:* degree to which staff agree on the goals and objectives of the center.

♦ *Task orientation:* emphasis placed on good planning, efficiency, and getting the job done.

♦ *Physical setting:* extent to which the spatial arrangement of the center helps or hinders staff in carrying out their responsibilities.

♦ *Innovativeness:* extent to which the organization adapts to challenge and encourages staff to find creative ways to solve problem.

Supportive Work Space

Caregivers are more productive in work settings that support all aspects of their performance, including their thinking roles: team member, creator, planner, evaluator, and communicator. A staff room with teacher workspace, a conference room space for meetings and conferences, and a teacher nook or desk in the room with a telephone and ample storage are important. How is confidentiality possible without a private space for a conference? How can creativity flourish without storage?

Supervision

Good supervision is a fundamental element in quality. The fundamentals of good supervision are clear expectations of the employee, maximizing the employee's talent, ongoing evaluation, and follow-through with support.

Orientation and Training of New Staff

Orientation is the first step in establishing clear expectations. It is both a short and a long-term process. There is a temptation to pack everything the new staff person needs to know into the first few days of work, thereby creating overload that may prevent absorbing much information at all. A better strategy is to have a list of everything a new employee needs to know and then prioritize the items on the list, identifying those things that need to be learned at the beginning and those that can wait. The more information available in writing the better—job description, program handbooks, and policies and procedures. Written material still has to be supplemented with discussion with supervisors, however. (See samples on pages 309–312.)

Follow-Up with New Staff

Much of what has to be learned will be learned on the job. A program culture that encourages new staff to feel that they are free to ask questions, even seemingly simple or obvious ones is important. The director and homebase staff should continually communicate that they know that there is a lot to absorb and that questions are expected and welcomed. Having information to read or videos to watch, followed up by discussion, is an effective way to present information to new staff.

A Note to Parents and Staff: Living with Diversity

Diversity is essential to our program. We believe strongly in having a multiage, multicultural, female and male staff from a variety of ethnic backgrounds and a range of experience and training. We also enjoy serving families from all economic, ethnic, and cultural groups.

Understanding diversity means recognizing and accepting that people are not the same and that quality care comes in different forms. Individuals' caregiving styles are different, male and female styles are different, and cultural groups have different styles.

Differences are not deficiencies. It is inevitable that some of us—parents and staff—have trouble accepting this. And truthfully, probably all of us at times struggle with complete acceptance. Children, however, rarely have trouble because they have no expectation that we are all the same. Some adults are uncomfortable with male caregiving or with care that reflects differences in culture, class, or language. Often we characterize the issue as simply *their* competence, not any limitation in our own incomplete understanding of differences or our own struggle for tolerance. Competence is defined by *our* terms and reflects the style and practices we are familiar with and prefer.

A child care center is different from in-home care by a nanny, relative, or family child care provider. You have to put your trust in the whole center, not just in the person who happens to be your child's caregiver. Caregivers come and go: on vacation, on leave, on to other things. Trusting the center means trusting the administration to hire the best people available and the administration and lead teachers to be competent and conscientious supervisors. While staff come to us with a variety of training and experience, *everyone employed at our center meets the center's high standards.*

When we have substitutes with less training and experience, they work under close supervision. All staff have different strengths and weaknesses, some that parents are aware of, some that they are not. Staff have different personalities. Because we are all different, not all staff will be beloved by all parents (and vice versa). *But all children will receive excellent care and education and the entire center is responsible for seeing to that.* The diversity of our staff is an inherent aspect of our center's quality.

When a parent or a staff member has a concern about a staff member, we take it very seriously. We carefully check out the concern through observation and discussion with coworkers and other parents. When the concern is whether a particular teacher compromises the program's quality (such as limited English fluency, which is not harmful), we also research the issue with other child development authorities. Often the concern is with a behavior easily correctable through simple awareness, training, or occasionally, a timely restful vacation. In some cases, the real concern is instead about the style, language skills, or personality of the caregiver, although not always couched to us in that way. It is no accident that many of these cases concern staff from other cultures or ethnic groups or male staff. In other words, the concern is most often about caregiving different than the white, middle-class female norm.

In a good program, *adults also grow* as the children grow: we come to terms with some of our own stereotypes and narrow thinking. We probably all have these, whether we are willing to admit it or not.

Our center is a multicultural program committed to excellence. It has staff and families from all sorts of backgrounds. That is precisely what we want it to be.

Sample New Staff Orientation

Introduction to the Center

Center Tour and Center Information
    ___ Tour/Introductions

Personnel Information
    ___Personnel Forms
    ___Staff Handbook

Program Information
    ___Program Handbook
    ___NAEYC Accreditation Standards
    ___Program Forms
    ___Emergency Information

Introduction to the Homebase
    ___Homebase Information
    ___Homebase Forms

Training
    ___ About the Infant/Toddler Program with the Lead Teacher

Video Discussions
    ___ *My Kind of Place* video
    ___ *Training Toddler Teachers* video
    ___ *Seeing Infants with New Eyes* video
    ___ *Getting in Tune: Creating Nurturing Relationships with Infants and Toddlers* video

Books/Articles:
    ___ Gonzalez-Mena and Eyers, *Infants, Toddlers, and Caregivers*
    ___ Stonehouse, *Trusting Toddlers*
    ___ American Academy of Pediatrics, *Model Health Policies*
    ___ Dodge, Dombro and Koralek, *Caring for Infants and Toddlers*, volumes1 and 2

©1996 *Prime Times: A Handbook for Excellence in Infant and Toddler Care;* Redleaf Press, 450 North Syndicate, St. Paul, MN 55104. 800-423-8309.

Staff Handbook

Sample Table of Contents

continued on next page

Teamwork and Communication

A typical homebase has a staff team of two to five caregivers over the course of the day. No matter how sensitive or talented the individuals, several people "doing their own thing" will not result in good care. It is how they work *together* that counts for children and parents. Effective teamwork does not just happen, but is the result of effort, experience, lots of communication, and time. Good teamwork is like a dance, in which partners seem to understand what is happening, what will happen next, and how to fit with each other. Where people have worked together for a long time, little may have to be said—they just know. If one is sitting with a child helping her to eat, the other just knows she should get up and help the other children start clearing the table. If one is caught up with a child in distress, the other just knows she should keep a particularly watchful eye out for everyone else in the group.

The unspoken, intuitive support in good teams is not be confused with the silence that comes from mindlessly doing things the way they have always been done or "by the book." Staff often have strong views about certain dimensions of their practice, based on their own past work experience, their experience as parents, or from their own childhoods. "Mindless" or "by the book" is often a coping response that masks differences in beliefs and values. It is healthier to acknowledge and bring out in the open potential differences in order to reach consensus or compromises. While there is certainly room for diversity in care-giving practices, it is important that staff agree on basic principles and practices and speak to parents with one voice.

Good caregiving teams:

◆ understand that there is not usually one right way to do things.

◆ think, reflect, and discuss.

◆ pat each other on the back.

◆ share successes and accomplishments.

◆ share concerns and issues.

◆ share less desirable jobs.

◆ help all members improve

◆ give and receive help during difficult times.

◆ expect that there will be periodic tension and conflict to work through.

◆ communicate openly and directly.

◆ trust and respect each other and the work they are doing.

Teams come together over time as trust and understanding develop. Teamwork requires frequent communication, much of it on the run while people work with children, but there has to be time to sit down together to talk, evaluate, and plan. Group meetings can be supplemented by minimeetings of fifteen minutes or less, the exchange of written information in notebooks and white boards, and, perhaps increasingly, the use of audio messages and voice mail.

Empowerment

Much of what has been discussed has the intention of empowering staff, recognizing their capacity to make decisions and to take responsibility, to think as well as to do. Empowerment takes a number of forms:

◆ *Opportunities to be Heard*: structuring mechanisms for staff to be heard allows them to influence decisions and helps the center leadership to asses staff morale. In larger centers, a staff rep system, much like the parent rep system, allows staff a structured opportunity to raise centerwide issues, suggest ideas, and express appreciation. It gives the director, board, or owner an opportunity to hear from staff at all levels. Polling staff about particular issues or polling them on more general "What's on your mind?" questions provides staff with a way to anonymously present their views.

◆ *Opportunities for Recognition:* in comparison with working with over three year olds, caregiving for babies may seem fairly repetitive and routine after a time. Caregivers may lose sight of the importance and meaningfulness of what they are doing. The rewards of working with under threes are more subtle than those of working with older children. Caregivers need to be reminded regularly that theirs in a very important and highly skilled job. This recognition can take all sorts of forms, from director's notes to newsletter mention to simple, positive introductions to visitors by the director as he or she tours others through the program.

◆ *Opportunities for More Responsibility:* a good organization provides opportunity for employees (as they become interested and ready) to be involved in areas that extend beyond the group that they work with, for example, assisting in developing or reviewing center policies, presenting workshops or leading discussions with other staff, or representing the center on an outside committee.

◆ *Learning to Advocate:* one of the skills that early childhood professionals need is the ability to articulate their practice, that is, to be able to speak clearly, strongly, and dispassionately about children and what they do with children: the why, what and how of being good at their jobs. Infant and toddler care has traditionally been devalued even within the early childhood profession. It is important to assist staff to understand what they are doing and why it is good and to be able to talk about it with each other and, even more important, with parents.

Professional Development

No caregiver is a finished product. Regardless of the qualifications and experience brought to the job, ongoing professional development through workshops, conferences, coursework, and readings is important. Good programs have budgets that support staff libraries and assist staff in obtaining further education and training.

However, just as important as access to training is a center culture that establishes the center as a place for professional growth: consolidating previous learning, gaining new skills, facing challenges, reflecting critically on practice, and engaging in debate. If a center's culture has fixed "the way we do things here" or invests the director or other powers-that-be with unchallenged wisdom, eventually mindlessness and apathy sets in. If the atmosphere is one of constantly learning and becoming in order to do a better job, if caregivers can be open about problems or questions they have, and if there are channels for constructive criticism as well as praise, not only will people be more excited about their work but there will also be little defensiveness. Conflict must be accepted as inevitable and as potentially positive when it is dealt with constructively.

Professional development does not happen by the simple absorption of expertise modeled by more skilled for less skilled staff. Modeling has to be coupled with opportunities for discussion that result in directed attention and reflective analysis. The difference between good and not so good practice with children is subtle, and inexperienced staff may not know what to take from watching someone else. Very often the demonstration will be lost in the busy atmosphere. Suggestions and ideas for improvement must be made explicit.

Effective modeling requires that lead teachers and more experienced staff be perceived as credible but not be set up as models of perfection. Part of their credibility stems from their leadership and part from an atmosphere that emphasizes that everything is subject to constructive criticism. Successes as well as failures are used as a basis for discussion in order to improve practice.

Identifying professional development needs of staff individually and collectively should be built into the evolution of program and individual staff. Staff and program development plans should include the provision for in-center mentoring as well as for outside workshops and courses. Helping to train others is a very effective way of making staff aware of their own expertise and competence, as well as providing them with an incentive to grow in knowledge.

Staff Evaluation

Evaluation is an essential component of professional development and of encouraging high-quality individual performance. It is an ongoing element of good supervision, which also includes clarifying expectations, recognition and praise, critical analysis, suggestions for improvement and performance and professional development goal setting. Evaluation also offers an opportunity for meaningful two-way communication about the job, job performance, and supervision. (For sample forms to use during evaluations, see pages 319–330.)

The evaluation process has five parts:

◆ establishing the criteria for employee performance: job description, program handbooks, supervisor memos, employee goals.

◆ collecting data from multiple sources: employee self-evaluation and portfolio, parents, coworkers.

◆ analyzing, reviewing, and discussing the evaluation between employee and supervisor.

◆ identifying goals for job performance and professional development.

◆ evaluating supervision.

Performance evaluations are serious business that not only affect the nature and quality of the employee's work but also usually affect salary and promotion. The supervisor and the employee can maintain a good relationship and still have the honest, sometimes painful discussions necessary if clear expectations for performance and support are established. The following categories for levels of performance are useful for both supervisor and employee because they allow for more objective analysis:

◆ *Inadequate Performance*: does not perform according to the requirements of the position. Requires close supervision and a performance improvement plan beyond annual goals to improve.

◆ *Adequate Performance:* frequently requires close supervision and extra support to meet job requirements. Little evidence of growth, extra effort, or more than adequate achievement of responsibilities.

◆ *Good Performance*: understands and consistently implements the program objectives during daily interactions with children, parents, and coworkers. Some initiative shown for professional growth.

◆ *Exceptional Performance*: either extraordinary effort or extraordinary achievement and otherwise consistent professional performance. Evidence of commitment to the center as a whole and to professional growth. Understanding and commitment to the program philosophy and goals. Above average attendance at nonrequired center meetings and events.

◆ *Outstanding Performance*: extraordinary effort and extraordinary achievement. The employee "threw herself/himself into the job" with exceptional performance results. Provided leadership through role modeling, enthusiasm, professionalism, commitment, and performance with children, parents, and coworkers. Clear integration of the goals of the center into employee's own needs and values.

"Why Did You Stay?"—Creating Stayers Who Perform

"I have now been at the center for nine years: through two directors, at least eight coteachers, a facility renovation, biannual budget crisis, a divorce, and finally finishing my BA. There were times I wanted to quit, and times I can't imagine why I wasn't fired (I was so angry throughout my divorce that I was no fun to be with). But I'm glad I'm here—although I'd like to make a lot more money!"

Sherry, the teacher quoted above, is a stayer. Fortunately for the center, she now stays not out of lethargy or minimal job prospects but because she wants to. She stayed with the center and the center stuck with her through thick and thin—sometimes more thin than thick.

"I stayed and I think I grew because it was a place where I was respected and cared about and quality did count—which was sometimes painful if the push for quality meant that I had to shape up. We went through a lot and accomplished a lot, and it felt like "we" did it —particularly accreditation. Over the years, I learned a lot about working with adults (parents and staff)—that was always the hardest part, and how to take things in stride."

Staff stay when it feels like a good place to work and the center makes a long-term commitment to them.

A Final Word: Change Takes Time

Improving as a workplace takes a center as much time as improving as a place for children and parents. But accomplishing the second requires the first. It is important to keep pushing along, writing and improving job descriptions and handbooks, and making time for meetings and training.

When it all comes together, children and families will benefit and staff will inevitably demonstrate the following:

◆ belief in the work they are doing. It is not "just day care" but rather a potential positive influence on children and families.

◆ a sense of themselves as growing, learning, "becoming" professionally, no matter what their training and how long their experience.

◆ confidence and trust in themselves and the children they care for—the attitude that "We know each other, we like each other, we can live well together, we can handle any situation."

◆ the work is fun (much of the time) and always worth it.

EXERCISES

1. Evaluate the expectations of performance found in your job description and staff handbooks for clarity and comprehensiveness.

2. Develop a new staff orientation list and prioritize it into the following categories: first day, first week, first month, first three months.

REFERENCE

Bloom, Paula Jorde. *A Great Place to Work.* Washington, DC: NAEYC, 1988.

RESOURCES

Bloom, Paula Jorde. *A Great Place to Work.* Washington, DC: NAEYC, 1988.

——————. *Avoiding Burn Out: Strategies for Managing Time, Space, and People in Early Childhood Education.* Lake Forest, IL: New Horizon, 1982.

Bloom, Paula Jorde, Sheerer, Marilyn, and Britz, Joan. *Blueprint for Action: Achieving Center-Based Change Through Staff Development.* Lake Forest, IL: New Horizons, 1991.

Carter, Margie, and Curtis, Deb. *Training Teachers: A Harvest of Theory and Practice.* St. Paul, MN: Redleaf Press, 1994.

Honig, Alice, and Lally, Ron. *Infant and Toddler Caregiving: A Design for Training.* Syracuse, NY: Syracuse University Press, 1981.

Jones, Elizabeth. *Growing Teachers: Partnerships in Staff Development.* Washington, DC: NAEYC, 1993.

——————. *Teaching Adults: An Active Learning Approach.* Washington, DC: NAEYC, 1986.

Employee Counseling Procedure

The Director should be fully aware of unsatisfactory job performance and must review and approve written communications before they are given to an employee.

Stage I: Recognition of the Problem

A. Description
In this informal communication stage, the employee and supervisor identify the problem and make plans for improvement. Supervisor usually means the immediate supervisor; thus, the teacher for associates, lead teachers for teachers, and so on. The Director/Assistant Director is informed of this situation.

It is optional for a third person to be present during Stage I discussions with the employee. The presence of a third person is a protection for the supervisor and a form of due process for the employee.

B. Direct Supervisor Conveys Nature of the Problem to Employee
Consult with Director/Assistant Director prior to discussion with employee.

It is possible that the employee will not understand or agree; with the evaluation; the supervisor must be extremely clear and

◆ convey why it's a problem in terms related to program philosophy, personnel practices/policies, or job description
◆ be very specific about examples of the problem performance.

Identify the correct or desired performance.

C. Develop a Plan for Achieving Success
Outline steps and time frames to achieve appropriate performance. Coach and counsel with goal of success.

D. Documentation and Communication
Despite informality of steps 1.B and 1.C, notes on the process should be maintained. Include date, time, and content. A copy of these notes is kept in the employee's personnel file.

The supervisor shares notes and discussion of steps 1.B and 1.C with the Director/Assistant Director.

Stage II: Put the Problem in Writing

A. Description
When the problem persists despite the coaching, counseling, and communication, a formal written record of specific efforts to achieve success now becomes necessary. This record must be acknowledged in writing by the employee.

If the employee refuses to acknowledge the written record, the refusal and reasons are noted on the document in lieu of a signature.

B. Develop a Meaningful Paper Trail
In consultation with the Director/Assistant Director, the supervisor creates a document/memo with a clear statement of the problem as follows:

Include an introduction and summary that enable a third party to understand the problem

Do not editorialize. State the facts clearly and concisely with a minimum of adjectives.

Include specific expectations and time frames.

Include a written summary of all meetings or activities related to handling this problem (refer to specific dates as appropriate).

Employee signs all documents to acknowledge receipt. The original goes to the employee, with copies to the file, and one copy to the Assistant Director/Director.

If the employee achieves the expected level of success, the process ends with a note confirming satisfactory resolution. Again, original goes to employee and signed copies to file and to the Director.

Stage III. Probation

A. Description
If the desired improvements do not occur as a result of continued coaching, counseling, and formal statement of the problem (stages I and II), the employee is told that her/his job is in jeopardy.

B. Probation Document
Consult the Director/Assistant Director regarding the terms of probation.

In coordination with the Director/Assistant Director, the direct supervisor prepares a memo that states the following clearly:

- Your job is in jeopardy
- Identified goals must be achieved by a specific date
- The documents that set the standards for the issue (e.g., personnel policies, staff handbook, NAEYC materials, etc.)
- the center reserves the right to terminate the employee at any time during the process if behavior jeopardizes the program.

Be sure the employee has enough trials at the desired behavior to become successful. In most matters two weeks is reasonable. If the matter is something very directly remediable (lateness, dress, signing in, etc.) one week is sufficient. The employee must understand that improvements must occur within the designated time period and for duration of employment.

Employee must sign the probation document to acknowledge receipt. The original goes to the employee, and copies to Assistant Director/Director and the file.

In general, the employee must agree that s/he is indeed committed to improvement. If not, resignation or termination (not probation) is the logical next step.

Stage IV: Termination

Steps for Successful Termination

Once termination is decided upon, the Director/Assistant Director and a third party meet with the employee. (The third party may be the direct supervisor, or, if the Director/Assistant Director is the direct supervisor, another third party will be selected.)

The Director/Assistant Director completes the termination process using the center's "Resignation/Termination of Employment Checklist." This checklist is filled out and filed in the employee's personnel file at the center to confirm that all steps have been completed.

©1996 *Prime Times: A Handbook for Excellence in Infant and Toddler Care*; Redleaf Press, 450 North Syndicate, St. Paul, MN 55104. 800-423-8309.

Resignation/Termination of Employment Checklist

Name: _____ Date: _____

Position: _____ Status: _____

Last day of Employment: _____

_____ If termination, a meeting with the employee was held with

_____; _____ was a witness.

_____ If resignation, the letter of resignation was received and filed.

Final paycheck will include (this information is sent to payroll):

Salary for the period from _____ to _____.

Severance pay from _____ to _____.

Deduct _____ paid days taken in advance. Add ____ unused, accrued vacation days.

Confirmed address and phone to which last paycheck will be sent:

The following steps were completed by the last day of employment listed above:

_____ Returned to employee any personal property brought to the center.

_____ Notified staff.

_____ Notified other _____.

_____ Notified parents (____ by phone on _____ or ____ by attached memo)

_____ Collected the following items:

    ____ ID   ____ personnel policies

    ____ key   ____ staff handbooks

    ____ other center or sponsoring company property

Comments:

Signed _____ Date _____

(This completed form should be filed in the employee's personnel file at the center.)

©1996 *Prime Times: A Handbook for Excellence in Infant and Toddler Care;* Redleaf Press, 450 North Syndicate, St. Paul, MN 55104. 800-423-8309.

Teacher Evaluation

Name _____   Supervisor's Name _____   Date _____

Goal   The teacher manages the homebase and its resources, staff, and interactions with parents in order to provide for the well-being of the children.

Major Areas of Responsibility

	Seldom	Sometimes	Frequently	Always	Comments
I. Homebase Management					
A. Assures the safety and well-being of each child under the supervision of the lead teacher.					
B. Keeps furnishings, equipment, and materials in good repair and fair supply.					
C. Develops an environment that allows for individual and group activities.					
D. Maintains an orderly learning environment.					

©1996 *Prime Times: A Handbook for Excellence in Infant and Toddler Care*, Redleaf Press, 450 North Syndicate, St. Paul, MN 55104. 800-423-8309.

	Seldom	Sometimes	Frequently	Always	Comments
II. Relationships with Children					
A. Plans and carries out a curriculum that meets program standards.					
B. Maintains an awareness of each child's level of development.					
C. Interacts with and guides children in an age-appropriate and positive manner.					
D. Provides for the development of each child in the following areas: 1. physical					
2. intellectual					
3. social					

	Seldom	Sometimes	Frequently	Always	Comments
4. emotional	___	___	___	___	___
5. cultural	___	___	___	___	___
E. Includes the following activities in a manner consistent with center policies:					___
1. rest	___	___	___	___	___
2. toileting/diapering	___	___	___	___	___
3. meals	___	___	___	___	___
F. Keeps appropriate records for each child.	___	___	___	___	___

	Seldom	Sometimes	Frequently	Always	Comments
III. Staff Management					
A. Under the supervision of the lead teacher, works closely with other homebase staff persons, including associate teachers, part-time and hourly workers, and substitutes.	___	___	___	___	___
1. assures that homebase staff members function as a team.	___	___	___	___	___
2. conducts evaluations of other homebase staff as required.	___	___	___	___	___
3. keeps staff informed of homebase plans and center happenings.	___	___	___	___	___
B. Assigns primary caregiver responsibilities, if appropriate.	___	___	___	___	___

	Seldom	Sometimes	Frequently	Always	Comments
C. Becomes involved in professional development and shares information with homebase staff.					
D. Includes associate teachers in homebase planning.					
E. Schedules homebase staff and areas of responsibility for the full day, if appropriate.					
F. As appropriate, shares information about homebase or child-related problems with homebase staff members and supervisor.					

IV. Parent Relationships
A. Establishes a positive, ongoing relationship with parents.

	Seldom	Sometimes	Frequently	Always	Comments
1. keeps parents informed of their child's activities.	—	—	—	—	_____
2. arranges parent conferences.	—	—	—	—	_____
B. Makes homebase information available to parents.	—	—	—	—	_____
C. Completes child assessment forms as required.	—	—	—	—	_____
V. Other Duties A. Represents the center and strictly maintains confidentiality about its clients and business.	—	—			_____
B. Complies with regulations and procedures found in the center's handbooks and manuals.	—	—	—		_____

	Seldom	Sometimes	Frequently	Always	Comments
C. Completes other duties as assigned by the leader teacher, assistant director, or director.	___	___	___	___	___

VI. Professional Behavior

	Seldom	Sometimes	Frequently	Always	Comments
A. Maintains a good attendance record.	___	___	___	___	___
B. Is punctual and prepared for work.	___	___	___	___	___

Review period successfully completed: _____ Yes _____ No

If no, review period extended until _____. At the end of the extended review period, another review will be conducted to determine progress made in achieving suggested areas for development.

Comments:

Major Accomplishments:

329

Areas and Strategies for Improvement:

Goals for the Coming Year:

Objective and Timeline:

_____   Date   _____   Date
Director   Immediate Supervisor

_____   Date
Evaluated Employee

Part 6

Staying Good: Evaluation and Quality Control

Chapter 16

....

Ongoing Program Evaluation and Change

excellence

Active intelligence—a culture where there is ongoing monitoring of program outcomes experienced by children and parents and evaluation of the program's purpose, philosophy, goals, and objectives.

It should be clear from the preceding chapters that good programs always employ a range of formal and informal monitoring and evaluation strategies. There is a program culture that encourages continual critical appraisal with an eye to improving, and a "Why not?" culture that welcomes ideas, suggestions, and constructive criticism from staff and parents. "What's happening?" "How are we doing?" "Should we be changing?" are not only heard during periods of crisis but are continuously asked questions representing a state of mind shared by staff and parents. Much monitoring and evaluation takes place informally when staff and parents observe and discuss the program, children, and staff actions. There is time set aside to meet and discuss approaches and issues, resources available to read and watch, professional development opportunities that spur growth, and opportunities for parents to discuss issues and concerns.

NOTE: It is important to distinguish between monitoring the outcomes experienced by children and child assessment that monitors child development. Child assessment studies their development: their behavior and abilities. This may be desirable in programs with staff trained in child development and assessment, but it is different from program evaluation. Program evaluation looks at program policies and practices: what is actually occurring in the program and what is experienced by children, parents, and staff. Is the program that exists on paper (the policies and stated practices in brochures and handbooks) a reality? Are the program goals being achieved?

....

Assessing Quality

Quality also requires a more systematic approach to monitoring and evaluation.

Monitoring is the process of identifying *what is really happening*: what is the actual experience of children, parents, and staff? Wait a minute, don't we know what is happening anyway? After all, we are right there ourselves. Yes and no. We know what *we* see and feel, what we pay attention to, but what about all the things we don't see and feel—the perspective of others? We naturally enough see from our own vantage point and filter our perceptions through our values and beliefs. Good programs systematically monitor the outcomes experienced by the people involved, ensuring a more complete picture. Monitoring involves directing attention and collecting perceptions from both children and adults.

Evaluation is the process of valuing *what is happening*: deciding what we think about what has been uncovered through monitoring and whether change is necessary. For example, monitoring tells us that the children in a two-years-old room spend a lot more time on indoor art than on outdoor sand and water. In our evaluation process, we determine whether we think that this is a problem and what might be done about it.

The basis for evaluation are the goals and objectives that underlie the program and the assumption about what constitutes good practice spelled out in this handbook and other program materials. Evaluation requires knowledge and perspective: knowledge of child development, families, and the cultures represented; and understanding of the perspectives of parents in the program.

A Culture of Responsibility, Not Blame

Evaluation can be threatening. It's hard not to be nervous if you or your homebase is the subject of scrutiny. What runs through your mind? "First, let me explain," "You are just focusing on what's wrong," and "It's not my fault." Establishing a culture of responsibility, not of blame, can eliminate much of the threat.

Child care is difficult and complex. The caregiver's actions take place in a context. Responsibility for outcomes should be shared. For example:

♦ *In the Bluebell room, it was not uncommon to find staff yelling at children from across the room. While they were not being particularly harsh, their actions set a loud, bossy, negative tone. "No," "Stop that," "Please come over here" rang out frequently, and even positive redirection came across as negative because it was done loudly at a distance. Obviously, it was a staff performance issue and the staff needed to change—they needed to stop yelling.*

Staff performance was the issue but not staff wrongdoing, ignorance, or indifference. In fact, for the most part, they were not aware of how much was happening. Why were they yelling? A number of reasons:

◆ It was a loud room with lousy acoustics.

◆ The room had fourteen active toddlers and two staff.

◆ It was not a "Yes" space; no one had helped them with room environment, and the caregivers had little training.

◆ Staff were valiantly trying to create more individualized, small-group learning centers and activities and to spread out and use the whole room.

The efforts to correct the problem illustrate the shortsightedness of blaming staff and putting all the responsibility on them. The director approached the yelling as a homebase issue, not just a staff in the homebase performance problem. She became as responsible for change as the caregivers. Caregivers were made aware of the yelling and worked together to break the habit. They got some training and some help planning a "Yes" environment, and they were promised a long-range plan to reduce the ratio and group size and to put in an acoustic ceiling.

Evaluation is positive when it is part of a process of improvement that everyone has responsibility for.

Monitoring

There are a number of ways to systematically monitor what is going on at the center: through observation and polling—asking parents, staff, and children about their experience.

Directed Observations

You can see a lot by watching.
—Yogi Berra

Yogi was right. If you watch, you will see what's happening with children and adults. One of the best ways of evaluating the daily program is to encourage staff to observe children as they work with them: their experiences in the environment, skills, strengths, interests, and also what they *do not* do—the experiences, parts of the environment or people they avoid. This seems obvious: it happens all the time, of course, but much of the time we are only *seeing* a limited amount. Often we focus more on the event (our actions—the caring or learning activity), than the outcome (their experience—the care or learning experienced). A teacher, when asked how her day went, replied: "Oh, really well, really smoothly, no problems, we all had a good time." This meant no major tantrums, the activities didn't fall apart, no one ate the paste or each other—in sum, "*My* day was smooth." But Johnny's day may have been chaotic, Nicole struggled with separation, Barney wandered about, Sarah learned ten new things, and so on.

Directed observations are used most often when we are struggling with a child's behavior like biting or a difficult time of the day when chaos periodically erupts, such as a transition time. Directed observations structure our looking; we focus on specific children, activities, interactions, aspects of the environment, or time periods. Recording those observations provides the raw material for discussion as a team. Caregivers can help each other to see a fuller, less egocentric picture by intentionally observing from different perspectives (e.g., the perspective of a particular child or parent) and sharing their perceptions.

For staff to remain motivated to use directed observations as a frequent tool, information has to be used effectively; there must be mechanisms for sharing the information and translating it into implications for practice. Homebase meetings are a good time for this. But not enough time to "talk about the kids" is a common lament when meetings are taken up with announcements, planning, or staff issues.

When meeting time is short, touch-base times, minimeetings, and short staff conferences between primary caregivers are valuable.

Sampling   Sampling is a useful way to structure observations:

- *Event sampling* involves recording behaviors of the child or children being observed during a particular period of time. If Anne is having difficult separations, recording all her behaviors during the period of arrival (the "event") until she is engaged in the program should reveal a lot. Recording the behaviors of her parents, staff, and even other children would add to the picture.
- *Time sampling* records behavior observed and recorded at regular timed intervals. For instance, recording a child's behavior every five minutes or recording the behavior observed at a location (e.g., the book area) every ten minutes.

Both methods of sampling force us to see in a more rigorous and complete manner. We may notice patterns of behavior and events we weren't aware of—for example, a lack of activity choices that engage Anne in that particular situation.

Snapshots   Snapshots (see sample below) are another way to structure observation and are particularly useful in observing how children use the environment. The goal is to capture what is happening at a given moment in time. This can be done literally with a camera or simply by charting, using a room map. A snapshot may reveal adults or children bunching up, incomplete use of the room, or problems with supervision. Used with time sampling, e.g., taking a "snapshot" every ten minutes, the technique may focus caregivers' attention on the flow of children or the actions of particular children.

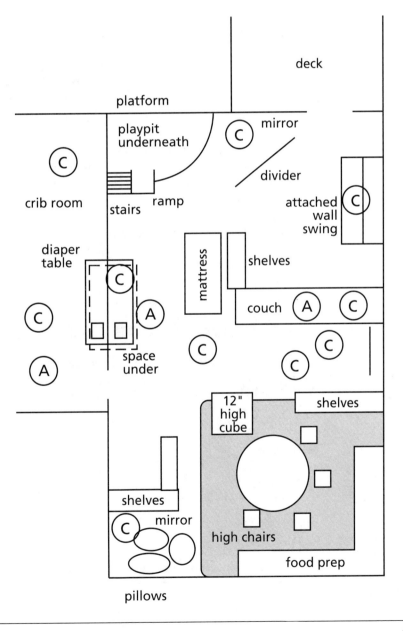

Anecdotal Records Typically, this involves caregivers writing down what they feel is significant: interactions, events, behavior, in a journal or log. It is important to record the information as soon as possible to include details and ensure accuracy. Also important is distinguishing between a description of the behavior, which should be objective and detailed ("Joey threw the blocks"), and your feelings or conclusions about the behavior ("Joey disrupted the block area and ruined the morning"). Discussing the anecdotes may lead others to different interpretations of the behavior.

Checklists Checklists are another method of structuring observations: when something happens, we check it off. Behavioral checklists can be devised for individual or groups of children around any behaviors the staff are concerned with, e.g., language use, exploration, distress, aggression, or withdrawal. A primary caregiver may devise a checklist in cooperation with a worried parent to track a child's emerging motor skills.

Polling Polling is just another name for systematically asking someone to tell you what he or she is thinking or feeling, either by interview or questionnaire. In chapter 14, we provided examples of questionnaires for new parents; in chapter 15, we gave an example of a survey for staff.

Polling can be long and comprehensive or short—a single question of the day. It can be done on a computer at the front desk, with Post-It notes, or the old-fashioned way. Almost anything to do with the experience of child care can be a topic for parents and staff. There is one important consideration, however. People tire of being asked their views if they don't see any result. Polling has to be followed by dissemination of the results, discussion, and, if called for, publicized change.

The Two-Minute Poll of the Week

Please take a moment to answer these two questions:

1. What was the best thing you noticed this week that happened at the center?
2. What would you change if you could?

Name _____ (optional)

Program Evaluations

Evaluation should extend beyond the homebase to periodic consideration of all aspects of the center: mission, philosophy, administrative and programming policies, and procedures. There should be regular opportunities for staff and parents to see if practice matches policy, if old policies need revising, and if new policies need developing.

Many centers are subject to outside evaluations or audits by funding sources, external administrators or owners, or regulatory agencies. These often identify problems and propel changes, but they are rarely comprehensive and may not provide the information that center staff need to grow and change.

NAEYC Accreditation

Accreditation by the National Academy of Early Childhood Programs, sponsored by The National Association for the Education of Young Children, is an excellent means of program evaluation because it forces you to look into nearly every nook and cranny of your center's operation. It is a voluntary process that includes extensive self-study and on-site recognition by the academy that your program meets a superior national standard for early childhood education and care. Standards cover a comprehensive range of program issues around caring, learning, parents, and staff, as well as administration procedures. The process involves all staff and parents in monitoring the program. Accreditation is for a three-year period.

Accreditation has been in existence only since 1985 and is gaining momentum as the recognized standard of quality. Accreditation standards and processes are very high but not perfect. Developing a national standard that applies to a wide range of early childhood programs results in compromises and some controversy. Some standards may be too vague or too precise. Those programs that become accredited may still be too opinionated and "by the book" or too loose. But accreditation is critically important for the child care industry, and all good programs should seek to be accredited. Without an established quality standard, the widespread public perception that meeting minimal licensing standards is the equivalent of quality will continue to plague child care and devalue real quality.

"Accreditation Is Like Flossing—A Bother, but Worth It. You Clear Out Some Stuff You Didn't Realize Was There."

"You know, doing accreditation was a lot harder and a lot more rewarding then I thought it would be," said a director whose center had just been accredited. "We were surprised both by some things we thought were happening that weren't and some things that were happening that were just sloppy. We were good, but accreditation made us get better."

"But the best byproduct was that it made us proud of ourselves and really educated the parents. It set us apart, and parents now understand better what they are getting (and we raised our fees without that much of an outcry)."

Other Routes to Program Evaluation

One effective method of structuring regular program evaluation is to develop a three-year calendar for reviewing center materials: personnel policies and staff handbook, center brochure and parent handbook, program handbook and environment and program checklists, and administrative operations materials. As each document is reviewed, polices and practices are subjected to scrutiny by staff and parents and revised as necessary.

A Final Word: Quality Takes Commitment and Time

The process of becoming a quality program is demanding, slow, and often frustrating. Usually our recognition of what quality is and our desire to attain it outpace our efforts to produce it. Evaluation can easily become a source of frustration: we identify more concerns, more blemishes, and more things to do. It doesn't have to be that way. Evaluations can and should uncover all that is right with the program: all those positive interactions, satisfied parents, learning children, and hard-working staff.

It goes back to the program culture. When evaluation is seen as a natural process, improvement as an ongoing need, and responsibility shared by a staff working together, programs will achieve the highest quality their resources allow.

EXERCISES

1. Observe one child during three different transition times. Record as many of the child's behaviors as you can. What can you say about the child or the transition?

2. Observe a learning center for three days during the same thirty-minute period. Describe who used the center, how materials were used, how children engaged and disengaged from the center, language used, social interactions. What similarities and differences did you observe between children in their use of materials, entry and exit, and social behavior?

3. Develop a checklist based on daily goals for a primary-care child and parents.

Resource List

BOOKS

American Public Health Association and the American Academy of Pediatrics. *Caring for Our Children, National Health and Safety Performance Standards: Guidelines for Out-of-Home Child Care Programs.* Washington, DC: American Academy of Pediatrics, 1992.

Bloom, Paula Jorde. *A Great Place to Work.* Washington, DC: NAEYC, 1988.

——. *Avoiding Burn Out: Strategies for Managing Time, Space, and People in Early Childhood Education.* Lake Forest, IL: New Horizon, 1982.

Bloom, Paula Jorde, Sheerer, Marilyn, and Britz, Joan. *Blueprint for Action: Achieving Center-Based Change Through Staff Development.* Lake Forest, IL: New Horizons. 1991.

Brazelton, T. Barry. *Infants and Mothers.* New York: Dell Publishing, 1972.

——. *Toddlers and Parents.* New York: Dell Publishing, 1974.

——. *Touchpoints* Reading, MA: Addison-Wesley, 1992. [book and video]

Carter, Margie, and Curtis Deb. *Training Teachers: A Harvest of Theory and Practice.* St. Paul, MN: Redleaf Press, 1994.

Cryer, Debbie, Harms, Thelma, and Bourland, Beth. *Active Learning for Infants.* Menlo Park, CA: Addison-Wesley Publishing Company, 1987. (Additional volumes for *Ones, Twos, and Threes.*)

Erickson, E. *Childhood and Society.* New York: W.W. Norton, 1950.

Galinsky, Ellen. *Six Stages of Parenting.* Reading, MA: Addison-Wesley Publishing Company, 1987.

Gonzalez-Mena, J. *Dragon Mom.* Palo Alto, CA: Mayfield, 1993.

Gonzalez-Mena, J., and Eyer, D. *Infants, Toddlers, and Caregivers.* Palo Alto, CA: Mayfield, 1993.

——. *Multicultural Issues in Child Care.* Palo Alto, CA: Mayfield, 1989.

Greenman, J. *Caring Spaces, Learning Places: Children's Environments That Work.* Redmond, WA: Exchange Press, 1988. Chapter 13.

Honig, Alice. *Playtime Learning Games for Young Children.* Syracuse, NY: Syracuse University Press, 1982.

Honig, Alice, and Lally, Ron. *Infant and Toddler Caregiving: A Design for Training.* Syracuse, NY: Syracuse University Press, 1981.

Jones, Elizabeth. *Growing Teachers: Partnerships in Staff Development.* Washington, DC: NAEYC, 1993.

——. *Teaching Adults: An Active Learning Approach.* Washington, DC: NAEYC, 1986.

Kendrick, Abby; Kaufmann, Roxanne; and Messenger, Katherine. *Healthy Young Children: A Manual for Programs.* Washington, DC: NAEYC, 1988.

Miller, K. *More Things to Do with Toddlers and Twos.* Beltsville, MD: Gryphon House, 1989.

———. *The Outside Play and Learning Book.* Beltsville, MD: Gryphon House, 1989.

———. *Things to Do with Toddlers and Twos.* Beltsville, MD: Gryphon House, 1989.

Pennsylvania Chapter of the American Academy of Pediatrics. *Model Child Care Health Policies.* Washington, DC: NAEYC, 1993 [book and disk]

Segal, Mariliyn, and Adcock, Don. *Your Child at Play.*(Series) New York: New Market Press, 1985, 1985, 1985, 1986.

Stonehouse, Anne W. *How Does It Feel? Childcare from a Parent's Perspective.* Redmond, WA: *Child Care Information Exchange,* 1995.

White, Burton. *The First Three Years of Life.* Englewood Cliffs, NJ: Prentice Hall, 1975.

VIDEOS

The Program for Infant/Toddler Caregovers. A seris of training videos produced in three languages (English, Spanish, Chinese) on infant/toddler policies, environments, play and learning and interaction. Available from WestEd, Sausalito, CA (415)331-5277.

Carter, M. *Time with Toddlers.* Produced by Jan Reed and Charlie Hinkley. 22 minutes. Kidspace, 1991.

Greenman, J. *Best for My Baby.* Produced by Jim Greenman and Ann Follett. 31 minutes. Greater Minneapolis Day Care Association, 1990.

———. *My Kind of Place: Identifying Quality Infant and Toddler Care.* 26 minutes. Greater Minneapolis Day Care Association, 1989.

PERIODICALS

Child Care Information Exchange Magazine
Redmond, WA: Exchange Press
(800) 221-2864

For Special Needs Children:
Exceptional Parent Magazine
Council for Exceptional Children
1920 Associaition Drive
Reston, VA 22901
(703) 620-3660

CHILDREN WITH SPECIAL NEEDS
Clearinghouse on Disability Information
U.S. Departnment of Education
3330 C Street SW
Washington, DC 20202
(202) 732-1250

National Information Center for
    Handicapped Children and Youth (NICHCY)
PO Box 1492
Washington, DC 20013
(202) 893-6061

Equipment Resources
Bear Blocks: carpeted blocks, planks,
    and blocks to create everchanging spaces.
1132 School Street
Mansfield, MA 02048
(800) 424-2327

Fancy Foote-Works: custom-built infant environments,
    lofts, and play equipment.
549 Moscow Road
Hamlin, NY 14464
(716) 964-8260

Torelli-Durret: custom-built infant environments, lofts,
    and play equipment.
1250 Addison Street, Suite 113
Berkeley, CA 94704
(800) 895-3121

SafeSpace Concepts, Inc.: custom-built infant environments,
    lofts, and play equipment.
1424 North Post Oak
Houston, TX 77055
(800) 622-4289

Accreditation Materials
Bredekamp, Sue. *Developmentally Appropriate Practice in Early Childhood Programs Serving Children From Birth through Age 8.* Washington, DC: NAEYC, 1987.

Harms, Thelma, Cryer, Debbie, and Clifford, Richard M. *Infant/Toddler Environment Rating Scale.* New York: Teachers College, Columbia University, 1990.

Harms, Thelma; and Cryer, Debbie. *Video Observations for the Infant/Toddler Environment Rating Scale.* New York: Teachers College, Columbia University, 1991.